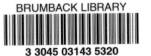

ESSENTIAL BOOK OF MARTIAL ARTS KICKS

LEARN TO UNLEASH A DEVASTATING BARRAGE OF KICKS TO THROW YOUR OPPONENT OFF-GUARD!

By MARC DE BREMAEKER and ROY FAIGE   Illustrations by SHAHAR NAVOT

89 KICKS FROM KARATE, TAEKWONDO, MUAY THAI, JEET KUNE DO, AND OTHERS

TUTTLE Publishing

Tokyo | Rutland, Vermont | Singapore

Published by Tuttle Publishing, an imprint of Periplus Editions (HK) Ltd.

www.tuttlepublishing.com

Library of Congress Cataloging-in-Publication Data

Bremaeker, Marc de.
Essential book of martial arts kicks / by Marc De Bremaeker and Roy Faige ; illustrations by: Shahar Navot ; photography by: Guli Cohen.
p. cm.
ISBN 978-0-8048-4122-1 (pbk.)
1. Martial arts--Training. 2. Self-defense--Training. I. Faige, Roy. II. Title.
GV1101.B74 2010
796.815--dc22
2010012444

ISBN: 978-0-8048-4122-1

Distributed by

North America, Latin America & Europe
Tuttle Publishing
364 Innovation Drive
North Clarendon, VT 05759-9436 U.S.A.
Tel: 1 (802) 773-8930; Fax: 1 (802) 773-6993
info@tuttlepublishing.com
www.tuttlepublishing.com

Japan
Tuttle Publishing
Yaekari Building, 3rd Floor
5-4-12 Osaki, Shinagawa-ku
Tokyo 141 0032
Tel: (81) 3 5437-0171; Fax: (81) 3 5437-0755
tuttle-sales@gol.com

Asia Pacific
Berkeley Books Pte. Ltd.
61 Tai Seng Avenue #02-12
Singapore 534167
Tel: (65) 6280-1330; Fax: (65) 6280-6290
inquiries@periplus.com.sg
www.periplus.com

First edition
14 13 12 11 10 6 5 4 3 2 1

Printed in Singapore

IN MEMORIAM

SENSEI SIDNEY (SHLOMO) FAIGE
1932–2007

A great human being, a real master.

Acknowledgments

Without the support of my parents and family, my martial arts career would have been much poorer. Without their encouragement, this book would never have come to life. To my mother and late father; to Aviva, the love of my life; and to Nimrod and Dotan, my incredible children: thank you!

A special thanks to Sensei Roy Faige, co-author on this work, for his advice, support and help. And for a life-long friendship!

Thank you to Shay Levy, Gil Faige, Tamir Carmi, Itay Leibovich, Nimrod and Dotan De Bremaeker and Ziv Faige, who posed for the photos. And to Guli Cohen, a fantastic photographer and so special human being.

Many masters have influenced my martial arts career. I should mention among many, of course Sensei Faige, but also Maitre Ravinet, Maitre Decantor, Maitre Caronia, Maitre Calmette, Sensei Myazaki, Sensei Sawada and Sensei Harada. I also owe a lot to many training partners along the years. I should mention among so many: Of course the five fighting sons of Sensei Faige, but also Yannick Pierrard, Serge Coucke, Rui Monteiro, and my brother Luc De Bremaeker.

Contents

Foreword

I started Judo at age 6, and have never stopped training since. In the early Sixties, Judo was *the* mysterious Oriental art which would allow you to vanquish a stronger opponent by using his own power against him. It was the beginning of the discovery of Oriental martial arts by the general Western public.

But about seven years later, I saw, by accident, my first Bruce Lee movie, and it was like a revelation! That was the martial art I wanted to be proficient in. The success of the Bruce Lee movies, and the ensuing kung fu phenomenon, are testimony to the fascination that the discovery of such fighting proficiency instilled into the Western masses. In my humble opinion, a great part of the interest it aroused lay in the sophisticated kicking moves that the bulk of the fight scenes consisted of. Kicking in fights was a novelty of sorts in Western culture, and it explains, in my opinion, the big martial arts boom of the Seventies and Eighties. I, for my part, then decided to look for a karate school, and took up Shotokan karate.

Shotokan karate is a very traditional martial art, very well organized didactically, and emphasizes hard training and basic work. However, it is not an art known for extravagant kicks, which was somewhat disappointing to me. Nevertheless, I never stopped practicing Shotokan, or a Shotokan-derived style, during all my athletic years.

In parallel to my basic and uninterrupted Shotokan training, I decided to explore other arts, a few years at a time, as opportunities arose. During all my career, I practiced seriously, among others, and relevant to this work: karatedo of the Wado-ryu, Shotokai and Kyokushinkai schools, full-contact karate, taekwondo, savate-boxe francaise and two styles of jujutsu. Less intensively, I also practiced capoeira and the soft styles of kung fu. This, all together, allowed me to have the basis for my own personal research and individual training into the art of kicking.

In 1983, my quest took me to the Shi-Heun school of Sensei Sidney Faige. Shi-Heun is a Shotokan-based style, with intertwined Judo practice, which emphasizes extreme conditioning, total fighting under various rules sets and the personal quest for what works best for oneself. It is basically a precursor to the much later phenomena of Mixed Martial Arts. A winning combination, no doubt, and it is no wonder that the direct disciples of sensei Faige roamed the tournament scene undefeated for years.

Points tournament fighting was mainly WUKO (World Union of Karate Organizations) those days, and a rather dull affair. It generally consisted of two competitors jumping up and down, waiting for the other to take the initiative, so as to be able to stop-reverse punch him. I think this situation did a lot to hurt the standing of Japanese karate, and it is to me no wonder that taekwondo became an Olympic sport, and karate not (yet). Uncharacteristically, when my name was called for a fight in one of those tournaments, there was spontaneous applause from the spectators, as they knew they were going to see some kicking, often spectacular. My point is: That is what people came for, and that is what they expected from "martial arts."

As mentioned, it is my strong belief that kicking is a big part of what made the appeal of Oriental martial arts. It is also my belief that kicking is more efficient than punching! I know this is going to make a few people jump up in disagreement, and that there has always been an ongoing debate about the subject. Therefore, I'll qualify my opinion: I strongly believe that kicking is more efficient than punching, but *proficiency takes much more work*. When put this way, I hope there will be much less opposition.

Kicking is more efficient than punching:

- because of the longer range;
- because the muscles of the leg are much more powerful than those of the arms;
- because kicking targets, unlike punching, go from the toes up to the head;
- because of the surprise effect: People always expect less to be kicked than punched.

Opponents of this axiom will point out that kicks are inherently slower than punches, can be jammed because they only work at long ranges, and cannot be delivered from many positions. It is my experience that, after a lot of dedicated work, kicks can be as swift as punches, and can be used at all ranges and from all positions.

During all my training years, I invested a lot of time, personal drilling and research in the kicking arts. I tried all training tips and tried out all kicks variations in actual fights and tournaments, and I so developed my personal kicking style. In my years of research, I came across many treatises, but very few actually dedicated to kicking. The few works I found about kicking, although generally very good, were usually style-restricted, or unorganized. As I never found the kind of book I would have liked to have when I started my martial arts career, I decided to write it myself: There has never been an attempt, to the best of my knowledge, to compile and organize, all the different basic kick types and variations, in order to offer a basis of personal exploration or to serve as a reference work. I will try to achieve this, however imperfectly, and I hope that this work will be built upon to provide the sorely needed basic encyclopedia of the realm of martial arts kicking.

And now, a last word about punching! It is important to emphasize to the reader that the strong views expressed in this foreword are not meant in any way or form to denigrate punching arts. As mentioned, martial arts are a whole with different possible emphases: A complete martial artist should be proficient in punching, kicking, throwing, evading, and more; with his own preferences and particular skills, of course. More than that: There is no kicking without punching proficiency! Punching is necessary for closing the gap, feinting, setting up a kick, following up, and more. This will be clear from most of the applications described in this work. And punching is sometimes the best or the only answer in some situations. I have known some extraordinary punching martial artists, using kicks only as feints and set-ups. On the other hand, great kickers, like Bill "Superfoot" Wallace, were extremely skilled punchers as well! (I remember well, in one of his seminars, doing more push-ups in an hour than in the whole previous month). In other words: well-rounded practice is the key!

A last word before we can proceed with our exploration of the realm of martial arts kicks: I would not want the preceding introduction to be misunderstood as an appeal to always kick and especially high-kick in a fight. Not only is it not suitable for all morphologies and mindsets, but even the best kicker in the world should *not* deliver a high kick just because he *can*! A high kick should be delivered only when and because it is suitable for the fighter's specific situation.

—Marc De Bremaeker

Introduction

This book is not a "how to" book for the neophyte, but a reference work for the experienced martial artist. It presupposes the knowledge of stances, footwork, and concepts of centerline, guards, distance, evasions, and a good technical level in one's chosen style, including kicking. This book is intended as a tool for self-exploration and research about kicking outside one's specific style. Therefore, the description of the different kicks is very succinct and the typical applications are only briefly explained. We rely more on the illustrations to exemplify his point and let the reader expand on their own.

This is also why we have preferred drawings over photographs: The key points can be clearly emphasized in the drawings, when photos can sometimes hide important cues.

The experienced reader will immediately understand that our basic background is Japanese karate. This is unavoidable, but not purposeful. This work tries to be as "style-less" as possible, as its purpose is to bridge across the different schools on the basis of the common immutable principles. We consider the martial arts as an interconnected whole, where styles are just interpretations of some principles and strategies, and their adaptation to certain sets of rules, cultural constraints, or morphologies: It is the same thing, but with different ways to focus on it. It is purposeful that, in the pictures and illustrations, the reader will see technical differences, in order to underline the style-less point of view of the treatise. Sometimes the foot of the standing leg is flat on the floor, as required in traditional Japanese styles, and sometimes the heel is up as in certain deliveries of Korean arts. The biomechanical principles are identical for trained artists and those differences of emphasis are meaningless. This book does not present an axiomatic way to kick! In the same vein, arms during kicking are sometimes close to the body in hermetic guard, and sometimes loose and counterbalancing the kicking move. Hands can be open, or fists tight.

This Japanese background, though, and more precisely Shotokan karatedo, is probably beneficial, as it tends to encourage strong technical work from relatively low stances, which is important for basic description. It also encouraged the organization and classification that we imperfectly attempted.

It has proved very difficult to name and divide the kicks in groups: Many compromises had to be made. We have given the techniques descriptive names in English, whenever possible the most commonly used names. But the more complex and exotic kicks, and the hybrid kicks, have sometimes several different appellations in use, while being difficult to describe. The names given could be therefore disputed by some, and improvements can definitely be made: This is the first time such an exhaustive effort at compilation has been made, and we hope it will be the base for improvement. For the basic kicks common to all styles, we have added the respective original foreign names. Here again, we apologize in advance to the purists of all styles: It is clear that the description of a technique cannot be in all details valid for all styles. For example, the basic front kick is taught differently in Shotokan karate than in taekwondo; And we gave both names to our front kick. This writing license of ours tends to underline the basic common factors and principles in the sea of small nuances of execution. The original foreign names in Japanese or Korean are just there as an indication for further research by the reader. It should also be noted that some techniques have different names in different schools of the same art!

For the more complex or exotic kicks, we have purposely omitted original names. Only when a kick is especially typical of a certain style, did we mention it, as a tribute to the specific school.

We also apologize in advance for the transcription of foreign names, as purists could dispute the way it is done: There are several ways to transcribe foreign sounds, and we have chosen a way arbitrarily.

Our efforts at classification proved even more difficult, and resulted in many arbitrary decisions. Again, we hope that our work will be the basis for many comments, discussions and finally improvements. The way we divided the kicks for easier presentation has no technical importance. It is based on the common way to describe kicks. Moreover, many kicks do belong to two or more categories. We've arbitrarily decided in which of the two or more categories a specific kick should be described, as it suits better the flow of the narrative or the logic specifically presented. A kick belonging to several categories will be presented fully in one, though, it will also be itemized and briefly cited in the other categories it could belong to. This book only covers *basic kicks*. Advanced kicks like flying kicks, ground kicks, feint kicks, stop kicks, low kicks, double kicks and joint kicks are beyond the scope of this work. Moreover, not all possible basic kicks are described for a variety of reasons.

Some kicks have been omitted, as we felt we had to draw the line somewhere. Again the decision was arbitrary, and could be considered as open for discussion. First, the wide range of nuances of given kicks have been omitted—as already mentioned, the same basic kicks are delivered in slightly different ways in all different styles and schools. The small differences come from the different emphasis of each style, and do not alter the basic principles.
We therefore described the kicks in the ways that their own experiences dictate as best, and each reader can adapt it to his own personality.

Second, hybrid kicks variations have been omitted, as the infinite number of intermediate possible deliveries in between two kicks would make this endeavor ridiculous. For example, many possible hybrids of front and roundhouse kicks could be presented here, each one with different levels of emphasis on the "front" side and the "roundhouse" side.

Kicks combinations, and kick-punch combinations are infinite in numbers. Therefore, only the basic and well-known kicks combinations, and those with some relevance, will be presented here.

Knee strikes, although very effective and versatile, will not be presented: For the purpose of this work, they will not be considered as kicks.

Finally, the kicks which we feel are already in the realm of acrobatics and aesthetics have been omitted, and out of the scope of effective martial arts. Some of the over-complex flying kicks of some Korean arts or some acrobatic kicks of capoeira come to mind. This was a judgment call which in no way seeks to denigrate any of those arts: Some of those acrobatic kicks, when performed by very skilled students of these styles, are probably very effective, but still out of the range of feasibility for most martial artists outside of these schools.

The kicks presented in this work are generally presented in a prescribed manner: after a brief general introduction and the description of the kick (mainly by illustrations), the key points to remember for a good execution will be noted. Please remember that the book is intended for conversant martial artists. The relevant targets to be kicked in most applications will be mentioned, although only general targets will be mentioned: The specific and precise vulnerable points are out of the scope of this volume. Following the discussion of targets an example of typical application will be detailed and illustrated. The typical application will generally be, unless irrelevant, a detailed use or set up of the given kick in a tournament-type situation. This will generally be a combination based on alternating different attack angles or/and levels (For example: high-low-high, and/or outside/inside/outside), or the Progressive Indirect Attack principle as it is called by jeet kune do artists. The tactical principle involved will not be detailed or presented systematically though, as it is beyond the scope of this volume. Of course, those applications will also usually be relevant to real life situations and training work. Whenever possible, specific training tips to improve the given kick will be detailed. The specific training section will be brief and will only deal with the very specific characteristics of the kick and the ways to perfect them. Last, and in order to widen the scope of applications, an additional example of the use of the kick will be presented, generally more suitable to a self-defense or mixed martial arts application.

CHAPTER ONE

Front Kicks

The basic front kick is generally the first kick taught to martial arts novices, as it is relatively easy to deliver and a more natural movement than the other kicks. It is therefore the perfect base for the beginner to build upon in order to develop his kicking proficiency. This is where to start your kicking career.

Front kicks in most of their variations are also the perfect kicks for real life situations: being easier to deliver and master, they are appropriate for every level of proficiency while being very safe and effective. Front kicks, in one version or the other, are really the bread and butter of fighting: they are used in combination attacks, as feints, as distance closers, and of course, when mastered, as decisive single attacks.

Many variations of the basic front kick will be presented in this chapter, to allow for most possible dynamic situations in sports or everyday life.

1.1 The Penetrating Front Kick

Mae geri kekomi (Shotokan karate), *Jik tek / Tshe the / Quan bian jiao* (kung fu), *Ahp chagi / Ahp cha tzirugi* (taekwondo), *Bênção* (capoeira), *Gyaku geri* (Shorinji kempo), *Chuong tieu cuoc / Truc cuoc* (viet vo dao)

General

This front kick is very powerful and very fast. We named it "penetrating," to differentiate it from the upward front kick described later in the chapter. Unlike the upward front kick, the penetrating front kick travels in parallel to the floor into the target. On the other hand, the upward front kick strikes targets like the chin or groin from below. The skilled martial artist is well aware of the fact that there are many variations between the two extremes and front kicks can be a combination of both the upward and forward movement. But only the two extremes of the range will be described in this work.

It is interesting to note that, because of the rules of competition, front kicks are not practiced in savate-boxe française. Fighting in savate drives home the point about how important the front kick really is.

On the other hand, the front kick is probably the most-used kick in traditional karate katas, although much more in its upward form. The penetrating aspect of the kick is, for example, emphasized in the traditional *Unsu* kata of the Shotokan-ryu style. The relevant kata sequence is presented in the kata excerpt shown in Figures 1.1.1 through 1.1.5, as an illustration of the concept of penetration.

Figure 1.1.1

Figure 1.1.2

Figure 1.1.3

Figure 1.1.4

Figure 1.1.5

This kata excerpt shows a combination that includes a penetrating front kick.

The kick is usually delivered to connect with the ball of the foot (In Japanese: *tshusoku*, *koshi*, *josokutei*). Sometimes the whole plant of the foot is used. In some styles, the stiffened toes (In Japanese: *tsumasaki*) are used against very specific anatomical points, for example the *Sokusen geri* of Uechiryu karate, or ninjutsu kicks.

In Wado-ryu karate, there are even names for combinations including the ubiquitous front kick. For example, *Kette Jun-tsuki*: high lunge punch, rear leg front kick and front jab while landing forward (See Figures 1.1.6 through 1.1.8)

Figure 1.1.6

Figure 1.1.7

Figure 1.1.8

The ubiquitous front kick is often included in combinations such as the *Kette Jun-tsuki* combination (high lunge punch, rear leg front kick and front jab while landing forward) shown here.

Description

In fighting stance (see Figure 1.1.9), raise the knee of the back leg as quickly and as high as possible (Figure 1.1.10). Extend the leg in such a way that the foot travels directly to target from the chambered position, nearly in a motion parallel to the floor (Figure 1.1.11). Nearing the impact, the hips push forward for the penetrating effect. Immediately after the impact with the ball of the foot, the leg is retracted as quickly as possible into the chambered position with the knee high, as a protection. The foot is then lowered either (a) in front, in fighting stance (Figure 1.1.12), or (b) back where it came from (Figure 1.1.13).

Figure 1.1.9

Figure 1.1.10

Figure 1.1.11

Figure 1.1.12

Figure 1.1.13

These images show the execution of a penetrating front kick, with the kicking leg optionally lowered to the front or the rear.

Figures 1.1.14 through 1.1.20 show the execution of the kick, with the kicking leg lowered in front.

Figure 1.1.14

Figure 1.1.15

Figure 1.1.16

Figure 1.1.17

Figure 1.1.18

Figure 1.1.19

Figure 1.1.20

These images show the execution of a penetrating front kick, with the kicking leg lowered in front.

Figures 1.1.21 through 1.1.26 show the execution of the kick while landing back.

Figure 1.1.21

Figure 1.1.22

Figure 1.1.23

Figure 1.1.24

Figure 1.1.25

Figure 1.1.26

These images show the execution of a penetrating front kick, with the kicking leg lowered back to the starting position.

Key Points

- The foot you're standing on must be flat on the floor to offer support for the forward hip movement (Figure 1.1.27).
- To avoid knee injury, do not overextend the kicking leg.
- Lift your toes when kicking: the kick connects with the ball of the foot (Figure 1.1.28).

Figure 1.1.27
Keep the foot that you're standing on flat for best support.

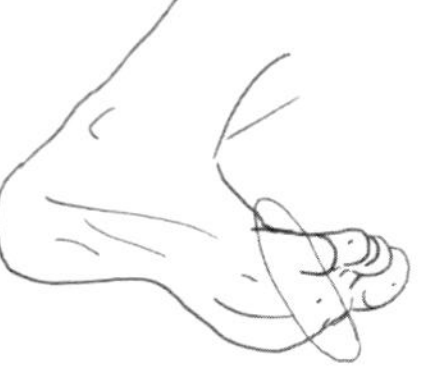

Figure 1.1.28
The parts of the foot that make contact during the penetrating front kick.

Targets

The targets include the solar plexus, the groin, and the ribs. The throat could be a worthy target, but a more difficult one to achieve. Because of the penetrating direction, the kick is rarely used higher than the solar plexus.

An interesting target is the front of the thigh of the rear leg of an opponent in fighting stance in front of you. The target is further away than the trunk, which allows for a full development of the kick if you are close. The kick will cause temporary paralysis of the leg and extreme pain extending to the hip joint. This is a special technique of Sensei Faige, of the Shi Heun style (See Figures 1.1.29 through 1.1.32)

Figure 1.1.29

Figure 1.1.30

Figure 1.1.31

Figure 1.1.32

These images show an example of targeting the front of the thigh of the rear leg of an opponent in opposite fighting stance in front of you.

Typical Application

From fighting stance (Figure 1.1.33), lunge forward with a high punch toward your opponent's eyes. Try to catch or control the hand he'll instinctively raise to block, or at least leave your hand in front of his face (Figure 1.1.34). Kick in the lower abdomen, while keeping control of his forward hand. If you have caught it, pull the hand toward you while delivering the penetrating kick (Figure 1.1.35). Finish up, while lowering the kicking leg forward, by punching his face with your (now) lead hand (Figure 1.1.36).

Figure 1.1.33

Figure 1.1.34

Figure 1.1.35

Figure 1.1.36

These images show a typical application of the penetrating front kick.

Specific Training

- Kick above a chair placed in front of you, with the seat toward you (Figures 1.1.37 and 1.1.38).
- Tie a belt just below the knee of the standing leg, hold parallel to the floor while blocking the path of the kicking leg. This will force you to lift the knee high first, before being able to develop the kick (Figures 1.1.39 through 1.1.41).

Figure 1.1.37 Figure 1.1.38

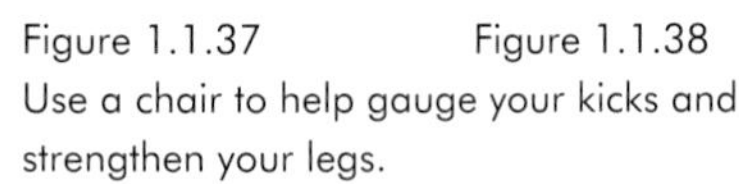
Use a chair to help gauge your kicks and strengthen your legs.

Figure 1.1.39

Figure 1.1.40

Figure 1.1.41

Have a partner help you use a belt to train yourself to lift your knee high before delivering a kick.

- Squat and kick. And repeat with other leg. Then repeat (See Figures 1.1.42 through 1.1.47).

Figure 1.1.42

Figure 1.1.43

Figure 1.1.44

Figure 1.1.45

Figure 1.1.46

Figure 1.1.47

The squat and kick exercise will help develop explosive strength in the legs.

- Kick over a partner on all fours in front of you, to force you to high chamber the leg (Figures 1.1.48 and 1.1.49).
- Practice the kick with exaggerated chambering: hit your own backside with the heel of the kicking foot before getting to chambered position and kick, in one continuous smooth movement.
- Practice the whole *Unsu* kata, or the sequence illustrated in Figures 1.1.1 through 1.1.5.
- Lift the knee explosively to chambered position, then lower. Perform in front of partner doing the same, and try to beat him at speed.
- In chambered position, resist a partner's downward push to the count of ten (isometrics). See Figure 1.1.50.
- Kick the padded target cushion held by a partner (Figures 1.1.51 and 1.1.52).

Figure 1.1.48

Figure 1.1.49

Kick over a partner to train yourself to raise your knee high before kicking.

Figure 1.1.50

Isometric exercise with a partner to strengthen the leg.

Figure 1.51

Figure 1.52

Kick a padded target to develop impact strength.

Self-defense

This is an extremely powerful kick, especially in a self-defense situation with shoes on.

Throw keys, wallet or any object toward the eyes of the assailant (Figure 1.1.53) and kick groin, abdomen or ribs when he instinctively lifts his hands (Figure 1.1.54). Lower back the kicking leg and let the foot rebound on the floor (Figure 1.1.55) for the launch of an *upward* front kick to his bent-over head (Figure 1.1.56).

Figure 1.1.53

Figure 1.1.54

Figure 1.1.55

Figure 1.1.56

Throw an item to distract your opponent, and then rapidly launch two successive front kicks.

When a penetrating front kick scores to the groin or the abdomen, it will always result in your opponent bending forward to alleviate the pain, and therefore setting him up for specific follow-ups. Figures 1.1.57 through 1.1.64 show one possible follow-up action.

Figure 1.1.57

Figure 1.1.58

Figure 1.1.59

Figure 1.1.60

Figure 1.1.61

Figure 1.1.62

Figure 1.1.63

Figure 1.1.64

The use of an overhead sacrifice throw as a follow-up to a penetrating front kick to the lower abdomen delivered as a "timed" counter to a lunge punch.

Figure 1.1.65

Figure 1.1.66

Examples of the penetrating front kick. (R. Faige)

1.2 The Upward Front Kick

Mae geri keage (Shotokan karate, *Kin geri*, if directed to groin), *Teng toi* (kung fu), *Ahp Chagi-Ahp Cha pusugi* (taekwondo), *Sepak sekop* (pencak silat), *Kinteki sokushi geri* (ninjutsu), *Ponteira* (capoeira)

Figure 1.2.1
A demonstration of the upward front kick.

General

As already mentioned, the upward front kick hits the target from down under. As such, it is shorter and less powerful than the penetrating version. The groin being a preferred target, it is, however, a very effective kick in self-defense situations. The upward front kick to the groin, given with the front of the ankle joint, is called in Japanese karate: *Kin geri*, *Kogan geri* or *Kinteki geri*, and is learned as a specific kick, on top of the regular upward front kick (*Mae geri keage*) delivered to all other targets (See Figure 1.2.1).

The differences between upward and penetrating are clear from the comparison of the arrows in Figures 1.2.2 and 1.2.3. As mentioned before, there is an endless range of nuances between those two extremes, and the martial artist will choose the right amount of "upward-ness" and "penetration" that suits him and the particular situation.

Figure 1.2.2 Figure 1.2.3
Notice the difference between the penetrating front kick (left) and the upward front kick (right).

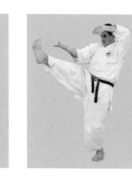

The upward front kick is the most common kick to be found in traditional karate katas. This kick is presented in the kata excerpt shown in Figures 1.2.4 through 1.2.8, from a basic Shotokan karate form.

Figure 1.2.4

Figure 1.2.5

Figure 1.2.6

Figure 1.2.7

Figure 1.2.8

This kata excerpt includes an upward front kick.

Description

Lift the knee of the back leg high into the same chambered position (Figure 1.2.9), but this time, extend the leg naturally from below (Figure 1.2.11). As soon as the target is hit, with the ball or the top of the foot (*Kin geri*—karate), retract to the chamber position (Figure 1.2.12) and lower the leg in front or back. The push of the hips is much less pronounced in this kick than in the penetrating one, but the leg extension and retraction are more "whippy."

Figure 1.2.9

Figure 1.2.10

Figure 1.2.11

Figure 1.2.12

These images show the execution of an upward front kick.

Figures 1.2.13 and 1.2.14 show the use of the kick to hit the armpit of a hand you control.

Figure 1.2.13 Figure 1.2.14
These images show the execution of an upward front kick to the armpit.

Key Points

- The upward movement should not tempt you to lift the body before and during the kick, so as to retain power and avoid telegraphing your intentions.
- The target is hit with the ball of the foot (for the chin or armpit) or the upper part of the foot/ankle (for the groin). See Figure 1.2.15.

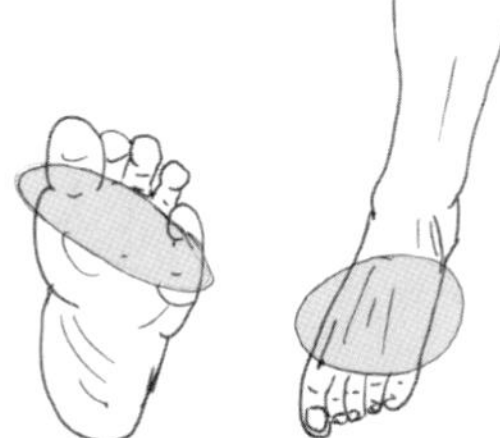

Figure 1.2.15
The striking areas of the foot used in the upward front kick.

Targets

The targets for the upward front kick are the chin, armpit (Figure 1.2.16), and groin.

The face and the abdomen are valid targets when the opponent is bent forward, for example from a previous strike or an armlock.

Figure 1.2.16
An upward front kick to the armpit.

Typical Application

No man on earth is able to keep his cool with something on a direct trajectory to his groin! This is true in competition as well as in real life. Use this subconscious instinctive reaction to get your opponent to lower his guard for a double punch: from an opposite stance (Figure 1.2.17), fire a real and clear upward front kick toward your opponent's groin (Figure 1.2.18). Jab to his face as soon as his hands start to go down, even if only slightly, while lowering your leg forward (Figure 1.2.19). And then throw a powerful reverse punch (cross). See Figure 1.2.20. Remember: the simplest things work best! After your reverse punch, you can hook his front leg and pull it to his forward (*Ko uchi gari*—judo) to throw him to the floor (Figure 1.2.21).

Figure 1.2.17 Figure 1.2.18 Figure 1.2.19 Figure 1.2.20 Figure 1.2.21
A simple but very effective combination starting with an upward front kick to the groin.

Specific Training

- Kick with a chair (with the back turned to the side) in front of you to force high knee chambering (Figures 1.2.22 and 1.2.23).
- Same over-a-belt-kicking than penetrating front kick.
- Squat and kick.
- Practice the whole *Heian Yodan* kata, or the sequence described in the kata excerpt shown earlier in this discussion.
- Practice on a padded target pad held by a partner to simulate armpit or chin height (See Figure 1.2.24).

Figure 1.2.22 Figure 1.2.23
Use a chair to improve your chamber height.

Figure 1.2.24
Kick at a padded target to practice full strength strikes.

Self-defense

An assailant grabs your sleeve from the side (Figure 1.2.25). Immediately immobilize his fingers by pushing his grabbing hand onto your arm, while circling his grabbing hand from the outside with your grabbed arm (Figure 1.2.26). Do not let go of his hand and use your whole body while completing the circle around his hand and getting him bent-over in a wrist lock (Figure 1.2.27). As soon as he bends over, kick him in the face with an upward front kick (Figure 1.2.28).

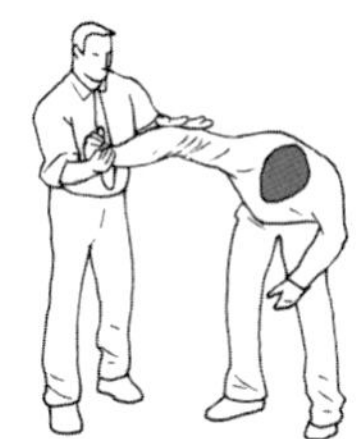

Figure 1.2.25 Figure 1.2.26 Figure 1.2.27 Figure 1.2.28
Turn an opponent's grab against him by using leverage on the grabbing arm to bend him over into position for an upward front kick to the face.

1.3 The Straight-leg Upward Kick

Mae keage (karate), *Ahp ohlligi* (taekwondo), *Ponteira esticada* (capoeira)

General

This kick is not very much used in most Japanese styles, as it is more difficult to place effectively than the regular upward front kick. Flexible fighters will like it, though, and it can be a very surprising kick. It is naturally followed by, or can be considered as the set-up for, the downward heel (hatchet) kick (See Chapter 6, Section 5).

This kick is very much practiced in most styles as an exercise for warm-up, and for flexibility work to improve general kicking performance.

Description

From the fighting stance (Figure 1.3.1), bring the rear leg forward while keeping it totally straight (Figure 1.3.2). Lift it in front at maximum speed, aiming for the chin (Figure 1.3.3).

Figure 1.3.1 Figure 1.3. 2 Figure 1.3.3
These images illustrate the execution of a straight-leg upward kick.

The power of the kick comes from the centrifugal force. It is useful to slightly pivot on the standing foot. Opening the foot outwards, like for roundhouse kicks, opens the hip and allows more speed and flexibility. Usually the leg is brought down as a downward hatchet kick on any target available (head, shoulder, arm). In training, lower straight leg forward or back to rear position, as of the start. The trajectory of the kick is clearly shown in Figure 1.3.4. Compare the straight leg-upward kick to the other front kicks (Figures 1.3.5 and 1.3.6).

Figure 1.3.4 Figure 1.3. 5 Figure 1.3.6
The image on the left shows how your straight leg-upward kick should move upward toward the opponent's chin.
Compare this movement to the two kicks illustrated on the right: the penetrating front kick and the upward front kick, respectively.

Key Points

Speed is the key to the success of this kick.

Targets

Targets are the chin or face, if the opponent is tilted forward.

Typical Application

This kick can be used as a counter for a roundhouse kick for example, utilizing the forward momentum of the attacking opponent. Start the upward motion of the leg when the roundhouse connects with your block. Your kick will contact with his chin while he chambers the knee and is carried forward by his momentum. See Figures 1.3.7 through 1.3.9.

Figure 1.3.7 Figure 1.3. 8 Figure 1.3.9
Counter your opponent's intent to deliver a roundhouse kick by intervening with a swift straight leg-upward kick.

Specific Training

Front splits: flexibility is the secret of speed, especially for straight leg kicks.

Self-defense

This is the perfect kick to hit an opponent bending over from a previous kick or punch. Because of the centrifugal force of the kick, even if the opponent manages to place his hands before his face, he will be hitting himself in the face from the speed of the upward kick. For example, when attacked by an overhead strike with a stick (Figure 1.3.10), evade with a small outside step (Figure 1.3.11), while keeping the back hand up for control. Kick the opponent groin from the outside with a small roundhouse kick (Chapter 3, Section 2). See Figure 1.3.12. Retract the leg while he doubles over (Figure 1.3.13), and launch a straight leg upward kick with the same leg, to his face (Figure 1.3.14). If possible, use your hand to keep or drive his head down toward the rising kick.

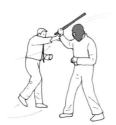

Figure 1.3.10 Figure 1.3.11 Figure 1.3.12 Figure 1.3.13 Figure 1.3.14
Evade your opponent's strike and move him into position for a devastating two-kick combination.

1.4 The Front Leg Front Kick

Surikonde mae geri (Shotokan karate), *Oi geri* / *Okuri geri* (Shorinji-ryu kenkokan), *Ahp-bal ahp-Chagi* (taekwondo), *Jun geri* (Shorinji kempo, Sankukai karate)

General

Front leg kicking is a fast way to close the distance with the opponent, but it results in less powerful kicks. All kicks can be made with the front leg, and the description here is relevant to all kicks described: penetrating, upward, straight leg, and more.

Front leg kicking can be used statically, as a stop-kick, or it can be used sliding toward the opponent. The front leg stop-kick is beyond the scope of this book, so we will talk here only about the sliding front leg kick. Figures 1.4.1 through 1.4.4 show an example of the static front leg front kick to stop an opponent followed by a "shoot" (Lunge for a double leg takedown).

Figure 1.4.1 Figure 1.4.2 Figure 1.4.3 Figure 1.4.4
The static front leg front kick can be used to stop an opponent long enough for you to execute a "shoot."

Description

Bring the back leg forward without moving the upper body, so as not to telegraph your slide (Figure 1.4.6). The legs are slightly crossed. You then lift the formerly front leg (that was slightly behind—see Figure 1.4.7) with the knee high, and you now develop the kick just as you would if it was a rear leg kick (Figure 1.4.8).

Figure 1.4.5 Figure 1.4.6 Figure 1.4.7 Figure 1.4.8
These images illustrate the execution of a front leg front kick.

As you become proficient with the kick, you can begin to proceed as shown in Figures 1.4.9 through 1.4.11. The rear leg does not cross forward anymore, but the back foot comes forward and sort of replaces the front foot. This is made possible because the front knee lifts a few milliseconds before the back leg lands.

Figure 1.4.9 Figure 1.4.10 Figure 1.4.11
As your footwork improves, the execution of this kick will change to the configuration shown above.

Figures 1.4.12 through 1.4.14 show the front leg front kick used statically, after a backward evasion into cat stance (*Neko ashi dachi* in karate), where the front leg is largely free of body weight.

Figure 1.4.12 Figure 1.4.13 Figure 1.4.14
These images show a static front leg front kick being launched from a cat stance.

Key Points

- All key points of back leg front kicks are relevant here.
- It is imperative to keep the upper body free of any movement, especially upward movement.
- The feet are moving very close to the floor—there is no jumping or hopping; only sliding.

Targets

The targets for the front leg front kick include the solar plexus, ribs, and groin.

Typical Application

Again, the simplest things work best! Lunge with jab toward your opponent's eyes (Figure 1.4.15) and keep your hand there a few seconds to block his vision, while replacing your front foot with the rear one (Figure 1.4.16). Lift the knee and kick the open ribs with the front foot (Figure 1.4.17). This is a serious kick, but you can finish the combination with a power roundhouse from the other leg (Figure 1.4.18).

Figure 1.4.15 Figure 1.4.16 Figure 1.4.17 Figure 1.4.18
Block your opponent's vision while you shift your feet, and follow up with a two-kick combination.

The front kick, especially when delivered with the front leg, often causes a push-away of the opponent. One of the preferred follow-ups in these cases is the flying knee strike to the body or the head, as presented in Figures 1.4.19 through 1.4.22.

Figure 1.4.19

Figure 1.4.20

Figure 1.4.21

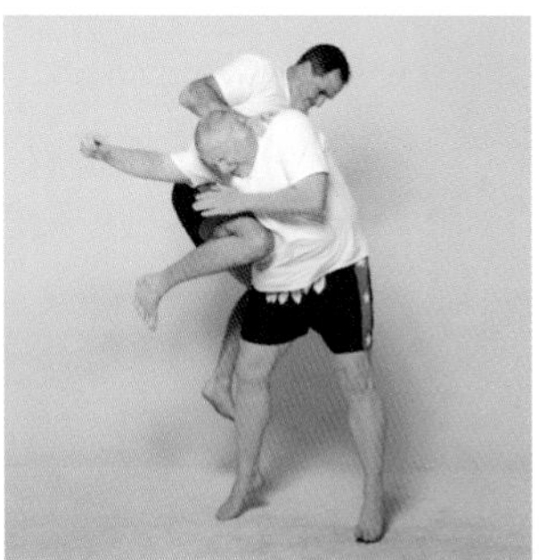
Figure 1.4.22

A flying knee strike follow up to a front kick allows you to keep up the pressure on your opponent after the force of your initial kick pushes him backward.

Specific Training

- In front of a mirror, check for the elimination of upper body movement and head height bobbing.
- Mark the position of the front leg on the floor and do the kick while trying longer and longer slides for reach.

Self-defense

Suppose your opponent has practiced martial arts, and is attacking you with high roundhouse kicks. Open yourself with a fake half jab, to lure him into another one. When he chambers the leg for his next roundhouse, hop forward while lifting the knee and replace your lead hand in protection (Figure 1.4.24). Kick his groin with a front leg/upward front kick, while he delivers the high kick that leaves him unprotected (Figure 1.4.25). Hit him with your lead hand when landing, with a palm strike to the nose for example (Figure 1.4.26).

Figure 1.4.23

Figure 1.4.24

Figure 1.4.25

Figure 1.4.26

Stop an onslaught of roundhouse kicks with a front leg front kick, and follow up with a strike from your lead hand.

1.5 The Side Front Kick

Yoko geri (Wado-ryu karate), *Yoko sokugyacku geri kekomi* (ninjutsu)

General

This is an important variation of the front kick, which is practiced in the Wado-ryu style of karate, a style that emphasizes hip movements, evasions and dodging. This is simply a front kick, penetrating or upward (or other), performed together with a turn of the hips. At full kick extension, the upper body does not face the opponent but is perpendicular to him (Figure 1.5.1). This allows for greater penetration, while giving less target surface area for the opponent's retaliation. It also allows kicking while evading an incoming kick or strike to the body's centerline. It's interesting to note that

Figure 1.5.1

At full kick extension, your upper body is perpendicular to your opponent.

in the katas of the Wado-ryu style corresponding to a specific Shotokan kata, the side kick is basically this "side front kick," when the Shotokan kata sports a "real" side kick.

It is also interesting to note that a variation of this kick is present in the classical tai chi chuan sequence: two front kicks, in succession, which are not delivered at centerline, but obliquely at 45 degrees. This is not, of course, totally a side front kick, but half-way. The principles behind these kicks are the same, though. The relevant part of the form—*Fen jiao* or "Split the feet"—is presented in Figures 1.5.2 through 1.5.5.

Figure 1.5.2 Figure 1.5.3 Figure 1.5.4 Figure 1.5.5
This kata excerpt shows a variation of this kick in a classical tai chi chuan sequence.

Description

From the fighting stance (Figure 1.5.6), start by turning the hips while lifting the knee for the kick (Figures 1.5.7 and 1.5.8). Develop the kick just as any front kick type (penetrating, upward, heel), while the hips are already turned sideways to your opponent (Figure 1.5.10).

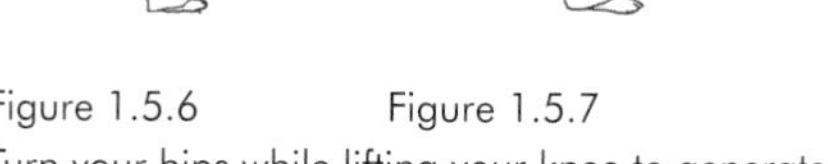

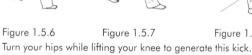

Figure 1.5.6 Figure 1.5.7 Figure 1.5.8 Figure 1.5.9 Figure 1.5.10
Turn your hips while lifting your knee to generate this kick.

The kick can also be practiced from a natural position, as a kick to the side (Figures 1.5.11 through 1.5.13).

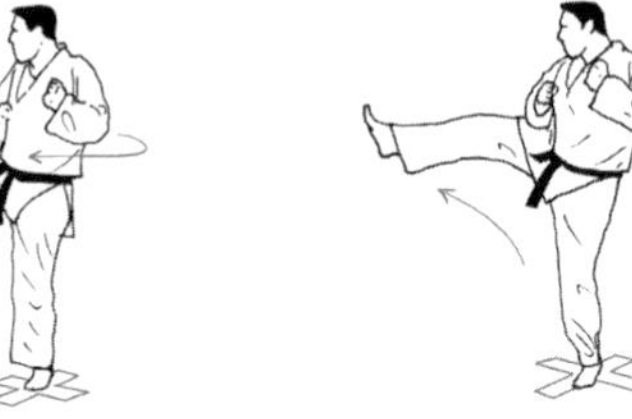

Figure 1.5.11 Figure 1.5.12 Figure 1.5.13
The side front kick, this time launched to the side.

Figures 1.5.14 through 1.5.16 show the use of the kick after an inside evasion from a punch.

Figure 1.5.14 Figure 1.5.15 Figure 1.5.16
The side front kick after an inside evasion from a punch.

Figures 1.5.17 through 1.5.20 show the practice of the kick as a "side" kick.

Figure 1.5.17 Figure 1.5.18 Figure 1.5.19 Figure 1.5.20
The side front kick used as a "side" kick.

Key Points

The hip movement is key, and some pivoting on the foot is needed to allow the motion of the hip.

Targets

The targets for the side front kick include the solar plexus, ribs, and groin.

Typical Application

The advantage of this kick is the simultaneous evading action of the body. While the kick is executed, the body pivots totally to the side and moves out of the line of a linear attack. This is illustrated here on a reverse punch attack (Figures 1.5.21 through 1.5.24), though it is valid for a front hand jab as well. Keep your back hand in guard while you pivot, move out of the line of attack and kick.

Figure 1.5.21 Figure 1.5.22 Figure 1.5.23
Move out of the line of attack while executing the side front kick.

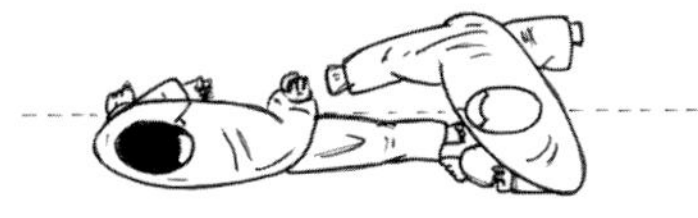

Figure 1.5.24
Overhead view of the side front kick.

Specific Training

- Have a partner hold a long stick pointed to your sternum, in the middle of the body. Execute the kick while evading contact. The stick forces you to turn your hips and rotate your body sideways while kicking. See Figures 1.5.25 through 1.5.27.
- Practice the hip movement in front of a mirror.

Figure 1.5.25 Figure 1.5.26
Have a partner help you practice moving your body out of the line of attack while delivering this kick.

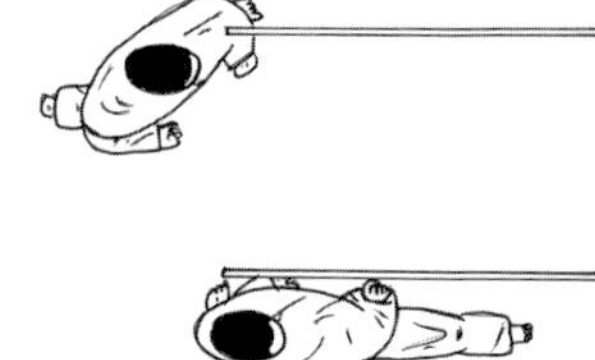

Figure 1.5.27
Overhead view of the side front kick training exercise.

Self-defense

When attacked from the side, especially if there is a second opponent in front of you, move slightly forward to get out of the line of attack and kick naturally to the side, quickly, without having to turn the hips and body. See Figures 1.5.28 through 1.5.30.

Figure 1.5.28 Figure 1.5.29 Figure 1.5.30
This kick is ideal when you are facing off against two attackers, with one approaching from the side.

Figure 1.5.31
The side front kick in counterattack. (R. Monteiro)

1.6 The Heel Front Kick

Mae kakato geri (Shotokan karate), *Tendangan depan* (pencak silat), *Teep trong* (muay thai), Sokugyacku geri (ninjutsu, *Ago kin geri*, if directed to chin)

General

This is simply a penetrating front kick but using the heel to connect. The kick is slightly different, because it requires more hip forward movement to complete. It is therefore more powerful, and ideal as a stop-kick. It is in its stop-kick version that it is very much in use in Thai boxing (muay thai) to keep the opponent at a distance: it is called a *teep* kick by Thai boxers. See Figures 1.6.1 through 1.6.3 for a *teep* stop kick followed by a full front heel kick.

Figure 1.6.1

Figure 1.6.2

Figure 1.6.3

These images show a "teep" stop kick followed by a full front heel kick.

The heel front kick is also a kick for people who instinctively avoid kicking barefoot because they subconsciously fear hurting their toes. Such an inhibition, even if mild, can be enough to subconsciously slow a kick's delivery.

A variation of this kick, with the foot tilted outward, allows for a powerful kick at closer range. Read about the tilted heel front kick in Section 8 of this chapter.

Description

The kick starts like a regular penetrating kick, with a high knee chambering (see Figures 1.6.4 through 1.6.7). The foot then travels even more in parallel to the floor than a regular penetrating kick, as the hips push strongly forward. This kick has a "pushing" feeling to it. The kick connects with the heel, of course (Figures 1.6.8 and 1.6.9).

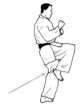

Figure 1.6.4 Figure 1.6.5 Figure 1.6.6 Figure 1.6.7
This kick starts like a regular penetrating kick, but connects with the heel.

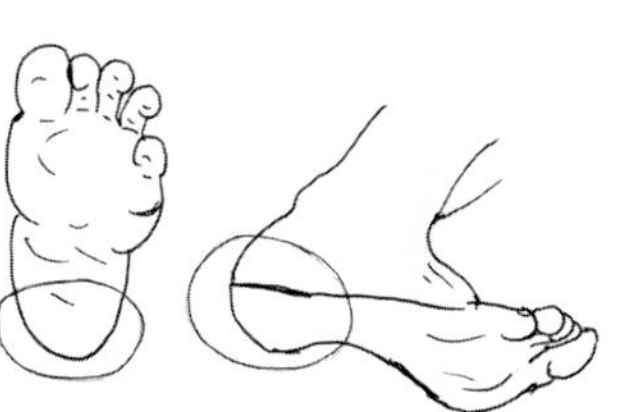

Figure 1.6.8
This image indicates the part of the foot with which to strike.

Figure 1.6.9
This image shows the foot properly making contact with a bag.

Figure 1.6.10 shows the kick at impact. Figures 1.6.11 through 1.6.13 show the application (*bunkai*) of the part of the *Unsu* Shotokan-ryu karate kata (form), where a penetrating heel front kick, while pulling on an arm, is delivered at low level.

Figure 1.6.10
The kick at impact.

Figure 1.6.11 Figure 1.6.12 Figure 1.6.13
A penetrating heel front kick being delivered in conjunction with an arm pull.

Key Points

- Strongly lift the toes and foot (Figure 1.6.14).
- The hips must be very forcefully pushed forward.

Targets

The targets for the heel front kick include the solar plexus, ribs, and groin.

Figure 1.6.14
The kick at impact.

This kick, because of the way it's done, also allows kicks to the head (See Figure 1.6.15 for a high front heel stop-kick).

Figure 1.6.15
A high front heel stop-kick.

Typical Application

Attack your opponent's front leg with a strong outside sweep kick that will put him off-balance and move his front foot toward his inside (Figure 1.6.16). Raise the knee into chambered position, immediately from the sweep impact, without touching the floor (Figure 1.6.17). Your opponent has now his back partly turned to you. Develop the front heel kick into his lower back (Figure 1.6.18). This is a very dangerous technique, which can damage the spine or kidneys—practice carefully.

Figure 1.6.16 Figure 1.6.17 Figure 1.6.18
A front heel kick to the spine or kidneys can be very dangerous—practice carefully.

Specific Training

- Kick over the chair with the back of seat close to you (Figure 1.6.19 and 1.6.20).
- Kick the bag with the heel at different heights: lower abdomen, chest, and face.
- Kick a padded target held by a partner: kick for penetrating power (See Figures 1.6.21 through 1.6.23).

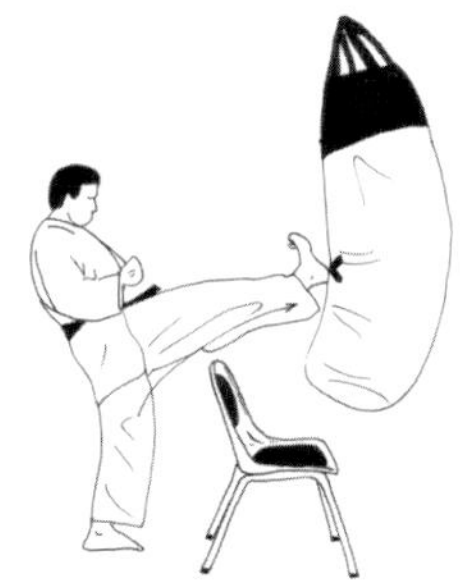

Figure 1.6.19 Figure 1.6.20
Use a chair to help train yourself to chamber the kick at the correct level.

Figure 1.6.21 Figure 1.6.22 Figure 1.6.23
Kick a pad held by a partner to develop penetrating power.

Self-defense

As soon as an assailant takes hold of your front wrist to control you (Figure 1.6.24), front heel kick with your back leg to his solar plexus (Figure 1.6.25), while pulling your arm (and therefore your assailant) toward you. It should be enough, but you can then have your kicking foot rebound on the ground for a forward knee strike (*Hiza geri*—karate) to his bent-over head as you also pull downward with your hands (Figure 1.6.27).

Figure 1.6.24 Figure 1.6.25 Figure 1.6.26 Figure 1.6.27

A front heel kick to the solar plexus should disable your opponent sufficiently, but you may choose to follow up with a knee strike to the head to eliminate any possibility of a continued threat.

1.7 The Hopping Front Kick

General

This is a regular rear-leg front kick, of any type, with a forward hop of the standing leg while the knee is up and the kick is developing. This allows for more distance to be covered while the kick is already being delivered. "Hopping" is somewhat misleading, because the movement is forward and not upward. This is a very useful way to deliver the front kick, especially when confronting an opponent who retreats when attacked.

Description

The rear knee is lifted just as for a regular front kick. Together with the knee lift and the development of the kick (Figure 1.7.2), a small hopping/sliding step is made forward. But when the foot connects, the standing foot is firmly on the floor (Figure 1.7.3).

Figures 1.7.4 through 1.7.8 show the execution of the kick, with the forward hop after the knee has been chambered. Figures 1.7.9 through 1.7.11 show the advantage of delivering such a kick to a retreating opponent; the gray line clearly shows the length of the hop.

Figure 1.7.1 Figure 1.7.2 Figure 1.7.3

The hopping front kick features a small hopping/sliding step forward before the kick connects.

Figure 1.7.4 Figure 1.7.5 Figure 1.7.6 Figure 1.7.7 Figure 1.7.8

These images show the hopping front kick in action.

Figure 1.7.9 Figure 1.7.10 Figure 1.7.11

The hopping front kick is an ideal way to keep the pressure on a retreating opponent.

A variation of the principle behind this kick is presented in Figures 1.7.12 through 1.7.15: a low kick given to the opponent's knee while putting oneself slightly off-balance forward. The full hop is replaced by some leaning onto the opponent's knee and a small hop into a "shooting" lunge.

Figure 1.7.12

Figure 1.7.13

Figure 1.7.14

Figure 1.7.15

These images show a variation on the hopping front kick principle, with the hops replaced by other tactics.

Key Points

- No body movement upward.
- The sole of the foot stays as close to the floor as possible.
- When the kick connects, the standing foot is firmly planted on the floor.

Targets

Typical targets include the solar plexus, the groin, and the ribs. See the corresponding penetrating front kick (Section 1 of this chapter) for additional details.

Typical Application

The best use of this kick is after tricking your opponent into believing that your front kicks are short, and therefore causing him to "learn" to retreat less when you kick and become overconfident. For example, and maybe after a few other "short" front kicks, deliver a front leg front kick (Figure 1.7.18), where your back leg takes the place of your chambering front leg. Immediately, lower your attacking foot in front (Figure 1.7.19), as far as is safe, and start delivering a long hopping front kick with the rear leg (Figure 1.7.20), covering much more distance than your opponent expects (Figure 1.7.21). Be careful for possible counter attack in between your two kicks. This is a great combination against a "retreater" fleeing back as soon as he discerns a move on your part. And never forget: nobody can run backward as quickly as you can run forward!

Figure 1.7.16

Figure 1.7.17

Figure 1.7.18

Figure 1.7.19

Figure 1.7.20

Figure 1.7.21

After lulling your opponent with a series of short front kicks, deliver a long hopping front kick to break through his defenses.

Specific Training

- Kick the heavy bag from an increasing distance. Mark the floor with your best distance to date and try to beat it next time.
- Repeat kick and hop without lowering the leg. Come back to a high-knee chambered position and repeat. Try twenty repetitions before switching legs.

Self-defense

This is the perfect kick to use on an assailant who is retreating or whom you have pushed away from you. For example: on an arms-free front bear hug, immediately clap your attacker's ears (Figure 1.7.23) and push his head away while kneeing his groin (Figure 1.7.24). Push him away vigorously with a step, from a low stance, to get him to a safe distance (Figure 1.7.25). Then, catch up with him with a penetrating front kick (Figure 1.7.27)—hopping style if necessary! You can follow up with a palm strike to the nose as you land your kicking foot forward (Figure 1.7.28). And then a full power "low kick" straight roundhouse to the outside knee or thigh (Figure 1.7.29).

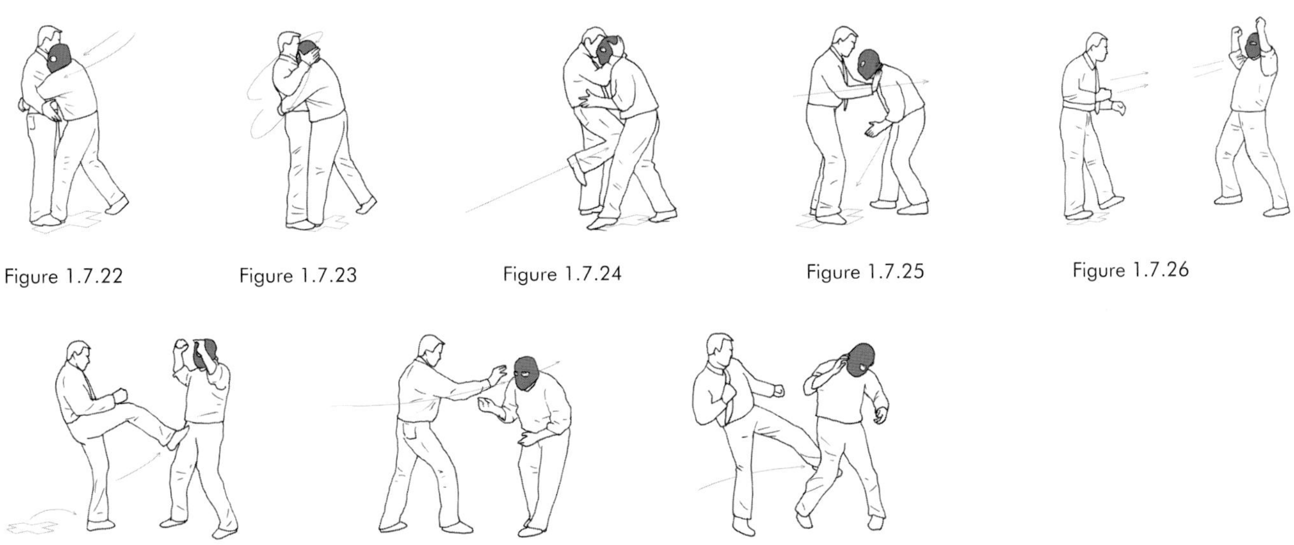

Figure 1.7.22 Figure 1.7.23 Figure 1.7.24 Figure 1.7.25 Figure 1.7.26

Figure 1.7.27 Figure 1.7.28 Figure 1.7.29

After breaking free of a bear hug and putting some room between you and your opponent, quickly turn the tables with a hopping front kick.

1.8 The Tilted Heel Front Kick

Sepak naga (pencak silat)

General

This is a variation of the heel kick, with the foot tilted outward. The kick is delivered just like the regular heel kick, but the tilt allows for power even if the kicking range is shorter. It also allows one to strike without the hindrance of the opponent's guard. The kick is delivered straight, but there is some feeling of "roundness," of going slightly around the guard. This kick is very surprising when well-executed. Its low version, attacking the knees, is very popular in many soft kung fu styles. (See Figure 1.8.1)

Figure 1.8.1
This image depicts the low version of the tilted heel front kick.

Description

While raising the knee, turn the foot outward at the ankle (Figure 1.8.3). Lift the knee high and kick straight, in parallel to the floor, with a goal of going over and around the guard (Figure 1.8.4). As soon as the heel connects deeply, the knee retreats to the chambered position.

Figure 1.8.2 Figure 1.8. 3
Side view of the tilted heel front kick.

Figure 1.8.4

Figure 1.8.5 Figure 1.8.6
Front view of the tilted heel front kick.

Figure 1.8.7
Overhead view of the tilted heel front kick.

Figure 1.8.9 shows the kick being used at low ribs level, and under the guard of the opponent. Figure 1.8.10 is a close-up of the kick at impact.

Figure 1.8.8
This is the correct angle of the foot when delivering the tilted heel front kick.

Figure 1.8.9 Figure 1.8.10
These images show the tilted heel front kick the kick being used at low ribs level.

Key Points

- Lift the knee high
- Strike "penetratingly"

Targets

Mainly the lower ribs. Also the solar plexus, and the higher ribs.

Typical Application

This is the ideal front kick when the distance from your opponent is short; for example, after an attempted lead or rear hand punch. Here is a description of a counter to a lead hand punch to the face: step 45 degrees forward out of the line of attack (Figure 1.8.12) while controlling the punch, and immediately chamber the (now) back leg for a tilted heel front kick (Figure 1.8.13). If possible grab the striking arm for control: pull and keep it up to "open" the ribs for the kick (Figure 1.8.14). You can follow up with an inside sweep of his front leg with your descending kicking foot, while pulling his arm down (Figure 1.8.15).

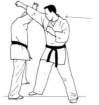

Figure 1.8.11 Figure 1.8.12 Figure 1.8.13 Figure 1.8.14 Figure 1.8.15
Control your opponent's arm and open the ribs for a tilted heel front kick.

Specific Training

Hit the heavy bag, as powerfully as possible, from shorter and shorter distances. This forces you to lift the knee high and kick in a straight fashion.

Self-defense

An assailant tries to get a hold of you and reaches for an arm grab or an arm lock (Figure 1.8.16). As he is close enough to grab you, he is too close for a regular full-fledged kick. Lift the foot immediately while tilting and kick the groin or the ribs exposed by his extended arms (Figure 1.8.17). As you are close, elbow him in the face while lowering the foot, with a full hip twist (*Mawashi empi uchi*—karate). See Figure 1.8.18.

Figure 1.8.16

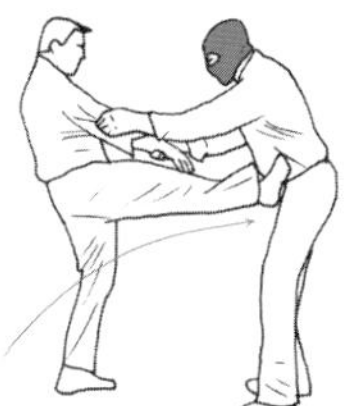
Figure 1.8.17

Figure 1.8.18

Control your opponent's arm and open the ribs for a tilted heel front kick.

1.9 The Outward-tilted Front Kick

Gyacku mawashi geri (Shukokai karate, Shorinji-ryu Kenkokan karate), Inverted hook kick (jeet kune do)

General

This kick is not to be confused with the tilted heel front kick: this is not truly a straight kick but, in some ways, a hybrid of a front kick and an outside crescent kick. This is not an extremely powerful kick, but sneaky and surprising. The surprise effect comes from the way that an opponent, who stands in fighting stance with his profile forward, feels that he is protected from front kicks. Well executed, it is a difficult kick to parry, and has brought this author many points in tournament karate. It is also very effective in real life if targeting the groin of an opponent who feels protected because he stands with his side forward. This is not a feint kick, as the change in trajectory comes at the end of the kicking motion, and there is no intention of provoking a reaction from the opponent. It is told that the technique, inspired by Chinese Arts, was introduced in Japanese karate by Nakayama Masatoshi, direct student of the founder of the Shotokan-ryu, Gishin Funakoshi. In Okinawan karate, it is often referred to as the "Dragon" kick.

Description

Lift the knee swiftly, like any regular front kick (Figure 1.9.2). From the chambered position, extend the leg while mildly changing the trajectory inward and turning the foot outward (Figures 1.9.3 and 1.9.4). The kick connects from inside out. The whole feeling of the kick is that of a front kick: the knee is the axis of the development of the kick, and the target is hit with the ball of the foot. There are many possible nuances in between the two kicks (front and outside crescent), but the change in trajectory and tilt of the foot should be just enough to skirt the obstacles in the way of the target, no more.

Figure 1.9.1

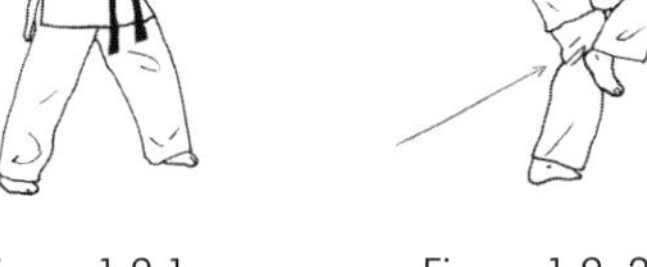
Figure 1.9. 2

Side view of the outward-tilted front kick.

Figure 1.9. 3

Figure 1.9.4

Figure 1.9.5

Figure 1.9.6

Front view of the outward-tilted front kick.

Figure 1.9.8 shows an application of the kick.

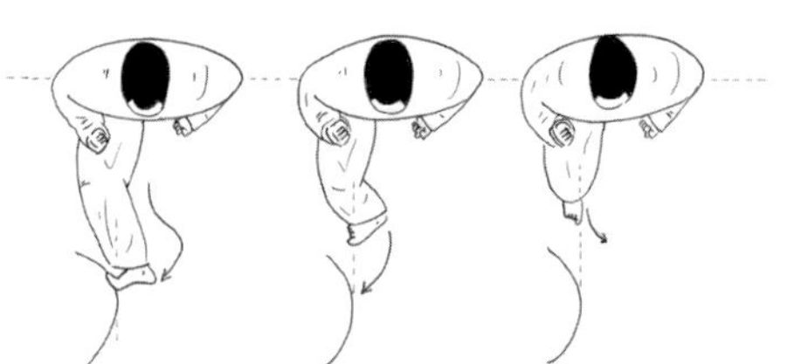

Figure 1.9.7
Overhead view of the outward-tilted front kick.

Key Points

- Up to the chambered knee, this is totally a straight front kick.
- Lift the toes and hit with the ball of the foot.

Targets

This is not as powerful as a penetrating kick, and therefore to be used only on soft targets: solar plexus, groin and lower ribs.

In tournaments, you should try to hit the abdomen below the guard (Figure 1.9.9), as low as possible within the rules framework: usually above the groin, but just below the belt. It is then extremely difficult to block.

Figure 1.9.8
This image depicts an application of the outward-tilted front kick.

Typical Application

This is again an ideal kick to trick an opponent who stands with his side toward you, by establishing a routine that you will break. After a few "regular" front kicks, your opponent will expect more of the same. Deliver a rear leg front kick that he will easily block (Figure 1.9.11). Land your foot back to the rear (Figure 1.9.12), and immediately throw a deep lunge/reverse punch to the outside of his head to force him to over-block and concentrate on his upper outside (Figures 1.9.13 and 1.9.14). The reverse punch will pull the rear leg into an outward-tilted front kick on his lower inside (Figure 1.9.15): kick the lower belly from the unexpected inside, as low as allowed by the rules.

Figure 1.9.9
A well-placed outward-tilted front kick is difficult to block.

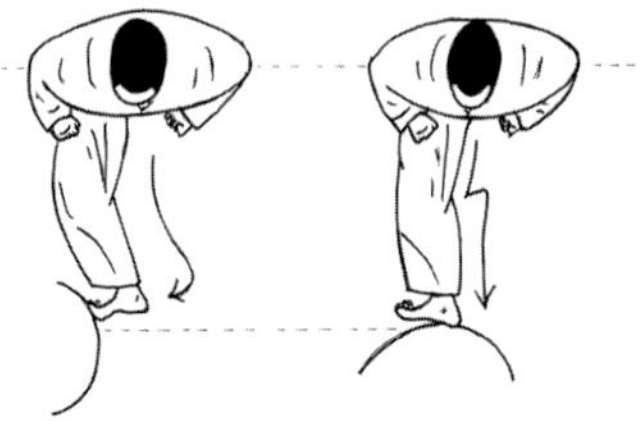

Figure 1.9.10
The overhead view of the outward-tilted front kick (left) compared with the tilted heel front kick (right).

Figure 1.9.11 Figure 1.9.12 Figure 1.9.13 Figure 1.9.14 Figure 1.9.15
Mislead your opponent with easy-to-block kicks followed by punches, then follow up with an outward-tilted front kick.

Specific Training

- Heavy bag kicking: stand in front, but hit the side of the bag, at a mark you have made at belt's level.
- Kick a padded target held sideways by a partner: drill for speed and power (See Figures 1.9.16 through 1.9.18).

Figure 1.9.16 Figure 1.9.17 Figure 1.9.18
Kick a pad held by a partner to develop speed and power.

Self-defense

When attacked by a front kick in matching stances, retreat with the front leg to get just out of range and control the kick. If possible, "pull" the kicking leg a little to cause your opponent to over-extend himself and be slightly off-balance when he lands forward (Figure 1.9.20). Immediately rebound forward with a rear-leg front kick. As he falls with his side facing you, an outward-tilted front kick, preferably to the groin, will catch him unawares (Figure 1.9.21). Chamber the leg back while using the front hand to hit his face and then go down to control his forward arm (Figure 1.9.22). Lower the leg while reverse punching him (Figure 1.9.23).

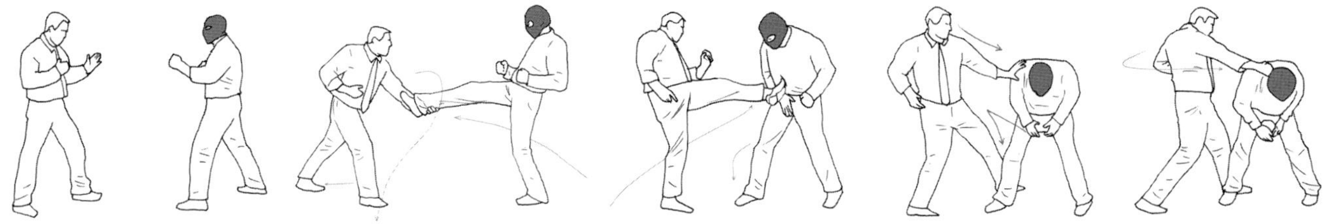

Figure 1.9.19 Figure 1.9.20 Figure 1.9.21 Figure 1.9.22 Figure 1.9.23
Off balance your opponent during his attempt to kick you. Follow up with an outward-tilted front kick, and conclude the encounter with a punch to his head.

1.10 The Inward-tilted Front Kick

General

This is the mirror image of the previous kick: a front kick with a change in trajectory at the end, this time from outside inwards. This kick could be considered a hybrid of the front kick and the well-known small roundhouse kick (Chapter 3, Section 2). Again, this is not a very powerful kick, but it is surprising to an opponent who stands very much on his side and feels protected from straight kicks. Well executed, this is a very effective kick, although the effect of surprise is somewhat less than with the outward tilted front kick: a kick coming from the outside inwards is always more expected than the other way around.

Description

The kick starts with a regular straight high knee chambering (Figure 1.10.2). While developing the kick, the leg tilts mildly outward and the foot turns inward (Figure 1.10.3). The trajectory of the front kick changes slightly to allow the ball of the foot to connect from outside inward. Again, the whole feeling of the kick is of a front kick, and not a roundhouse.

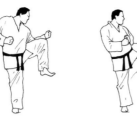

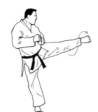

Figure 1.10.1 Figure 1.10. 2
Side view of the inward-tilted front kick.

Figure 1.10. 3

Figure 1.10.4

Figure 1.10.5 Figure 1.10.6
Front view of the inward-tilted front kick.

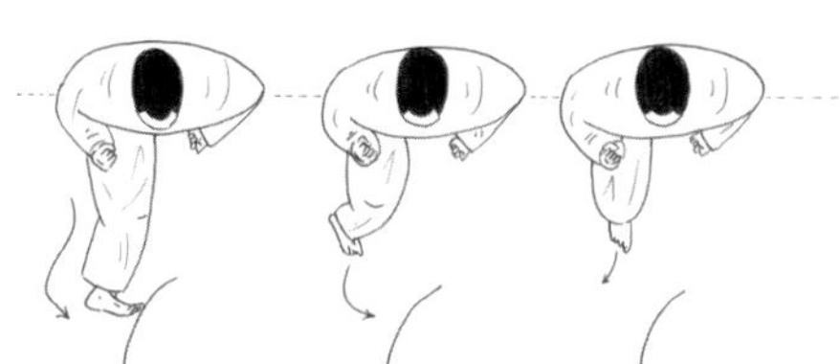

Figure 1.10.7
Overhead view of the inward-tilted front kick.

Figure 1.10.8
This is the correct angle of the foot when delivering the inward-tilted front kick.

Figure 1.10.9 shows an application of the kick.

Key Points

- Lift the knee straight and high like any regular front kick.
- Hit with the ball of the foot.

Targets

Solar plexus, lower ribs, groin.

In point tournaments, you should try to hit as low as possible within the rules: above the groin, but just below or on the belt. Well executed, it is very difficult to block (Figure 1.10.10).

Figure 1.10.9
An inward-tilted front kick.

Typical Application

Again, it is wise, before executing this technique, to get the opponent used to seeing regular front kicks. This technique is especially useful to score against opponents in opposite stance (other foot forward) and who stand very much on their side to give as little target as possible. Lunge with a lead jab/reverse punch combination, but make sure you hit slightly toward the outside of your opponent's head (Figure 1.10.11 and 1.10.12). Make sure you keep your fist on the outside of his face a few seconds more than necessary, while you chamber your back leg for an inward-tilted front kick. Develop the kick while keeping the upper body as relaxed as possible, so as not to betray your intentions. This kick is faster and much less telegraphed than a roundhouse.
Try to hit as low as possible within the rules. See Figure 1.10.14.

Figure 1.10.10
A well-placed inward-tilted front kick is difficult to block.

Figure 1.10.11 Figure 1.10.12 Figure 1.10.13 Figure 1.10.14
Mislead your opponent with easy-to-block kicks followed by punches, then follow up with an inward-tilted front kick.

Specific Training

- Accuracy is very important: mark the heavy bag on the side, at your belt's level.
- Kick fast, while concentrating on bursting out without telegraphing any move.

Self-defense

The inward-tilted front kick is the kick of choice when you find yourself slightly on the outside of your assailant. For example, if grabbed by the hair from behind (Figure 1.10.15), press both hands forcefully on your assailant's hands and pivot under his arm and slightly outside (Figure 1.10. 16). You can release your head because of the lock on your opponent's arm and kick his groin from the outside with an inward-tilted front kick (Figure 1.10.17). Lower the kicking leg and immediately deliver a roundhouse kick, regular or preferably straight-legged, to his exposed back at kidneys level (Figure 1.10.18).

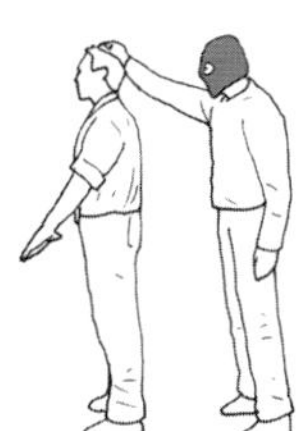

Figure 1.10.15 Figure 1.10.16 Figure 1.10.17 Figure 1.10.18
Use of the kick in a release from a hair grab from behind. Turn the tables on your assailant by controlling his arm and delivering an inward-tilted front kick to his groin.

1.11 The Foot Blade Front Kick

Mae sokuto geri (karate)

General

This is very simply a regular front kick, penetrating or upward, that connects with the blade of the foot (*Sokuto*, or *Ashi gatana* in Japanese) instead of the ball of the foot. It requires turning the foot inward during the development of the kick, but the basics of the kick are just like a regular kick. This is an excellent way to execute the front kick as a stop-kick, as it is quicker than a side kick executed with the same "foot blade." This is also a good technique for those who kick more slowly in a real fight, because of a subconscious fear of hurting their toes.

Description

Chamber the knee as usual with a regular front kick (Figure 1.11.2). Only when the leg is extended and the kick develops do the foot and the hip start to turn inward (Figures 1.11.3 and 1.11.4). The kick connects with the edge (the "blade") of the foot, just as the hips finish their push forward, and the leg retracts to the knee-high chambered position.

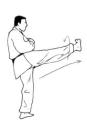

Figure 1.11.1 Figure 1.11. 2 Figure 1.11. 3 Figure 1.11.4
Side view of the foot blade front kick.

Figure 1.11.5 Figure 1.11.6 Figure 1.11.7
Front view of the foot blade front kick.

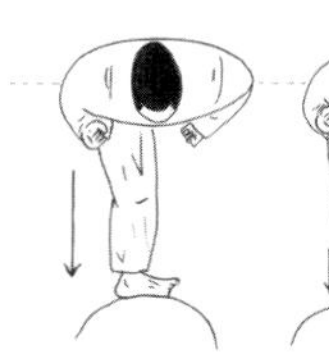
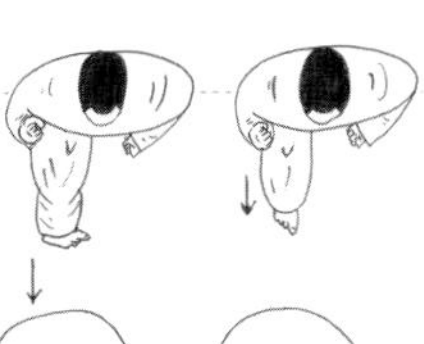

Figure 1.11.8
Overhead view of the inward-tilted front kick.

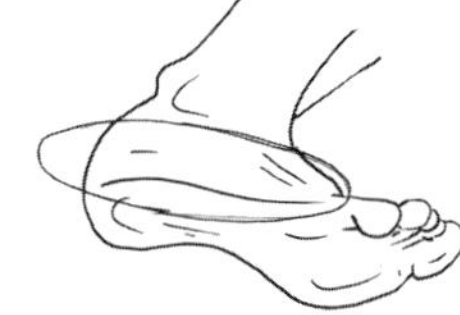

Figure 1.11.9
This is the portion of the foot that makes contact during the execution of a foot blade front kick.

Figure 1.11.10 shows the use of the kick as a stop kick at sternum height.

Figure 1.11.10
This image depicts the execution of a foot blade front kick.

Key Points

- Push the hips forward, like a regular front kick, while turning them simultaneously slightly inward to allow the pivoting of the foot itself
- It is a straight kick.

Targets

It is generally a stop-kick; therefore the lower abdomen and the ribs are prime targets.

The way the kick is delivered allows also for high front kicks, to the throat for example.

Typical Application

As mentioned, this is a typical stop-kick, fast to execute from the front or the rear leg. Figures 1.11.11 through 1.11.13 illustrate the foot blade front kick as a rear-leg stop to a lunge punch.

Specific Training

It is important to familiarize oneself with the kick by hitting a real target, like a heavy bag.

Figure 1.11.11 Figure 1.11.12 Figure 1.11.13
Apply the blade of your foot to stop a lunge punch.

Self-defense

The following images illustrate a front leg stop kick, against a high roundhouse. You are threatened by an assailant with obvious martial arts training. Retreat into a fighting stance to keep your distance (Figure 1.11.14). When your opponent starts developing a high roundhouse kick (Figure 1.11.15), close the distance as needed with a short hop of the rear leg, while chambering the knee for a foot blade front kick to his open groin area (Figure 1.11.16). Follow-up with a knee strike to the pulled-down head (Figures 1.11.17 and 1.11.18). You can slip to his outside for a hook kick to the back of the head with the same leg that just kneed him (Figure 1.11.19).

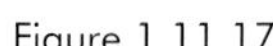

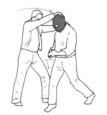

Figure 1.11.14 Figure 1.11.15 Figure 1.11.16 Figure 1.11.17

Figure 1.11.18 Figure 1.11.19
Interrupt an experienced opponent's developing roundhouse with a quick foot blade front kick to the groin. Follow up with a knee strike to his lowered head and finish with a hook kick to the back of his head.

1.12 The Oblique Front Kick

General

This is a regular front kick, but delivered about 45 degrees on your inside, while pivoting on the standing foot. The kick is described here because of the exhaustive nature of this chapter. All skilled martial artists know kicks can be fired from various angles during a fight. The practice of this kick is an important training building block toward proficiency in kicking in all situations. As will be described in the *Typical Application* subsection that follows, this kick is extremely efficient in scoring a full power front kick to an adversary presenting a very closed guard, with his side toward you; or to an adversary trying to evade you on the outside.

Description

It is useful to practice the kick after a small step with the front leg. Chamber the knee high and straight, just like a regular front kick (Figure 1.12.3). While extending the leg, pivot inward on the standing foot (Figure 1.12.4). The kick is delivered straight, exactly like a regular front kick. Pull the leg back before landing the foot.

Figure 1.12.1

Figure 1.12.2

Figure 1.12.3

Figure 1.12.4

Side view of the oblique front kick.

Figure 1.12.5

Figure 1.12.6

Comparison of a regular (open) guard and a closed side guard. The oblique front kick is ideal for penetrating a closed side guard.

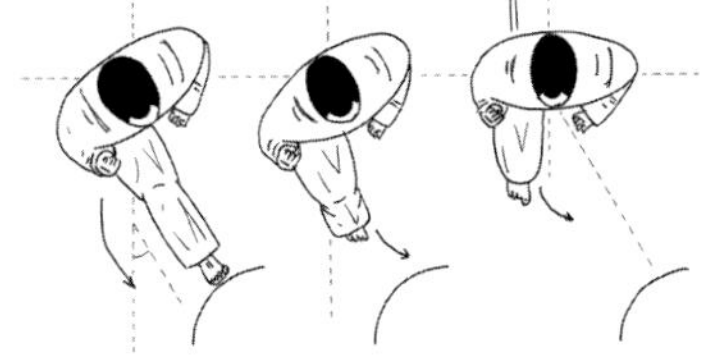
Figure 1.12.7
Overhead view of the oblique front kick.

Figures 1.12.8 through 1.12.11 show the use of the kick after an inside evasion of a penetrating front kick.

Figure 1.12.8

Figure 1.12.9

Figure 1.12.10

Figure 1.12.11

These images show the oblique front kick being used after evading a penetrating front kick.

Key Points

Turn on the standing foot after raising the knee, so as not to telegraph your move.

Targets

Typical targets for the heel front kick include the solar plexus, ribs, and groin.

Typical Application

Your opponent is in a very closed guard (Figure 1.12.12), with his side toward you, and initiates a full-step lunge punch. Do a quick lunge step forward at 45 degrees to your inside (Figure 1.12.13). Immediately chamber the knee of the rear leg while pivoting back toward your opponent, from an angle this time (Figure 1.12.14). Kick (Figure 1.12.15).

Figure 1.12.12

Figure 1.12.13

Figure 1.12.14

Figure 1.12.15

Execute the oblique front kick quickly to minimize your exposure to the risk of counterattack.

The step and pivot must be sudden and fast as they put you momentarily in a dangerous position. The best way to initiate such a kick is presented in the images that follow: for an opponent with same foot forward, initiate a lunge punch to his face while stepping in and forward (Figure 1.12.17). Keep your fist in front of his eyes while pivoting and kicking to his open ribs (Figure 1.12.18). If possible, take control of his blocking hand.

Figure 1.12.16

Figure 1.12.17

Figure 1.12.18

Distract your opponent with a lunge punch to the face before pivoting in with an oblique front kick to the ribs.

Specific Training

- Hit the heavy bag when facing 45 degrees from it.
- Kick a partner evading a jab from your outside.

Self-defense

The same principles are valid when dealing with a kick. Suppose your opponent throws you a front kick. The technique stays basically the same, whichever leg he uses to kick you. You block his kick at its maximum with an outside "spoon" block (*Sukui-uke*—karate): sweep his leg to the outside while catching its underside (Figure 1.12.20). Then lift slightly and pull the leg toward you and your outside, in order to overextend your opponent and put him off-balance. The catch is very short: release his leg and he lands in an overextended stance, half-way with his back toward you (Figure 1.12.21). In order to deliver a powerful front kick from your rear leg into his exposed kidneys, you'll need to perform an oblique front kick (Figure 1.12.22). You can finish him off with a stomp kick into the back of his knee (Figure 1.12.23). Note that had he kicked you with his other leg, the same technique would have brought him to you off-balance and with his front open to your oblique kick!

Figure 1.12.19

Figure 1.12.20

Figure 1.12.21

Figure 1.12.22

Figure 1.12.23

Deflect an incoming kick, spinning your opponent to the outside, and then follow up with an oblique front kick to his kidney. Finish off the confrontation with a stomp to the back of his knee.

1.13 The Instep Angular Front (Lotus) Kick

Sokuchi geri (ninjutsu), Lotus kick (common name), *Ponteira lateral* (capoeira)

General

Sometimes called the lotus kick, this is a true hybrid between an upward front kick and an outside crescent kick. It is basically a very short outside crescent kick that starts from a front kick chambered knee. An outside crescent kick starts from the floor with an extended leg and makes a large circular movement in order to gain the centrifugal speed that will give it its power. The instep angular front kick is much less powerful, but very fast and surprising. As it climbs up very close to the opponent's body, it is rather undetectable until it is too late. Because of its lack of power, it needs to be aimed at the soft spots of the head. The kick is not to be mistaken for the inward-tilted front kick, which is not a straight leg kick.

This kick is one of those kicks suitable for close combat, because of its short range and surprising effect. Most people do not expect to be kicked at close range.

Although the classic kick is delivered with the rear leg, such a delivery is detrimental to the element of surprise. It will therefore be described in the application examples as a fast front leg kick.

Description

Bring the rear knee to chambered position, while turning the foot inward (Figure 1.13.2). Straighten the leg while keeping the straight upward movement (Figure 1.13.3). Start pushing the leg out, like an outside crescent kick, but only when the leg is straight and close to the target (Figure 1.13.4). Hit with the blade and the top of the foot. Chamber the knee back (Figure 1.13.5).

Figure 1.13.1 Figure 1.13. 2 Figure 1.13. 3 Figure 1.13. 4 Figure 1.13.5
Side view of the instep angular front kick.

Figure 1.13.6 Figure 1.13.7
Front view of the instep angular front kick.

Figure 1.13.8
This is the portion of the foot that makes contact during the execution of an instep angular front kick.

Figures 1.13.9 through 1.13.11 show the use of the kick in close combat after a rear hand block of an incoming punch.

Figure 1.13.9 Figure 1.13.10 Figure 1.13.11
The instep angular front kick can be used in close combat as well.

Key Points

Keep the upper body straight, relaxed and as immobile as possible, so as not to telegraph your movement.
The leg travels outside the vision range of your opponent!
This kick is about speed and surprise.

Targets

- The head and its soft points: chin, temples, ears, and nose.
- The lower ribs if the opponent is open and extended.

Typical Application

This is a very surprising kick for use when you are close to your opponent, and the skilled artist can score many points with it. If your opponent is in opposite stance, jab to the outside of his face to force him to over-block and keep his attention there. In this example, the outside jab comes in a continuous deceiving movement starting toward his groin (Figures 1.13.12 and 1.13.13). Keep your hand on the outside of his face while delivering your instep angular front kick with your front leg to the other side of his face (Figure 1.13.15). As he is very close, once the kick is delivered, chamber back, and be ready to punch him in the face with your front palm, for example (Figure 1.13.16).

Figure 1.13.12

Figure 1.13.13

Figure 1.13.14

Figure 1.13.15

Figure 1.13.16

Distract your opponent before delivering a surprise instep angular front kick.

Should your opponent be in the same stance as you, punch to the inside of his face and kick him from his outside.

Specific Training

- Hit the heavy bag when starting from a fighting stance in which your front hand touches the bag (Figure 1.13.17). Practice rear leg and front leg kicking (Figure 1.13.18).
- Practice the kick while chambering over a chair.

Figure 1.13.17 Figure 1.13.18
Start with the heavy bag at arm's length, then practice rear and front leg instep angular front kicks.

Self-defense

Evade to the outside of a reverse punching assailant, while controlling the punch with your lead hand (Figure 1.13.20). Lift the knee of the front leg and deliver the instep angular front kick to his open ribs (Figure 1.13.21). Hit with the tip of the shoe into the lower ribs.
It would be natural to conclude the technique with a low side kick into his inside knee! See Figure 1.13.22.

Figure 1.13.19

Figure 1.13.20

Figure 1.13.21

Figure 1.13.22

Evade your opponent's punch before delivering an instep angular front kick to his ribs. Finish the confrontation with a side kick to his knee.

1.14 The Switch Front Kick

General

This is again a kick that is presented here because of the exhaustive nature of this chapter. The experienced martial artist is aware of, and proficient in, the different patterns of footwork, which are applicable to all kinds of kicks. The switch front kick is simply a regular front kick, generally penetrating, but executed after a switch of the legs, made more or less in place where you are standing. The kick allows for the use of the front leg of your stance, while having the power of a rear-leg kick—the best of both worlds! Of course, this is not a kick to use in pursuit of a retreating opponent. It is in fact a stop-kick par excellence. It is an extremely powerful kick, not only because of the rear leg power, but also because the kicking leg that is brought backward rebounds off the floor for the kicking motion. It also is a surprising kick, as the switching legs will baffle your opponent.

During the small hop to switch legs, the distance must be adapted to the circumstances: on the same spot, a little closer to the opponent, or a little further away if the opponent is approaching quickly.

Description

From the fighting stance (Figure 1.14.1), hop as close to the floor as possible, and switch legs fast, while adjusting for distance (Figures 1.14.2 and 1.14.3). The kicking foot, formerly of the lead leg, rebounds off the floor, and lifts up to its high-knee chambered position. Kick as usual, preferably a penetrating or heel front kick (Figure 1.14.4). Recoil the leg and lower foot.

Figure 1.14.1

Figure 1.14. 2

Figure 1.14. 3

Figure 1.14.4

Side view of the switch front kick.

Figures 1.14.5 through 1.14.8 show the delivery of the kick, in place. The height of the jump is exaggerated in the photos!

Figure 1.14.5

Figure 1.14. 6

Figure 1.14. 7

Figure 1.14.8

These images show an example of the switch front kick.

Key Points

- Suppress unnecessary upper body movement.
- Stability and a strong foundation while kicking is of the utmost importance. Foot switch as close to the floor as possible—there is no jumping up.

Targets

This is a stop-kick. The lower abdomen, ribs and solar plexus are typical targets, although the face is another possible target.

Typical Application

As a stop kick, it is nearly applicable to all attacks launched with a high forward momentum. It is an excellent technique to launch after a few exaggerated retreats. Your opponent will expect you to flee backward again, and will find you much closer before he can develop his attack to a viable momentum. For example, in Figures 1.14.9 through 1.14.13, We show such a move on an opponent seeking to close the distance with a long lunge jab, to set up his favorite spinning hook kick. Switch legs while he lunges, moving slightly backward, and kick his back while he still rotates to prepare his spinning kick. You can then punch him with the lead hand while landing, or grab him and sweep the leg on which he is standing.

Figure 1.14.9 Figure 1.14.10 Figure 1.14.11 Figure 1.14.12 Figure 1.14.13
The switch front kick is an excellent stop kick that can be effectively used to surprise an opponent whom you've lulled into expecting a retreat.

Specific Training

Mark a spot on the floor and practice the kick while trying for the three possible distance adjustments while switching: on the spot, as backward as possible, as forward as possible.

As with all stop-kicks: get a training partner to lunge toward you with protective gear or a padded target.

Self-defense

The switch front kick is also a great move to evade an attack on the low front leg—a sweep or a front kick, for example. If you switch while your opponent develops his sweep (or kick), he will miss your front leg, and probably the other one too. Even if he connects with the switched previously rear leg, it will not be where he expected it to be: the impact will be weaker and your opponent will be off-balance. Figure 1.14.15 illustrates a fully committed sweep into the void while you switch and deliver a powerful penetrating kick to your off-balance assailant (Figure 1.14.16). In this example, you then land on his outside, and deliver a hook kick to the back of his head (Figure 1.14.18).

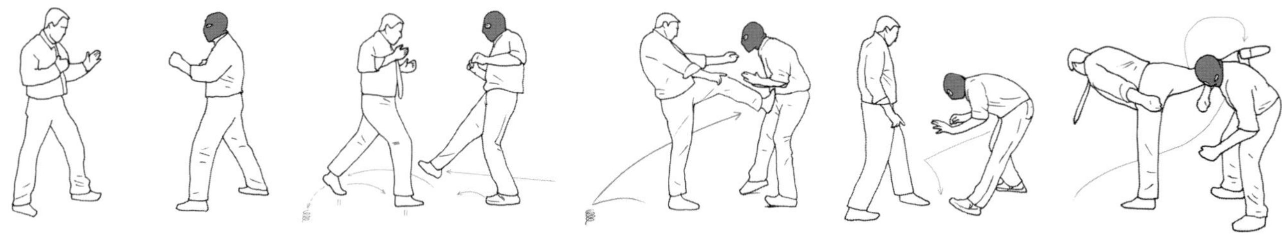

Figure 1.14.14 Figure 1.14.15 Figure 1.14.16 Figure 1.14.17 Figure 1.14.18
Switch your legs to interrupt your opponent's attempted leg sweep, and follow up with a penetrating front kick. End the confrontation with a hook kick to the back of your opponent's head.

1.15 The Lift Kick

Scoop kick (common name, jeet kune do)

General

This is a deceptively simple kick typical of the soft styles of kung fu. This is a very simple lift of the leg that targets, because of its lack of power, only soft targets: mainly the groin, and sometimes the sacrum. This is a close range kick, which must be delivered swiftly and with no telegraphing moves in order to be effective.

Description

See Figures 1.15.1 through 1.15.3. In a fighting stance with more weight on the back leg (*Ko kutsu dachi*—karate), simply raise the front leg—as it is, with no chambering—into your opponent's groin.

Figure 1.15.1 Figure 1.15.2 Figure 1.15.3
Side view of the lift kick.

Figures 1.15.4 and 1.15.5 show the way the kick is executed, with as little telegraphing as possible.

Figure 1.15.4 Figure 1.15.5
To be effective, this simple kick must not be telegraphed.

Key Points

- The effectiveness of the kick lies with the surprise effect: disguise as much as possible the fact that your weight is on your rear leg and that the front leg is "weightless."
- Avoid any telegraphing move: don't look at the target and keep the upper body relaxed and still during the kick.

Targets

- Typical targets include the groin, from the front or the back.
- Sometimes the sacrum.

Typical Application

Evade a step-through punch on the outside (Figure 1.15.8), pivot and lift-kick to your opponent's sacrum or testicles from behind (Figure 1.15.9).

Figure 1.15.6 Figure 1.15.7 Figure 1.15.8 Figure 1.15.9
The simple lift kick can have devastating effect.

Specific Training

- Work on a heavy bag hung at a level where the bottom hangs at groin level.
- Practice with a totally relaxed upper body.
- Train in front of the mirror to check for "tell tales."

Self-defense

You are being challenged from very close. Retreat obliquely on your assailant's inside with one leg while controlling his lead hand (or blocking his punch). See Figure 1.15.11. Immediately lift the front leg, now "weightless" because of your rear step, into his groin (Figure 1.15.12). You can hammerfist the back of his neck as he bends forward from the pain of the kick, while moving away (Figure 1.15.13).

Figure 1.15.10 Figure 1.15.11 Figure 1.15.12 Figure 1.15.13
Evade the punch while shifting your weight to your back leg, and then flick this kick into the opponent's groin.
Follow up with a fist to your opponent's head while he's doubled over from the kick.

1.16 The Phantom Groin Kick

General

This is also a close-range groin kick, with effectiveness reliant upon the surprise of a "no-clues" delivery. In fact, this is a version of the previous lift kick, but for even closer-range fighting. When in a close-quarters scuffle, simply lift the front foot from where it is directly into your opponent's groin, bending the leg as much as needed to adjust for distance. As with the lift kick, there should be no glancing at the target and no upper body move that would hint at the coming kick.

This kick appears, in our opinion, in one of the most traditional of Shotokan-ryu karate katas: *Tekki shodan*, a form entirely performed in a very low horse stance, on a straight line, as if with one's back to a wall. There are, of course, several possible interpretations (*bunkai*) of this move in the kata, but one of them is a phantom groin kick, delivered forward with no preceding body or leg movement. See Figures 1.16.1 through 1.16.6.

Figure 1.16.1 Figure 1.16.2 Figure 1.16.3 Figure 1.16.4 Figure 1.16.5 Figure 1.16.6
The phantom groin kick in the *Tekki* kata sequence.

Description

For the kick from a regular stance, see Figures 1.16.7 though 1.16.11. For a (higher) close-range fighting stance, simply lift the front foot to groin level while bending the knee and turning it outwards.

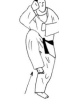

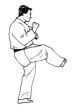

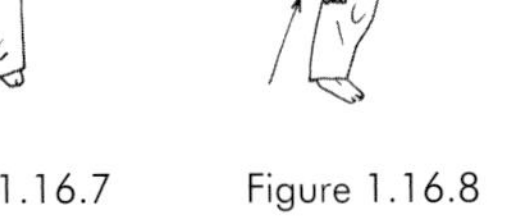

Figure 1.16.7 Figure 1.16.8 Figure 1.16.9
Front view of the phantom groin kick.

Figure 1.16.10 Figure 1.16.11
Side view of the phantom groin kick.

Figures 1.16.12 through 1.16.14 show the use of the kick in a close combat combination, following a jab.

Figure 1.16.12 Figure 1.16.13 Figure 1.16.14
The phantom groin kick is effective in close combat.

Key Points

- Do not look at the target.
- Keep the upper body relaxed and keep your opponent's attention on your hands.

Targets

- The groin.
- The face of a bent-over opponent.

Typical Application

This is obviously a kick for very close-range fighting. If you get very close to your opponent and exchange punches, just lift the closest leg to his groin (Figure 1.16.16), while keeping his attention riveted to hand control. You can follow up with an elbow strike (Figure 1.16.17).

Figure 1.16.15 Figure 1.16.16 Figure 1.16.17
Distract your opponent with upper body concerns before delivering the phantom groin kick, and then follow up with an elbow strike.

Specific Training

- Work on a heavy bag hung at a level where the bottom hangs at groin level.
- Practice delivering the kick without telegraphing.
- Practice in front of a mirror.
- Work on hip flexibility exercises. For example: yoga's cobbler's pose (See Figure 1.16.18).
- Drill for speed, explosiveness and power on a padded target held by a partner at groin level. See Figures 1.16.19 and 1.16.20 for a rear leg version.

Figure 1.16.18
The cobbler's pose (yoga).

Figure 1.16.19 Figure 1.16.20
Practice the kick with a partner holding a padded target to develop explosive power.

Self-defense

This is obviously a kick of choice for many self-defense situations. Remember: not telegraphing is key to success. Do not look at a target and keep your upper body relaxed. When attacked with a front choke, lift your joined hands in between your attacker's arms (Figure 1.16.21). Hit his right arm up and out, while lifting your foot to his groin (Figure 1.16.22). Hit his left arm with a full twist of the hips for power (Figure 1.16.23), and twist back with a hand strike to his face or neck, preferably a hand knife-edge strike (*Shuto-uchi*—karate). See Figure 1.16.24. Continue the twist of the hips in a powerful straight-leg roundhouse (Chapter 3, Section 7) to his ribs (Figure 1.16.25), and twist back with an elbow strike to the face (1.16.26).

Figure 1.16.21 Figure 1.16.22 Figure 1.16.23 Figure 1.16.24 Figure 1.16.25 Figure 1.16.26
Break free of a choke and launch a phantom groin kick to your opponent. Follow up with a twist to deliver a hand strike and finish the confrontation with a straight-leg roundhouse.

1.17 The Drop Front Kick

Chapa no chão (capoeira)

General

The dynamic version of this kick, from a standing position, is described here. The front kick from the floor, though very similar, is beyond the scope of this book.

This is a very surprising kick, and very powerful if delivered correctly. Japanese styles are generally not fond of sacrificing power and balance by going down to the floor, but whoever has met a *capoerista* understands how tricky it is to deal with a seasoned fighter hovering close to the ground.

Description

Although the execution of this kick is conceivable while going forward, it is more logical as a kick against an advancing opponent. Therefore, it will be described here as such. For the sake of deception, it is useful to start from a high fighting stance (Figure 1.17.1). Step back from your fighting stance and shift your body weight to your rear leg (Figure 1.17.2). Flex the legs while planting your rear hand on the floor behind you. Only then, plant the other hand on the floor behind you while you lift the knee for a regular penetrating front kick (Figure 1.17.3). Extend the leg while pushing with the hips for extra power (Figure 1.17.4). Connect with the heel or the ball of the foot and chamber the leg back immediately. Of course, once you are familiar with the execution of the kick, you can literally drop, falling down directly into chambered position, as in the application described in the *Self-defense* section to follow.

Figure 1.17.1 Figure 1.17.2 Figure 1.17.3 Figure 1.17.4
These images illustrate the execution of the drop front kick.

Figures 1.17.5 through 1.17.9 show the execution of the kick.

Figure 1.17.5

Figure 1.17.6

Figure 1.17.7

Figure 1.17.8

Figure 1.17.9
Drop and use leverage to propel your front kick with devastating force.

Key Points

- While going down, keep your front hand in front of you for defense.
- The push of the hips is at its maximum, just as the foot connects.

Targets

Of course the knee and the groin are the primary targets. The ribs and solar plexus are also in range. And if the opponent bends toward you, do not hesitate to target the throat, chin and face.

Typical Application

It is, of course an excellent kick when confronting an overpowering opponent running forward with high attacks.
You just disappear suddenly from his line of sight while he cannot stop his forward momentum. We present the example of a high-kicking opponent, storming forward with no control of his roundhouse/spinning back hook kick combination, and getting kicked in his open groin. See Figures 1.17.10 through 1.17.12.

Figure 1.17.10 Figure 1.17.11 Figure 1.17.12
When confronted with the advance of a high-kicking opponent, drop and drive a kick to his open groin when his momentum carries him into range.

Specific Training

- Practice, practice and practice, for speed.
- Power: execute the kick on the heavy bag, from a fighting stance positioned with your body touching the bag.
- Practice "falling" down into chambered position.

Self-defense

The example presented here is less technical, as can be expected in real life. You are suddenly attacked with a downward circular short stick attack to the head, and you try to evade the strike by going backward. You do not have the time to step back and put the hand on the floor, so you just let yourself drop into the chambering position (Figure 1.17.14).
Your attacker will be surprised by your change of plane, and you will be able to kick his groin (Figure 1.17.15), and later follow up with other ground kicking techniques.

Figure 1.17.13 Figure 1.17.14 Figure 1.17.15
Drop down and back into a chambered position as you avoid the swing of your opponent's weapon, and then launch your kick.

1.18 The Drop Twin Front Kick

General

Again, we will describe here the dynamic version of this kick that can be also delivered as a static kick from a ground position. The drop twin front kick is the two-legged version of the drop front kick described in the previous section. It is also a surprising kick and is highly suitable to deal with an opponent who overly commits himself to forward movement. The kick is very much used in, and typical of, exotic kung fu styles like the Monkey and Drunken style.

Description

From a high fighting stance (Figure 1.18.1), step back while swiftly lowering your body weight onto the retreating leg (Figure 1.18.2). Place the rear hand on the floor behind you while keeping your front hand in guard. Place your front hand on the floor behind you while sitting on your buttocks and lifting your cocked knees (Figure 1.18.3). Extend your legs powerfully, while pushing from your hands and involving as much hip thrust as possible (Figure 1.18.4).

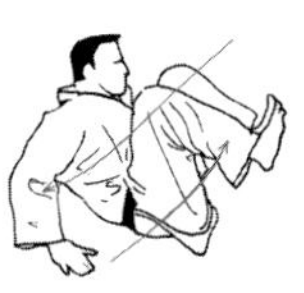

Figure 1.18.1 Figure 1.18. 2 Figure 1.18. 3 Figure 1.18.4
These images illustrate the execution of the drop twin front kick.

Figures 1.18.5 through 1.18.7 show an application of the kick, against a front kick, when downed. Figures 1.18.8 through 1.18.11 show the delivery of the kick against a high roundhouse kick.

Figure 1.18.5 Figure 1.18.6 Figure 1.18.7
Drop and use leverage to propel twin front kicks with into your opponent's groin.

Figure 1.18.8 Figure 1.18.9 Figure 1.18.10 Figure 1.18.11
The twin front kick is an effective response to an opponent's incoming roundhouse kick.

Key Points

- Keep your front hand up as long as possible.
- Your buttocks should "rebound" from the floor: the forward thrust comes immediately as you sit on the floor.

Targets

Primary targets are the groin, solar plexus, ribs, and knees. Figure 1.18.12 shows the use of the kick against the inner thigh of a kicking opponent.

Figure 1.18.12
If you're not confident that you can reach your opponent's groin, aim your kick at his inner thigh instead.

Typical Application

The premise of this situation is that you are being attacked by an opponent with an overwhelming barrage of punches. He is blasting forward with alternating punches to the head. This is a good move if you have been caught off-guard with the first punch and need to take back the initiative. You go back under the flurry of punches, and then suddenly drop down, preferably directly on your butt and hands, without passing through the classical intermediate position (see Figure 1.18.15). Double kick your opponent in the lower abdomen while he still has forward momentum (Figure 1.18.17). Although he impales himself on your feet, you still have to kick forcefully from the chambered position. Once he has been stopped, you must keep the offensive by kicking from the ground, at least until it is safe to quickly stand up without danger. For example, pivot onto your knee while you chamber the other leg for a ground side kick (Figure 1.18.18). Figure 1.18.19 depicts a kick to the body, but kicks to the knees and groin are easier and more effective.

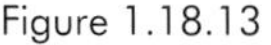

Figure 1.18.13

Figure 1.18.14

Figure 1.18.15

Figure 1.18.16

Figure 1.18.17

Figure 1.18.18

Figure 1.18.19

Re-gain the initiative by dropping under a flurry of punches to launch an attack of your own.

Specific Training

- Practice the drop for speed. Practice with and without the intermediate position.
- Start from a fighting stance in which you touch the heavy bag. Deliver for power.
- Practice with a padded lunging partner.

Self-defense

This is a perfect kick to execute when an assailant pushes you. Instead of resisting a push, drop down and let him push into the air and get off-balance. For example: an assailant has been pushing you, or has tried to, once (Figure 1.18.20). You retreat, but he again shows the intention of lunging at you (Figure 1.18.21). As he comes toward you, punching or pushing, you drop down, preferably directly into chambered position (Figure 1.18.22). Double kick into his forward momentum, in the abdomen or preferably the groin (Figure 1.18.23). You then roll on yourself and lie on your side, while hooking your foot behind his forward ankle, from the outside. Then you side kick or roundhouse kick the knee of his hooked ankle with a punishing joint kick (Figure 1.18.24). If necessary, keep kicking from the floor. Do not stand up before your assailant is disabled or out of range—you are more vulnerable while standing up.

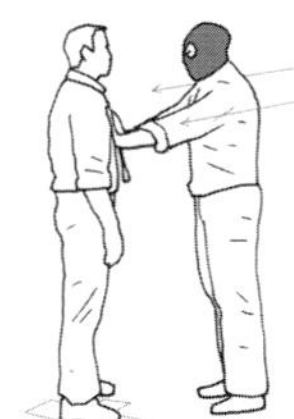
Figure 1.18.20

Figure 1.18.21

Figure 1.18.22

Figure 1.18.23

Figure 1.18.24

Drop beneath a push and initiate a twin front kick from the ground. Follow up with a joint kick and as many other kicks as are necessary to buy you enough time to safely get up off the ground.

An applied variation of the drop twin front kick.

More Advanced Front Kicks

What follows is a brief review of some more advanced kicks. They are not presented in detail here, as they are beyond the scope of this book.

The Double Front Kick

This is a classic way to deliver two front kicks in quick succession with the same leg, usually low, then high.

The Double Front Kick Combination

This is also a classic exercise, and the combination is very effective in combat. This is front leg front kick followed by a front kick by the other leg, switching legs virtually in the air.

The Flying Front Kick

This is the easiest of flying kicks, and can be delivered by jumping high or jumping far. This is simply a front kick leg delivery, but with forward momentum added by jumping.

A double flying front kick.

The Double Flying Front Kick Combination

This is a very classic and extremely effective combination, which is surprising and overpowering. It is recommended against a "fleeing" opponent who retreats quickly when you start an attack. It allows you to cover a lot of distance while delivering extremely powerful kicks. Again, it can be practiced jumping high or jumping far. The kick could also be considered first and foremost as a double kick.

The Roundhouse-chambered Front Kick

This is a great feint kick, and very successful when well delivered: make sure that your opponent expects a roundhouse kick by throwing a few half-hearted roundhouses. You then chamber the leg as a full roundhouse kick, start to deliver as a roundhouse, but progressively with the delivery, switch to a full hipped penetrating front kick.

The Soccer Low Front Kick

This is a very fast kick, difficult to block and extremely painful in self-defense situations. You simply kick in front of you, to your opponent's tibia, without chambering. This is the low kick par excellence, and is very useful as a stop kick.

A ground front kick.

The Low Front Kick

Simple and effective, this is a front kick with little chambering aimed at the legs, generally the lower leg.

The High Chambered Low (Stomp) Front Kick

The high chambered front kick delivered to the legs.

The Ground Front Kick

This is a front kick leg delivery, from a prone position, very much like the front drop kick.

Comparative Tables

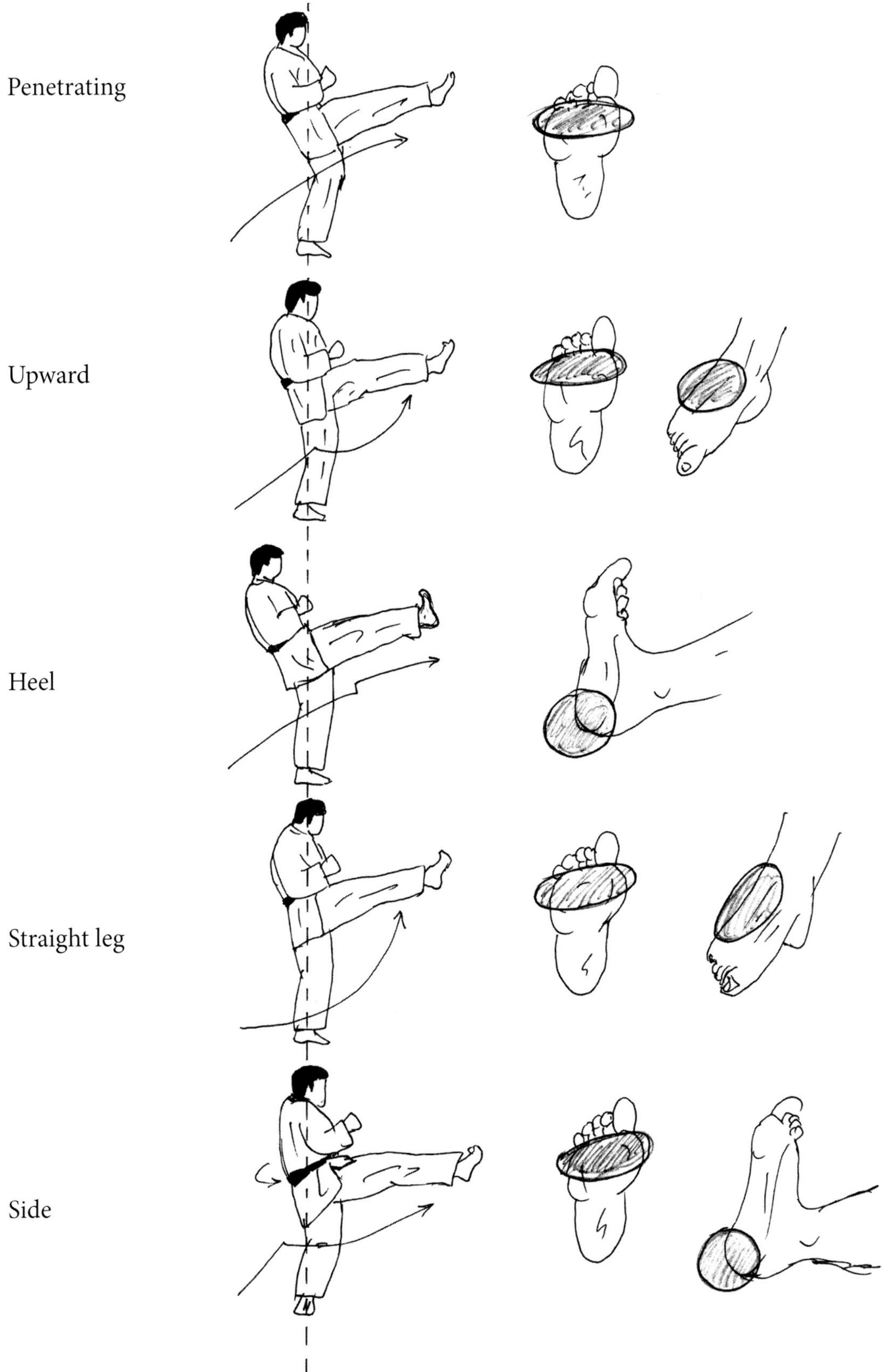

Table 1 — Comparative table of the trajectory and hip movement of the main front kicks.

Regular

Front leg

Hopping

Oblique

Lift and Phantom

Table 2 — Comparative table of the footwork in the main front kicks.

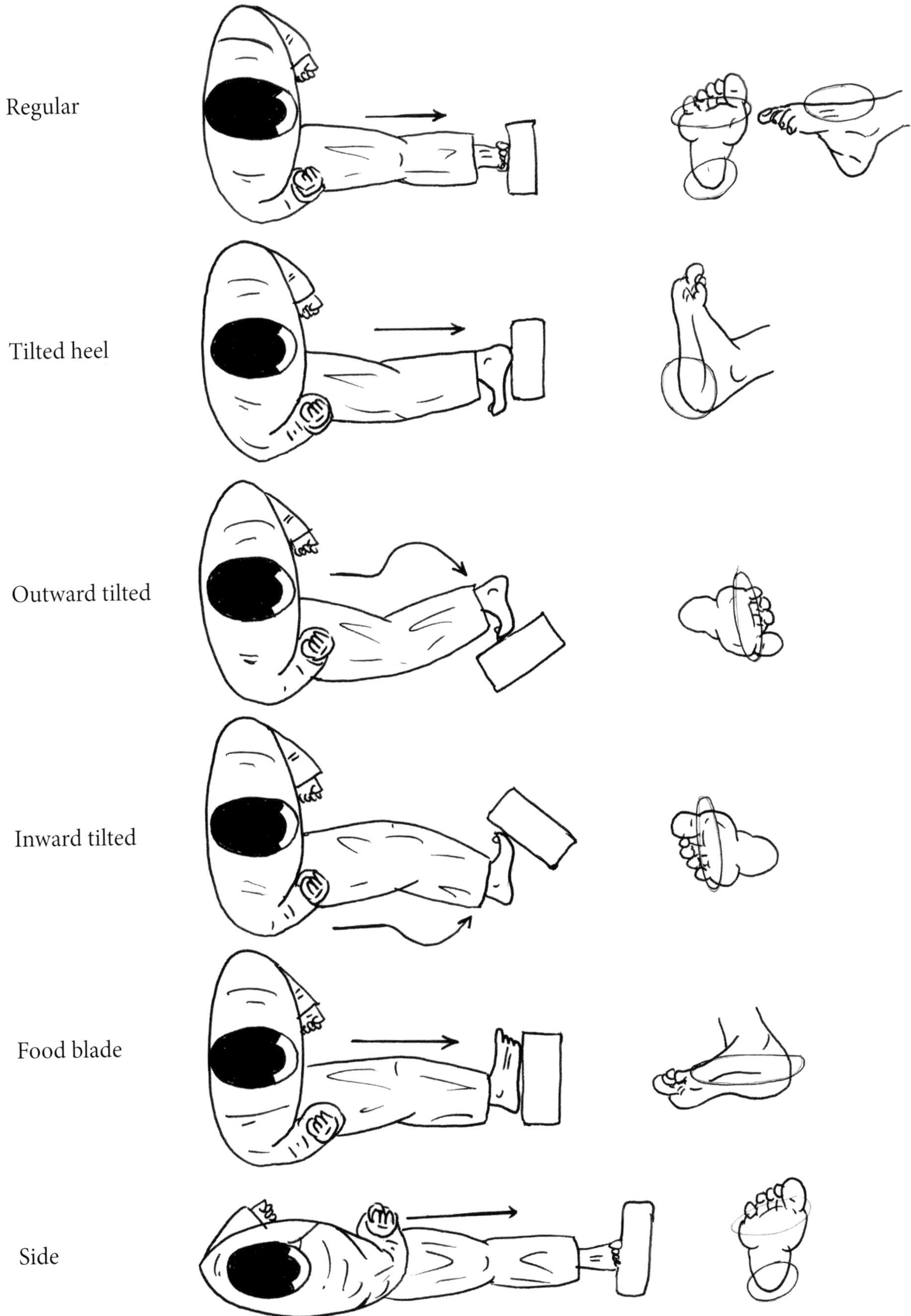

Table 3 — Comparative overhead view of the trajectory and leg position of the main front kicks.

CHAPTER TWO

Side Kicks

A penetrating side kick. (M. De Bremaeker)

The side kick is generally considered the most powerful of all kicks, its impact having been measured by sports researchers. Most will remember the scene in Bruce Lee's "Way of the Dragon," in the backyard of the restaurant, where his side kick sends his body shield-holding partner flying back in the air. This is the kind of power a well-delivered side kick creates.

Side kicks are slower to deliver than front kicks and require serious training. They will need a lot of drilling, but will teach the beginner to coordinate body and legs for power optimization. Side kicks allow for power and safe delivery and therefore exist in all styles and methods. The most important variations will be presented here: kicking with different footwork patterns, different targets, along different trajectories and with different emphasis of delivery.

2.1 The Penetrating Side Kick

Yoko geri kekomi (Shotokan karate), *Sokuto geri* (Wado-ryu karate), *Yop tshagy / Yup cha tzirugi* (taekwondo), *Tshuai thui / Juk tek / Jek tshan / Bang jiao* (kung fu), *Cruzado / Pisão / Chapa* (capoeira), *Bang thiet cuoc / Song cuoc* (viet vo dao), *Chassé* (savate–boxe française), *Tendangan rusuk* (pencak silat), *Teep khang* (muay thai).

General

The side kick is the most powerful kick of all, thanks to the necessary alignment between the leg and the body in a well-delivered kick. Because the kicking leg and the upper body are on one line during the kick, the hips can transmit the whole body power to the kick. No wonder it is a main kick of all existing systems. It is the preferred kick of Bruce Lee's jeet kune do, especially in its front leg version with the opponent's knee as a target. Because of its power and stability, it is also the most effective stop-kick, but with some slight differences in execution. It is interesting to note that the chambering part of the kick, with its pivoting on the standing foot, is in itself a block against an incoming kick or punch, from which the developing side kick becomes a counterattack (see *Self-defense* in Section 2.7)

Description

See Figures 2.1.1 through 2.1.4, which depict the rear leg version. Lift the rear knee forward while pivoting 90 degrees on the front foot. Your side is toward the target, and you extend the leg while pushing the hips and aligning your upper body and your leg. Immediately after impact, recoil the leg to the chambered position and pivot back toward your opponent while lowering your kicking foot in front or back to the rear.

Figure 2.1.1 Figure 2.1.2 Figure 2.1.3 Figure 2.1.4
Side view of the penetrating side kick (rear leg version).

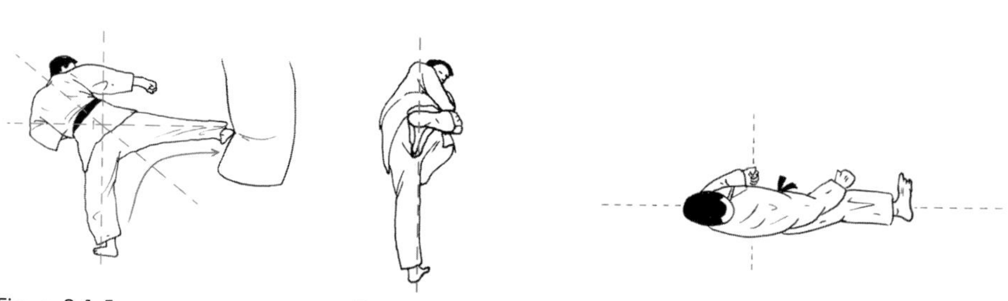

Figure 2.1.5 Figure 2.1.6 Figure 2.1.7
Side, front and overhead views showing the proper form of the penetrating side kick at impact.

You connect preferably with the edge of the foot, but the plant of the foot and the heel are also acceptable. See Figure 2.1.8.

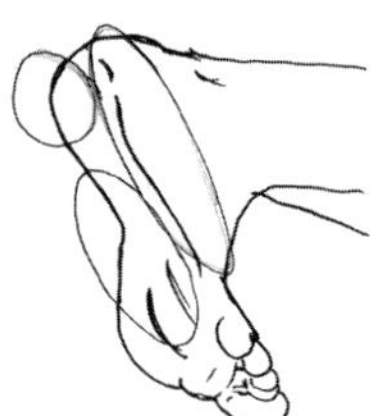

Figure 2.1.8
These are the parts of the foot that makes contact during the execution of a penetrating side kick.

Figures 2.1.9 through 2.1.11 show the execution of the kick mid-level from one side.

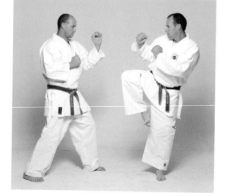

Figure 2.1.9 Figure 2.1.10 Figure 2.1.11
These images show a mid-level penetrating side kick in action.

Figures 2.1.12 through 2.1.14 show the kick delivered to a high level, as a stop-kick, and viewed from the opposite angle.

Figure 2.1.12

Figure 2.1.13

Figure 2.1.14

These images show a high-level penetrating side kick in action.

Key Points

- I cannot overstate that the kick is delivered with the hips, and body and leg are in a straight line.
- The standing foot is flat on the floor: no raising the heel.
- Chamber back quickly: the position you are in at impact, if your leg gets caught, is very dangerous as your opponent can have full access to your front, or worse, your back!

Targets

- The entire abdomen is a target: ribs, solar plexus, lower belly, underarm, kidneys, and lower back.
- Of course, the knee.
- The throat is a possible (lethal) target.

Typical Application

Although the kick from the rear leg may seem cumbersome at first glance, this author has found it an extremely successful kick for tournament scoring. After a lot of training, it becomes nearly impossible to block this kick, especially with a little hopping movement and if aimed at the lowest point of the belly allowed, usually the belt itself. Close the distance with a lunge and a high front/reverse punch combination (Figure 2.1.15), while using the hip turn of the reverse punch to "liberate" the rear leg and start the chambering of the knee (Figures 2.1.16 and 2.1.17). Hop slightly to close more distance if necessary, while chambering and kick (Figure 2.1.18).

Figure 2.1.15

Figure 2.1.16

Figure 2.1.17

Figure 2.1.18

The hard-to-block penetrating side kick is facilitated by and a short hop.

Specific Training

- This being a powerful kick, it must be practiced a lot on the heavy bag. Work from farther and farther away and explode into the kick.
- Deliver the kick over a chair on your side (Figures 2.1.19 and 2.1.20) and in front of you (see Figures 2.1.21 and 2.1.22), to force the necessary high chambering of the kick.

Figure 2.1.19

Figure 2.1.20

Figure 2.1.21

Figure 2.1.22

Use a chair while practicing the penetrating side kick to ensure high chambering.

- Practice the kick a lot from the ground with and without weighted ankles, until the burn is unbearable. This will develop all the important small muscles in the hip that are difficult to develop otherwise.
- Flexibility is key—practice all types of splits! Flexibility drills with a partner will be very helpful.
- Drill for penetration power on padded target held by partner. See Figure 2.1.23 through 2.1.25.

Figure 2.1.23

Figure 2.1.24

Figure 2.1.25

Practice the kick with a partner holding a padded target to develop penetrative power.

- Squat and kick (See Figures 2.1.26 through 2.1.29).

Figure 2.1.26

Figure 2.1.27

Figure 2.1.28

Figure 2.1.29

Adding squats to your practice will improve your strength.

Self-defense

Avoid a circular stick attack by retreating and leaning back (Figure 2.1.31). As soon as the stick has passed through, regain a forward momentum, now to the outside of your assailant while he still is carried away by his attack (Figure 2.1.32). Chamber the rear leg and side kick his ribs from his outside (Figure 2.1.33). Lower the leg directly into the back of his knee (Figure 2.1.34).

Figure 2.1.30 Figure 2.1.31 Figure 2.1.32 Figure 2.1.33 Figure 2.1.34
Lean back to avoid an attack, and then move forward into a penetrating side kick.

2.2 The Upward Side Kick

Yoko geri keage (Shotokan karate), *Yup cha ohlligi* (taekwondo)

General

Just as with the upward front kick/penetrating front kick comparison, this is the upward variation of the side kick: the hips are used much less in the kick, and the kick connects from down under upwards, usually with the armpit, the arm, the bent body or the chin. Of course, there are many variations and nuances of the side kick, with more or less "penetration" versus "upward-ness." The upward side kick is very fast, and quite painful when it hits the right targets. It is used, among other purposes, to disturb your opponent's guard by attacking the joints of the arms.

Surprisingly, it is the upward version of the side kick that is found in traditional karate katas: two examples are shown in the two kata excerpts that follow (Figures 2.2.1 through 2.2.10), from very basic Shatokan-ryu karate forms.

A straight leg version of this kick is sometimes called a "pendulum kick."

Figure 2.2.1 Figure 2.2.2 Figure 2.2.3 Figure 2.2.4 Figure 2.2.5 Figure 2.2.6

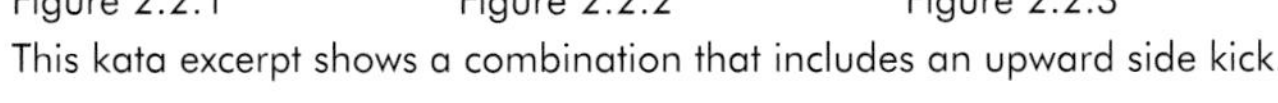

This kata excerpt shows a combination that includes an upward side kick.

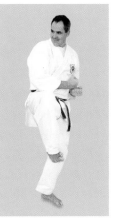

Figure 2.2.7 Figure 2.2.8 Figure 2.2.9 Figure 2.2.10
Another kata excerpt showing an upward side kick.

Description

The preparatory steps before the kick itself are identical to those of the penetrating side kick. Raise the knee and pivot sideways to your opponent (Figure 2.2.12). From there on though, the trajectory of the foot changes and you extend the leg upward, without pushing with the hips (Figure 2.2.13). After hitting your target from below, with the blade of the foot, chamber back immediately (Figure 2.2.14). The kick can, of course, be delivered with the front leg also (See the following section).

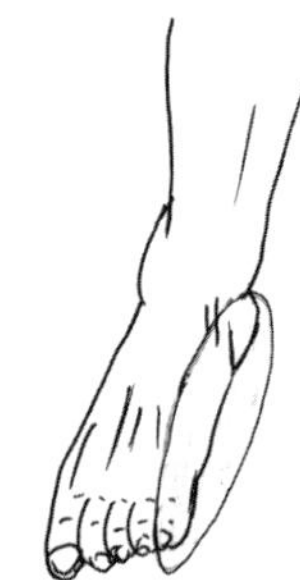

Figure 2.2.11 Figure 2.2.12 Figure 2.2.13 Figure 2.2.14
Side view of the upward side kick.

Figure 2.2.15
This is the part of the foot that makes contact during the execution of an upward side kick.

Figures 2.2.16 and 2.2.17 show the delivery of the kick to the armpit of a controlled arm. Notice that less hip thrust is needed in the upward version of the side kick.

Figure 2.2.16 Figure 2.2.17
Less hip thrust is necessary for the upward side kick.

Key Points

- Lift the knee high.
- In this kick, the upward development of the leg can start before the knee is fully chambered: as the momentum is upward, the end of the knee lift and the start of the upward leg movement should be simultaneous.
- The standing foot stays flat on the floor.

Targets

Only from down upwards: chin, arms, bent body or head. The armpit is a favorite, especially if you can get a hold of your opponent's hand and keep his arm up and extended.

Typical Application

As mentioned, this is an ideal kick to attack the arms or the guard of an opponent, especially if he tends to stand in high guard. It is surprising and painful and can open the opponent just long enough to allow for a more serious attack to go through. It is a great kick to hit a punch on its way to you, from below, although usually this is reserved for its front leg form. Here is an application that exemplifies the guard-opening angle: reverse punch to your opponent's face, while developing the upward side kick from your rear leg. Hit your opponent's elbow from below to open his guard and deliver pain (Figure 2.2.19). Chamber and immediately deliver a penetrating side kick to the unguarded ribs, if possible, without lowering the foot to the floor (Figure 2.2.21). If not possible, lower the foot and rebound off the floor to deliver the second kick, as illustrated. You can follow up by lowering your kicking foot behind his front leg, getting a hold of his shoulder or collar, and sweep him to the ground (*O soto gari*—judo). See Figure 2.2.22.

Figure 2.2.18 Figure 2.2.19 Figure 2.2.20 Figure 2.2.21 Figure 2.2.22
Open your opponent up with an initial upward side kick, then quickly follow up with a penetrating side kick. Finish the confrontation with a sweep that takes your opponent to the ground.

Specific Training

- This kick must be delivered precisely—therefore it should be practiced with a partner holding a target mitt facing down at arm and chin level.
- Kick over a chair beside you or in front of you, just like with the penetrating side kick (refer to Figures 2.1.19 through 2.1.22 in the previous section)
- Practice the whole *Heian Nidan* and *Heian Yodan* katas, or the sequences described previously.
- Squat and kick (refer to Figures 2.1.26 through 2.1.29 in the previous section).
- Stand on one leg and hold the other foot close to the belt knot, with the bent leg parallel to the floor. Pull on the ankle, and then explosively release the leg around the knee, as if in a low kick, in a typical *keage* upward movement.
- Work on your flexibility. For example, side leg raises while holding a dancing bar.

Self-defense

When suddenly attacked, you lift your arms, but your assailant gets a hold of your sleeve (Figure 2.2.23). Immediately chamber your front leg and try to get a hold of his hand to control it (Figure 2.2.24). Hit your assailant's extended arm or armpit from below (Figure 2.2.25)—this will be painful in any case, but if you have immobilized his hand, it will also damage the elbow joint. Keep control of his arm by catching his wrist with your front hand while you deliver a penetrating side kick with the same leg, directly from the chamber position, or after rebounding off the floor. Pull his arm toward you while kicking (Figure 2.2.27). You can follow up with a full-powered straight leg roundhouse to his exposed ribs (as you have kept pulling his arm). See Figure 2.2.28.

Figure 2.2.23

Figure 2.2.24

Figure 2.2.25

Figure 2.2.26

Figure 2.2.27

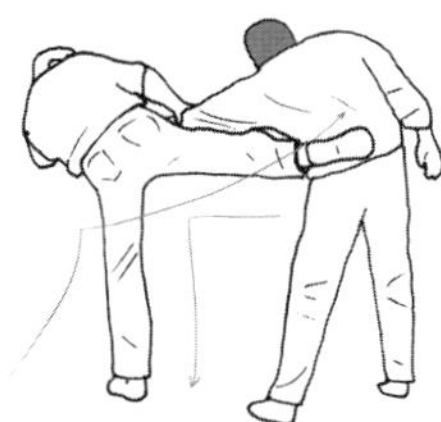

Figure 2.2.28

When an opponent has grabbed the arm that you lifted defensively after a sudden attack, three quick successive kicks (including the upward side kick) will free your arm and put him on the defensive.

2.3 The Front Leg Side Kick

Surikonde yoko geri (karate), *Pisaõ crusado* (capoeira)

General

The front leg version of the side kick is one of the bread-and-butter kicks of martial arts: fast, powerful and relatively easy and safe to deliver. It is less powerful than the rear leg version, but faster, and with the added advantage of guarding the body during delivery: the chambered leg keeps the side of the body covered, and there is always the leg between you and your opponent. It is basically a footwork variant only, and the kick itself could be penetrating, upward or any other type presented later.

The front leg kick with no forward movement, as a stop-kick or stationary kick, will not be presented here as it is beyond the scope of this book.

Description

We'll present the classic version first. Master this in order to clearly understand the principles of stability and power delivery of the kick. Bring your rear leg forward and cross your legs while pivoting on your front foot and presenting your side to your opponent (Figure 2.3.2). This is a classical cross-step. The rear leg comes behind the front leg, in order to clear an open pathway for the front leg to chamber and kick. Do not raise your body. The head stays at constant height. Do not stay cross-legged (ever!)—chamber immediately, bringing your knee as high as possible (Figure 2.3.3). Deliver the kick, in the form most suitable to the circumstances ("penetrating" is illustrated in Figure 2.3.4), and chamber back (Figure 2.3.5).

Figure 2.3.1 Figure 2.3.2 Figure 2.3.3 Figure 2.3.4 Figure 2.3.5

These illustrations show the side view of the front leg side kick.

Figures 2.3.6 through 2.3.10 show the kick used in the classic combination. Front hand backfist to lift the opponent's guard and front leg side kick to the exposed lower abdomen. Note the traditional delivery here with retraction of the backfist and cross-legged step; In modern or competitive fighting, it would be possible to leave the extended hand in front of the opponent's face for a few more seconds (beware of being caught), to hide the hopping step.

Figure 2.3.6

Figure 2.3.7

Figure 2.3.8

Figure 2.3.9 Figure 2.3.10
These images show the front leg side kick in action.

When you are proficient with the classic version, you can translate the same principles of stability, hip movement and unchanged head height into the very fast "hopping version." The rear leg hops forward, very close to the ground, to replace the front leg that is already going up to the chambering position (Figure 2.3.12), while the body is turning sideways. Kick (Figure 2.3.13) and chamber back.

Figure 2.3.11 Figure 2.3.12 Figure 2.3.13
These illustrations show the "hopping version" of the front leg side kick.

Key Points

- Standing foot must be flat on the floor on impact.
- Make sure you do not bob when surging forward: head stays at the same height.
- Never cross legs with kicking leg behind.

Targets

Targets vary depending on the type of side kick being delivered.

Typical Application

Here is the most typical use of the kick in its penetrating version. Don't forget that the old, simple and time-tested tactics do work. Lunge with a real and convincing backfist to your opponent's face, at eye level (Figure 2.3.15). It works even better if you can repeat and backfist twice. Keep your hand a few seconds more in front of your opponent's eyes while you close the lunging stance with your rear foot (Figure 2.3.16) and chamber. Kick to the ribs, opened by your opponent's raised hand (Figure 2.3.17). Follow-up with an additional backfist, downwards this time, while landing the kicking foot (Figure 2.3.18)—your kick has now caused his hands to lower! The combination works best if you stay on his inside.

Figure 2.3.14 Figure 2.3.15 Figure 2.3.16 Figure 2.3.17 Figure 2.3.18
Distract your opponent with a backfist while you chamber and launch a front leg side kick followed by a downward backfist when he drops his guard in response to the kick.

Specific Training

- Kick under a tense rope just over your head (Figure 2.3.19), to train yourself to minimize dropping your head height.

Figure 2.3.19
A partner holding a rope above your head as you kick will help you learn to keep your height more constant.

- Kick the heavy bag with the pathway of your leg blocked by a chair (Figures 2.3.20 through 2.3.22). Repeat from various distances.

Figure 2.3.20 Figure 2.3.21 Figure 2.3.22
Kicking over a chair will help you train yourself to chamber higher.

- Figures 2.3.23 through 2.3.26 show the drilling of the kick, with an exaggerated hop/slide, against a target pad held by a partner.

Figure 2.3.23

Figure 2.3.24

Figure 2.3.25

Figure 2.3.26
Improve focus and power by drilling with a partner holding a target pad.

Self-defense

This version of the kick is one where you attack a menacing opponent just as he prepares to attack you. This is not a stop-kick, which is usually delivered a little bit differently (with less chambering). As your opponent shows signs of initiating an attack toward you, do not retreat as he intuitively expects: surge forward with a front leg penetrating side kick (Figures 2.3.28 and 2.3.29). You'll catch him in mid-motion, as you have caused him to miscalculate his distance—in this case, with his arm raised. You can follow-up by landing, behind his front leg, on his outside, while hammerfisting the back of his neck (Figure 2.3.30). And then deliver a spin-back hook kick to his face from his blind side (Figure 2.3.31).

Figure 2.3.27 Figure 2.3.28 Figure 2.3.29 Figure 2.3.30 Figure 2.3.31
Interrupt your opponent's impending attack with a front leg side kick followed quickly by a downward hammerfist to his neck. End the confrontation with a spin back hook kick to his face.

2.4 The Universal Chamber Side Kick

General

The universal chambering position was popularized by Bill "Superfoot" Wallace, one of the best kicking artists ever. Wallace proved in points and full-contact competition the value of good kicking, and was able to score at will with incredibly fast and powerful kicks. He was generally using a front leg chambering position from which three possible kicks could be delivered interchangeably: a side kick, a hook kick or a roundhouse kick. We took the liberty to name this position: the universal chamber (see Figures 2.4.1 and 2.4.2). In this position, the body is protected by the leg and the groin by the foot. The leg is at 45 degrees, with the knee as high as possible, and the body slightly bent backward. From this position, all three kicks can be launched, and it is your opponent's best guess which one you'll ultimately deliver.

Figure 2.4.1 Figure 2.4.2
These illustrations depict a front and side view of the universal chamber.

Description

Bring your rear foot forward, close to your front foot (Figure 2.4.3) and lift into universal chamber position, with your knee as high as possible (Figure 2.4.4). Extend the leg as straight as possible into the target, with some hips push (Figure 2.4.5), and snap back to chamber (Figure 2.4.6). The kick is usually a hybrid of penetrating and upward, and is used high.

Figure 2.4.3 Figure 2.4.4 Figure 2.4.5 Figure 2.4.6
These illustrations depict a side view of the universal chamber side kick.

Key Points

- The knee must be as high as possible and the body slightly bent backward.
- The standing foot must be flat on the floor.

Targets

Typical targets include the face, throat, sternum and solar plexus.

Typical Application

A typical application would be to lure the opponent into believing that you will repeat the same attack from the same position. Attack your opponent with a high roundhouse from the universal position. If he blocks it, just repeat but this time side kick to his face or sternum. See Figures 2.4.7 through 2.4.11.

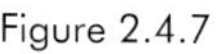

Figure 2.4.7

Figure 2.4. 8

Figure 2.4.9

Figure 2.4.10

Figure 2.4.11
Use the universal chamber position to launch a variety of kicks in quick succession.

Figures 2.4.12 and 2.4.13 show the delivery of a kick from the universal chamber. The opponent expects a roundhouse kick, but the side kick gets through.

Figure 2.4.12

Figure 2.4.13

These images show a kick being delivered from the universal chamber position.

Specific Training

- Get into universal chambering in front of the mirror. Practice both sides, and repeat endlessly.
- Deliver all three different kicks to the heavy bag, from the universal chamber, without lowering the leg.
- Squat and kick, emphasizing the universal chamber (See a similar exercise depicted in Figures 2.1.28 through 2.1.29 in the first section of this chapter).

Self-defense

Confront your assailant with a convincing rear leg roundhouse toward his groin (Figure 2.4.15). There is no way he won't lower his hands. From the roundhouse, chamber directly into universal position and side kick his face or throat, eventually with a hop (see Figure 2.4.17). You are thus attacking successively, both from a different angle and at a different level. You can follow up by attacking or feinting toward his face while lowering the kicking leg (Figure 2.4.18), and then using your rear leg to front kick his knee (Figure 2.4.19).

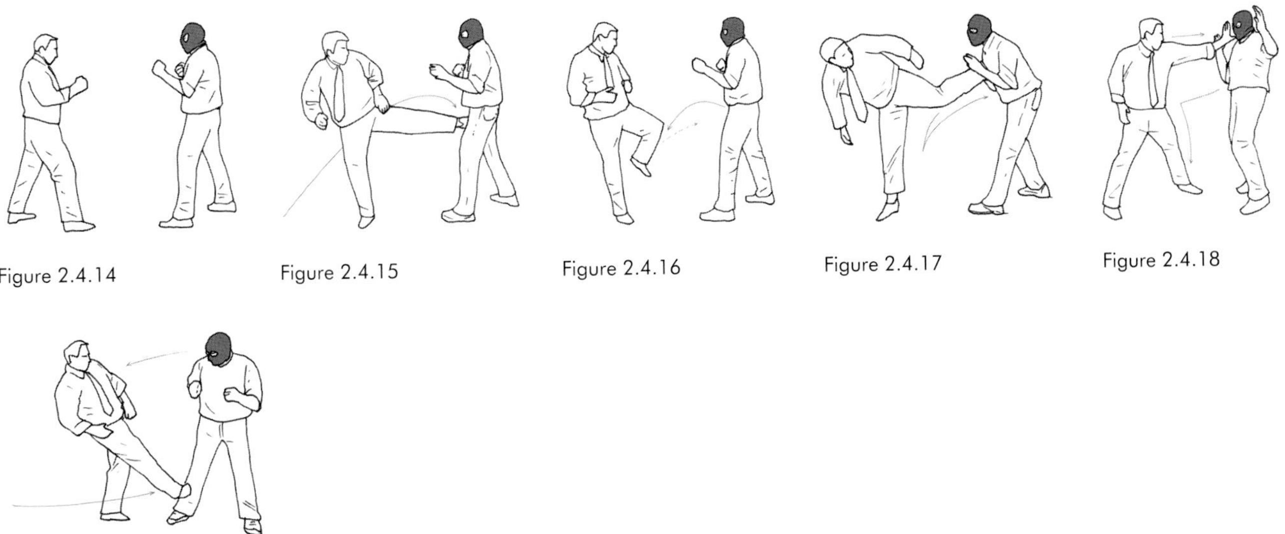

Figure 2.4.14 Figure 2.4.15 Figure 2.4.16 Figure 2.4.17 Figure 2.4.18

Figure 2.4.19
Quick, successive kicks from the universal chamber side kick will force your opponent to spend his time reacting to your offensive maneuvers, with little opportunity to launch his own attack.

2.5 The Bent-body Side Kick

General

This is simply a side kick performed with the upper body bent sideways much more than in the classic delivery, in order keep the face and body away from the opponent as much as possible. At the same time, the standing leg is bent, in order to allow more hip push in the kick, and therefore connecting from farther away. It is an excellent way to deliver the kick when you are dealing with an opponent waiting to counter or time your attack with a stop punch. It can also be of use when you are dealing with an opponent armed with a bladed weapon that you want to keep away from you as much as possible.

Description

The kick can be delivered from the front leg or the back leg, and it is the same up to the chambered position. Then, while delivering the kick, you bend the standing leg, lean sideways and away, and lengthen the hip as much as possible. Chamber back. It is often delivered with a small hop from the chambered position. See Figures 2.5.1 through 2.5.4.

Figure 2.5.1 Figure 2.5.2 Figure 2.5.3 Figure 2.5.4
These illustrations depict a side view of the bent-body side kick.

Figure 2.5.5 shows the kick delivered and its clear safety advantages.

Figure 2.5.6 shows the use of the kick as a stop kick, attacking the hip joint of an advancing opponent.

Figure 2.5.5
With the head positioned far out of range, the bent-body side kick has an obvious advantage.

Figure 2.5.6
The bent-body side kick being used as a stop kick.

Key Points

- Keep the hips into the kick for power.
- Lean back and bend the standing leg simultaneously.

Targets

Typical targets include the throat, solar plexus, ribs, and lower abdomen. The knee is also a target, especially as a stop kick.

Typical Application

This kick is effectively used as an attack against an opponent waiting to time you. In this scenario, you know your opponent is waiting for you to commit in order to reverse punch you. Start to deliver a front leg side kick. Bend back and bend the knee to keep out of range of the punch, while delivering the kick. See Figures 2.5.7 through 2.5.9.

Specific Training

- Hit the heavy bag from farther and farther away.
- Practice with an exaggeratedly low, bent leg (Figure 2.5.10). Repeat with a partner swinging a stick at chin level to ensure the body bend.

Figure 2.5.7 Figure 2.5.8 Figure 2.5.9
Outsmart an opponent waiting to catch you with a reverse punch after you commit. Deliver your kick while keeping your head well out of harm's way.

Figure 2.5.10
A partner swinging a stick over your head as you kick will help you learn to keep your head low.

Self-defense

Your assailant takes out a knife (Figure 2.5.11). Do not wait for him to get ready, but immediately side kick his knee, while staying as far away as possible (Figure 2.5.12). Repeat kick at low and mid-levels to keep him off-balance, injured and/or unwilling to keep fighting (Figure 2.5.13).

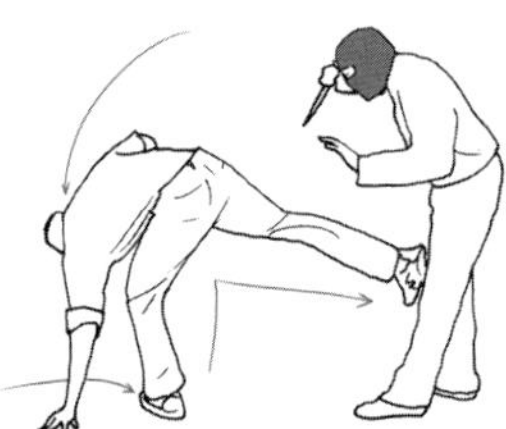

Figure 2.5.11 Figure 2.5.12 Figure 2.5.13
If faced with the last resort of fighting with someone wielding a deadly weapon, one strategy is to use the bent-body side kick early and often to keep your trunk and head as far out of range as possible.

2.6 The Front Chamber Side Kick

General

This is not a feint kick, but a faster way to get into a side kick, especially in sport competition. The kick is somewhat a hybrid between a front chamber and the way the side kick is delivered in Wado-ryu karate (*Sokuto*): less chambering but more hip push and a near back kick finish. The idea behind the kick is to perform the pivoting and turning of the hips—usually done during the chambering—during the delivery of the kick itself. It gives a faster kick with less telegraphing. The loss in power is compensated by more push of the hips.

Description

Chamber as a front kick and start pivoting on the standing foot and turning the hips together with the leg extension (Figures 2.6.2 and 2.6.3). Finish the kick at full extension with a strong push of the hips, which turns your back slightly toward the opponent (Figure 2.6.4). Chamber back.

Figure 2.6.1

Figure 2.6.2

Figure 2.6.3

Figure 2.6.4

These illustrations depict a side view of the front chamber side kick.

Figures 2.6.5 through 2.6.8 show the delivery of the kick: notice the front chamber and the progressive pivot and thrust of the hips.

Figure 2.6.5

Figure 2.6.6

Figure 2.6.7

Figure 2.6.8

These images show the front chamber side kick in action.

Key Points

This is a continuous movement: perform it seamlessly.

Targets

Typical targets include the throat, sternum, ribs, and lower abdomen.

Typical Application

This is a surprising kick because of its range, as the opponent tends to expect a much shorter front kick. Therefore, it is a good kick to perform after you have front kicked your opponent. Front kick (Figure 2.6.10), deliberately short, and retract the leg back to fighting stance (Figure 2.6.11). Repeat, with a break in rhythm, as you stay a millisecond more in front chamber position, to cause him to complete his block (Figure 2.6.12). As you have taught him the length of your front kick, he will probably not retreat enough to stay out of the range of your full-hipped side kick (Figure 2.6.14). You can follow up by keeping the pivot while landing the foot, to develop a high spinning hook kick (Chapter 5, Section 4). See Figure 2.6.15.

Figure 2.6.9 Figure 2.6.10 Figure 2.6.11 Figure 2.6.12

Figure 2.6.13 Figure 2.6.14 Figure 2.6.15

Train your opponent to expect another front kick, then chamber and hesitate half a beat for him to misplace his block before you drive home a side kick. Optionally follow up with a high spinning hook kick.

Specific Training

- Practice the kick on a heavy bag, with a belt tied to the knee of your standing leg to force you to front chamber (Figures 2.6.16 through 2.6.18).
- Kick in front of the mirror.

Figure 2.6.16 Figure 2.6.17 Figure 2.6.18

A belt tied to your knee and held by a partner will train you to front chamber before turning your hips for the transition into a side kick.

Self-defense

The principle of this application stays the same: this kick is deceptive about the range it can achieve. When confronted by an assailant, employ the advantage that wearing shoes gives you by kicking his shin with a low soccer front kick (Figure 2.6.20). Retract the leg directly into a front leg chamber (Figure 6.6.21): this is a totally natural movement. From the front chamber (which is also guarding your body), immediately start to develop the front chamber side kick, pivoting at the last moment with full hip thrust (Figure 2.6.22). If your assailant is out of range, add a small hop to close the distance. You can follow up with a low side kick to the front knee, directly from the chamber-back position, or after briefly lowering the foot to the floor (Figure 2.6.23).

Figure 2.6.19 Figure 2.6.20 Figure 2.6.21 Figure 2.6.22 Figure 2.6.23

Use the impressive reach of the front chamber side kick to dismay an assailant while you reach a target that would otherwise be impossible to hit with other front chamber kicks.

2.7 The Back Side Kick

Ushiro geri (Shotokan karate), *Yup duiro chagi* (taekwondo)

General

This is, very simply, a penetrating side kick with more back to the opponent: more powerful but from a less advantageous position and with less visual coordination. This is, in fact, the back kick (*Ushiro geri*) of the Shotokan school, more on the side than the back kicks of some other Japanese styles.

It is interesting to note that in Bruce Lee's jeet kune do, a distinction is made between a "basic" side kick without full hip thrust, and a more committed and penetrating side "rear" kick with more hip thrust and rotation toward the back.

Description

See Figures 2.7.1 through 2.7.4 The delivery is similar to the regular side kick, except near the end of the delivery, the hips push even more forward and the body pivots more, giving more back. The final position is just between full back and side toward the opponent, as illustrated in the overhead view (Figure 2.7.5).

Figure 2.7.1 Figure 2.7.2 Figure 2.7.3
These illustrations depict a side view of the back side kick.

Figure 2.7.4

Figure 2.7.5
Compared overhead view of a back kick, back side kick, and side kick, respectively.

Figures 2.7.6 and 2.7.7 clearly show the difference between the regular penetrating side kick and the back side kick.

Figure 2.7.6
The penetrating side kick.

Figure 2.7.7
The back side kick.

Key Points

The final pivot and push of the hips coincides with impact, as it gives the powerful penetration that is the hallmark of this kick.

Targets

Typical targets include the groin, lower abdomen, ribs, solar plexus, and chin.

Typical Application

This is the perfect kick when you find yourself in a position with your back partially toward the opponent. You attack your opponent's guard with a crescent kick (Chapter 6, Section 1): hit hard and aim for the elbow (Figure 2.7.9). The momentum leads you to lower your foot with your back partially toward your retreating opponent (Figure 2.7.10).

You immediately hop, closing the distance with your rear leg and delivering the back-side kick to your opponent's lower abdomen (Figure 2.7.11), without having to change your upper body's relative position (back half-turned toward your opponent). You can follow up by repeating the kick with the other leg! See Figure 2.7.12.

Figure 2.7.8 Figure 2.7.9 Figure 2.7.10 Figure 2.7.11

Figure 2.7.12
Use the momentum from a crescent kick to position yourself to deliver a powerful pair of successive back side kicks.

Specific Training

The purpose of the kick is to deliver more power, therefore: use the heavy bag.

Self-defense

This kick is also typical for use after having leg-blocked an attack with an inside knee sweep. You can follow up with a full-power backfist while lowering the foot, or after a small cross-step if necessary. See Figures 2.7.13 through 2.7.18.

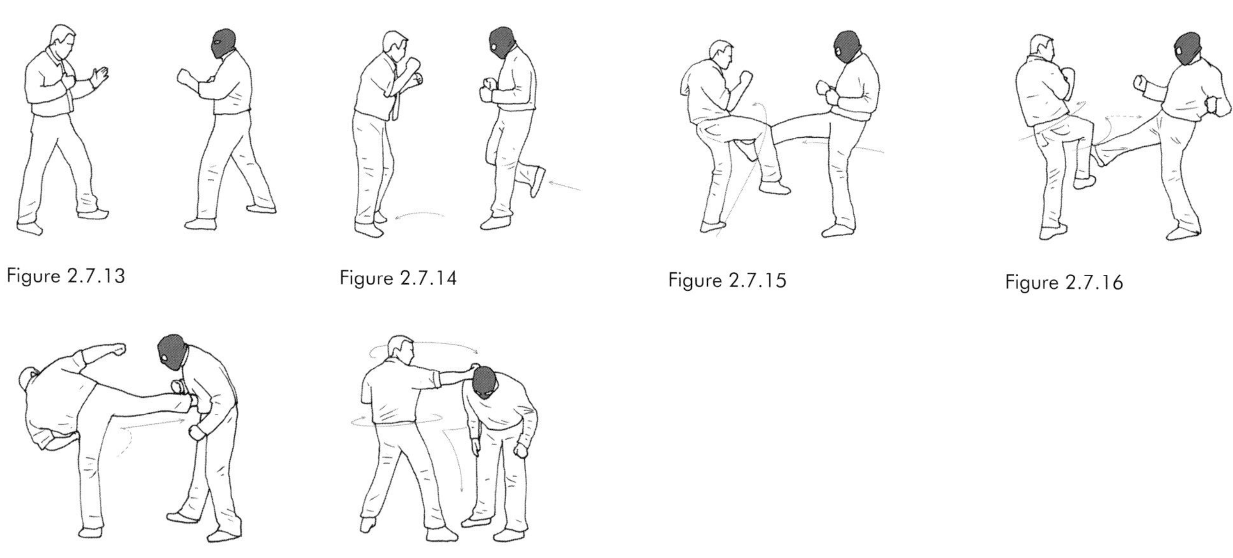

Figure 2.7.13 Figure 2.7.14 Figure 2.7.15 Figure 2.7.16

Figure 2.7.17 Figure 2.7.18
Use an inside knee sweep to block an opponent's kick, then propel a back side kick to his open midsection.
Follow up with a hammer strike to the back of his head or neck.

2.8 The Oblique Back Side Kick

General

This is the previous kick practiced with some footwork. Like the oblique front kick, the oblique back side kick allows you to attack an opponent with a very tight guard, who stands with his side toward you. You step out, and then just kick back in. Also, the kick in itself, as practiced, is an evasion that takes you out of a straight line of attack, as will be described in the applications.

The oblique back side kick is not a "curved" side kick, where the trajectory is not totally straight to avoid obstacles on the straight path; Rather, it is a straight kick, and the avoidance of obstacles is done by footwork!

The *curved* side kick is more of a feint kick; Figure 2.8.1 shows how a regular side kick traveling straight gets caught in the opponent's guard. The curved side kick—with exaggerated hop in this photo—goes around the guard in a trajectory that makes it a hybrid between a side kick and a hook kick (see Figures 2.8.2 and 2.8.3). Figure 2.8.4 shows the difference of range and trajectory.

Figure 2.8.1
A regular side kick is apt to get caught in the opponent's guard.

Figure 2.8.2

Figure 2.8.3
A curved side kick (with hop) avoids obstacles on the way to the target by taking a curved path.

Another way to circumvent the opponent's guard is the oblique back side kick described here.

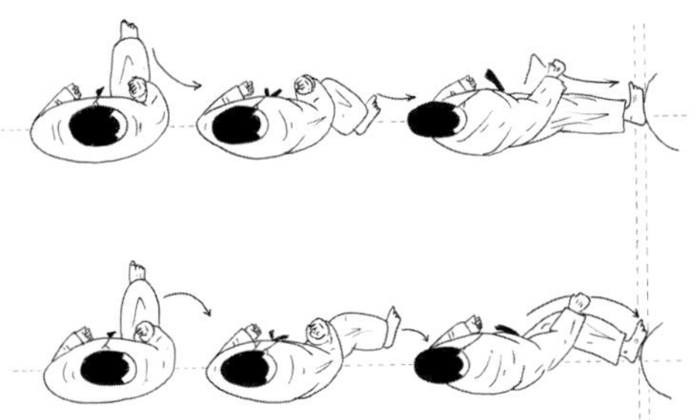

Figure 2.8.4
Overhead view of the regular side kick (above) and the curved side kick (below).

Description

In fighting stance, you step forward and in (Figure 2.7.6), giving half your back toward the straight line (and your opponent). You immediately slide your rear leg close to your front in the hopping footwork of all front leg kicks (Figure 2.7.7). But this time, you do not kick in the direction of your footwork momentum, but back toward the straight line (Figure 2.7.8). You are kicking your opponent 45 degrees on his unguarded inside.

Figure 2.8.5

Figure 2.8.6

Figure 2.8.7

Figure 2.8.8

These illustrations depict a side view of an oblique back side kick.

Figure 2.8.9
Overhead view of the oblique back side kick (left) and a diagram of the associated footwork (right).

Figures 2.8.10 through 2.8.12 show the execution of the kick against a same-stance jabbing opponent.

Figure 2.8.10

Figure 2.8.11

Figure 2.8.12

These images show the oblique back side kick in action.

Key Points

Giving your back to your opponent is always dangerous and must be a transient situation—you must perform the footwork and the kick in one swift and seamless movement.

Targets

All targets are fair game, from groin to face.

Typical Application

A typical application for this kick is as an attack against an opponent with a very tight guard. Attack your opponent's front leg with a sweep or a soccer low front kick (Figure 2.8.13). Keep the momentum of the kick and land forward and to your opponent's inside, about 45 degrees from the straight line (Figure 2.8.14). Preferably you should punch toward his face while landing to keep his eyes busy and prevent a counter. Step forward, obliquely, with your rear leg, which comes to replace the chambering front leg (Figure 2.8.15). From that point on, the direction of momentum changes by 90 degrees, and you side kick your opponent from the inside (Figure 2.8.16). Note that, when you start turning your back to a trained opponent, he will mistakenly expect a spin kick from the other leg and from the other direction. After landing your kicking foot, you can follow up with a spin-back outside crescent kick (Chapter 6, Section 8) with the other leg (Figure 2.8.17).

Figure 2.8.13

Figure 2.8.14

Figure 2.8.15

Figure 2.8.16

Figure 2.8.17
As you move into position to deliver an oblique back side kick, your opponent may mistakenly anticipate a spin kick from the opposite leg. Potentially follow up with a back spin outside crescent kick.

Specific Training

Practice the kick to the heavy bag over a straight line drawn on the floor. Get as far away from the line (and back) as possible while kicking in one move.

Self-defense

As an evasion from a straight attack. Your assailant rushes at to you with an overhead club strike. You evade the attack by stepping forward and obliquely to your inside, while punching toward his face (Figure 2.8.19). It is important to step forward, as well as aside, to cause him to miscalculate distance! Your rear leg then follows the front leg, doing a half step on its oblique trajectory. You are now fully out of the centerline. Deliver the side kick with the front leg (Figure 2.8.20). As you are on his inside, you must follow up, for example with a hammerfist to the groin, while landing and bending away from him (Figure 2.8.21).

Figure 2.8.18

Figure 2.8.19

Figure 2.8.20

Figure 2.8.21

Evade your opponent's overhead club strike, and deliver an oblique back side kick. Follow up with a hammerfist to the groin.

A stop spin back side kick.
(M. De Bremaeker)

2.9 The Spin-back Side Kick

Bandae yeop chagi / Momdollyo yeop chagi (taekwondo), *Pisaõ rodado / Chapa giratoria* (capoeira), *Teep glab lang* (muay thai)

General

This is a great way to deliver the side kick. The use of the centrifugal force of the pivot helps its power, though, of course much less than with a circular spin kick. The kick is very deceptive, as the spin back tends to prepare the opponent for a circular kick to come. The kick is excellent as a stop kick: just wait for your opponent to telegraph his starting attack, and "time" him.

Description

This is the version from a stationary position, timing your opponent or attacking a static opponent. Of course, all footwork variations are acceptable, stepping forward or backward before delivering. In fighting stance, you start by turning the head and then the shoulders back and around (2.9.2 and 2.9.3). You keep turning, pivoting with the hips now. Up to this stage, the feet have barely moved: It is like you have stretched an elastic band and are ready to let go. You then finish your 360 degrees turn while starting to chamber the knee in a regular side kick position (Figure 2.9.4). At this stage, unlike a spinning back circular kick, you have locked the hips and switch to a straight movement. You develop the kick by extending the leg and pushing the hips, just like a regular side kick (Figure 2.9.5). Chamber back.

Figure 2.9.1

Figure 2.9.2

Figure 2.9.3

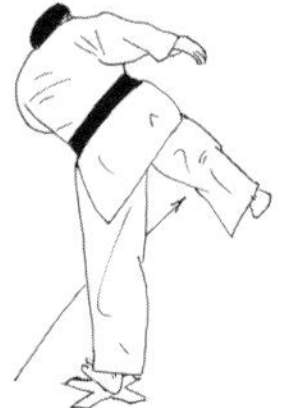
Figure 2.9.4

Figure 2.9.5

These illustrations depict a side view of the spin-back side kick.

Figures 2.9.6 through 2.9.9 show the execution of the kick from a static stance. Figures 2.9.10 through 2.9.13 show the kick delivered offensively after a forward step.

Figure 2.9.6

Figure 2.9.7

Figure 2.9.8

Figure 2.9.9

These images show the execution of spin-back side kick from a static stance.

Figure 2.9.10

Figure 2.9.11

Figure 2.9.12

Figure 2.9.13

These images show the execution of the spin-back side kick, delivered offensively after a forward step.

Key Points

- The key to success with this kick is the fast turning of the hips which stops and locks instantly as you reach the chambering position with your side toward your opponent.
- The spinning movement starts from the head, which "pulls" the shoulders, which in turn "pull" the hips. The hips keep turning without releasing the legs for as long as possible to hoard power and release it in one burst. The legs are crossed and twirled around each other until the body gets close to the kicking position.

Targets

All the body is a legitimate target, from knee to face.

Typical Application

Your opponent attacks you with a front leg high roundhouse kick (Chapter 3, Section 3), which you check with a front hand block while retreating slightly to keep your distance (Figure 2.9.15). You shuffle back just enough to stay in range and start pivoting inside into a spin-back side kick (Figure 2.9.16). The kick catches your open opponent in the body while he's still lowering his kicking leg (Figure 2.9.17). After lowering your kicking foot in front of you, you can follow up with a half pivot hook kick (Chapter 5, Section 7), to the face this time (Figure 2.9.18).

Figure 2.9.14 Figure 2.9.15 Figure 2.9.16 Figure 2.9.17 Figure 2.9.18

Use momentum from a front hand block to transition into a spin that culminates in a spin-back side kick to your opponent's body. Follow up with a half pivot hook kick to his face.

Specific Training

- Heavy bag kicking, making sure the kick comes in straight.
- Work the pivot and lock, while holding a stick on your shoulders (Figures 2.9.19 and 2.9.20).

Figure 2.9.19 Figure 2.9.20

Work on your pivot and lock, using a stick on your shoulders as a training tool.

- Figures 2.9.21 through 2.9.25 show how to drill the kick against a partner holding a target pad. Train for distance, power and speed.

Figure 2.9.21

Figure 2.9.22

Figure 2.9.23

Figure 2.9.24  Figure 2.9.25

Practicing the spin-back side kick with a partner holding a target pad will help you develop power and speed, and learn to quickly judge proper distance.

Self-defense

You confront your assailant and lunge punch toward his face (Figure 2.9.27). While he blocks, you immediately start your pivot and make use of your momentum to keep his hands busy around his head with a spinning backfist strike (Figure 2.9.28). You then lock your hips to stop your spinning movement and launch your side kick to his exposed ribs (Figure 2.9.29). This move can also be delivered to an opponent who counterattacks your lunge punch: you just change your spinning move from forward going to slightly backward going. You should practice both variations. As you have side kicked him to the body, you must follow up by sticking to him while he retreats from the momentum of the kick. Cross step with backfists until in range, then try to grab his front hand while front-leg hook kicking (Chapter 5, Section 3) him in the head (Figures 2.9.30 and 2.9.31).

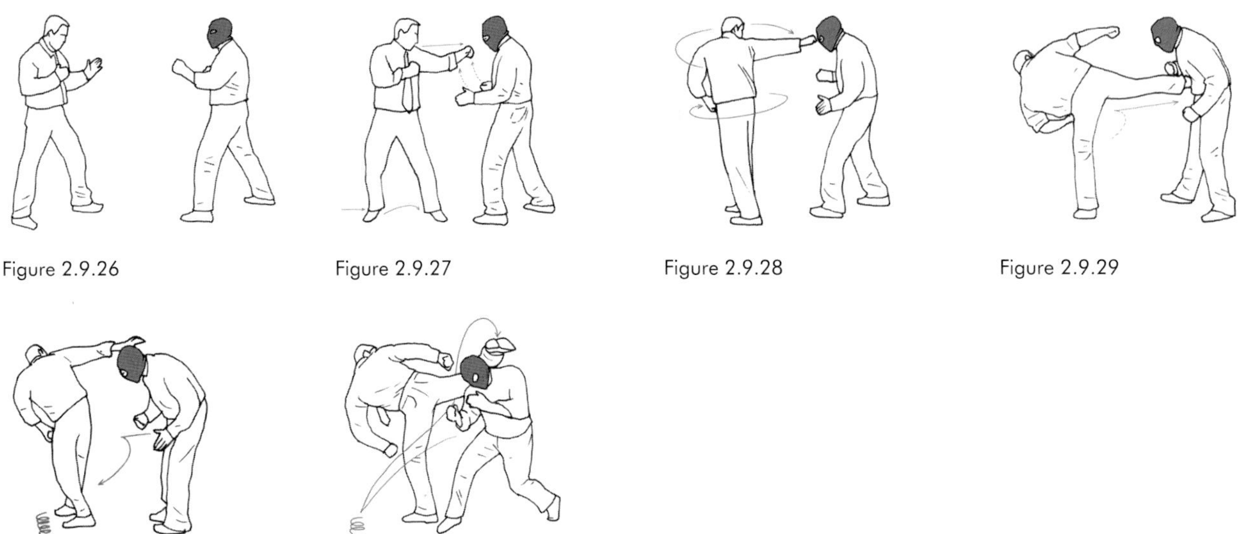

Figure 2.9.26 Figure 2.9.27 Figure 2.9.28 Figure 2.9.29

Figure 2.9.30 Figure 2.9.31

Preoccupy your opponent with a lunge punch to the face. Continue to keep him busy blocking while you line up a side kick to his ribs. Follow up with a front-leg hook kick to his head.

2.10 The Hand-on-the-floor Side Kick

Chapa no chão (capoeira)

General

We gave this kick its capoeira name, as it is very common in their practice, but it is a very interesting and easy way to perform the side kick in any martial art. The *capoeiristas* are trying to stay close to the floor at all times, and it is for them very natural. They also have a variation where both hands are on the floor, somewhat of a ground kick (*Escorão* or *Coice de mula*). For other martial artists however, this kick is a natural continuation of the principles of the body bent side kick (Section 5 of this chapter). In trying to keep the body away from the opponent, you bend the upper body even more, until you can place the opposite hand on the floor. This kick is very surprising and disorienting for a classical opponent.

Description

We will describe the kick in its attacking forward form, but footwork can be adapted to stop-kick or stepping backward or sideways situations. From the fighting stance, you cross your rear leg behind your front leg, while starting to bend your body to the side, away from your opponent (Figure 2.10.2). You then lift the leg, chamber half way and kick to the side like a regular side kick, while bending the body and placing the opposite hand to the floor (Figure 2.10.3). Because of the bending movement the chamber must not be with the knee as high as possible. While extending the leg, you are looking at your opponent from down under. Chamber back and, either keep going with other kicks, or get back into fighting stance. A *capoeirista* would probably use the hand on the floor for other kicks or to somersault or cartwheel.

Figure 2.10.1 Figure 2.10.2 Figure 2.10.3
These illustrations depict a side view of the hand-on-the-floor side kick.

Figure 2.10.4 shows the kick used as a stop kick against an opponent just about to initiate an attack.

Figure 2.10.4
This image shows the execution of the hand-on-the-floor side kick.

Key Points

- The hand touches the floor just as the foot impacts.
- The hand gives balance and power support to the kick: use it as such.
- Keep your eyes on your opponent at all times, while you bend from down under, not from the side.

Targets

The whole body is open to the kick, from shin to face.

Typical Application

You attack a counterattacking opponent with a convincing roundhouse kick at medium height (Figure 2.10.5) and you lower the kicking foot in front of the standing leg, purposely open to counterattack (Figure 2.10.6). Whether your opponent retaliates with a high punch or a kick is not important, as your upper body will get out of range. While your opponent develops his attack, bend away and lean on the floor, while side kicking (Figure 2.10.7).

Figure 2.10.5 Figure 2.10.6 Figure 2.10.7
Use a roundhouse kick as a pretense to get yourself into position, and then launch your hand-on-the-floor side kick.

Specific Training

Hit the heavy bag from different ranges: make sure your hand touches the floor simultaneously with the impact.

Self-defense

In this example, you stop-time your aggressor. As he starts his downward side stick attack (Figure 2.10.8), you step back, turning and crossing your front foot in front of the back. Simultaneously lower your upper body to get out of danger and put your hand on the floor (Figure 2.10.9). Side kick your assailant's ribs (Figure 2.10.10). Lunge punch at his face while you are standing up, back into fighting stance (Figure 2.10.11). Keep your forward momentum by reiterating the same movement, but this time as an attack: step forward by bringing your back foot behind your front foot, which will be delivering a second hand-on-floor side kick (Figure 2.10.12). Remember one of the golden rules of fighting, holding up both for sport tournament as well as real life: if you score with a technique and repeat it immediately, you will score again, because very few people can learn from their mistakes in the middle of a fight!

Figure 2.10.8 Figure 2.10.9 Figure 2.10.10 Figure 2.10.11 Figure 2.10.12
Two hand-on-the-floor side kicks are better than one! In the heat of a fight, you can deliver two of these kicks in succession with a high probability of landing both kicks.

2.11 The Kneeling-up Side Kick

General

This is a very interesting way to deliver the side kick: from a very low crossed knee position, very much in use in kung fu styles (*Lau Ma*) and Indonesian pencak silat. The use of the position itself is what makes this kick surprising. In the eyes of your opponent, you suddenly come down to burst up again with the kick. Going down is a footwork matter: you can step back, step forward or spin according to the situation. The kick is powerful because of the added effect of pushing up from the standing leg, but it is a kick that demands a lot of work to achieve proficiency. On the other hand, practicing the kick is an outstanding conditioning exercise.

Description

We describe here, as well as in the *Typical Application*, the kick from the low crossed leg position achieved by pivoting on the spot and turning a full 360 degrees without much movement of foot position. From the fighting stance, you turn the head and shoulders back to make a full turn (Figure 2.11.2), a little bit like a spinning kick (See Spin-back Side Kick—Section 9 in this chapter). While you execute the pivot you also lower yourself, with your upper body straight (Figures 2.11.3 and 2.11.4). How low you go depends on your flexibility, your training and the circumstances. It can be a relatively high crossed leg stance (*Kake dachi*—karate), or practically sitting on your bent leg, like in Indonesian styles. You then pop up, lifting yourself with the power of the front/upper leg, and lift simultaneously the back/lower leg into chambered knee (Figure 2.11.5). Side kick and chamber back (Figure 2.11.6).

Figure 2.11.1

Figure 2.11.2 Figure 2.11.3

Figure 2.11.4

Figure 2.11.5

Figure 2.11.6

These illustrations depict a side view of the kneeling-up side kick.

Figure 2.11.7
Side view of the low crossed knee posture

Figure 2.11.8
This illustration depicts a front view of the final movement of the kneeling-up side kick.

Key Points

- You have to spring up from the floor, rebound.
- The standing up and the kicking motions are simultaneous and must reach their apex together.
- Keep your hands up in guard at all times.

Targets

Typical targets include the groin, lower abdomen, ribs, solar plexus, throat, and chin.

Typical Application

This example is again based on the twisting motion to go down at the same spot you are standing. This is, in a way, an evasion, followed by a kick. While your opponent starts his lunging punch toward your face, you start pivoting back on yourself and going down into crossed leg low position (Figures 2.11.10 and 2.11.11). Your opponent pulls back his punch and you pop up, while keeping your front hand as a guard before your face (Figure 2.11.12). Side-kick from the high chambered position (Figure 2.11.13).

Figure 2.11.9 Figure 2.11.10 Figure 2.11.11 Figure 2.11.12 Figure 2.11.13
Evade a roundhouse punch by dropping beneath it, and into position to deliver the kneeling-up side kick.

Specific Training

- Practice standing up to the chambered position ten to twenty reps per leg.
- Practice the footwork variations of the crossed legs stance (See *Kneeling-up Roundhouse Kick*—Chapter 3, Section 17, *Specific Training*).
- Only after achieving smooth delivery in one move, start working on power on the heavy bag.
- The kick requires hip flexibility: work on splits and general flexibility.

Self-defense

In this case, we will illustrate a regular straight step back and crouching with no spin back and pivot. An assailant jumps on you with a lunging punch toward your face. Step back with your front foot behind the rear leg and "sit" down into position (Figures 2.11.15). As your attacker keeps coming on, and starts lifting his knee to kick, punch his groin with your front hand (Figure 2.11.16). You then lift up, while punching again to his face, and get his hands up, before side-kicking him in the ribs (Figure 2.11.17). You can follow up by punching his face again while lowering the kicking foot (Figure 2.11.18), and then spin-back back kicking (Chapter 4, Section 3) his body (Figure 2.11.19).

Figure 2.11.14 Figure 2.11.15 Figure 2.11.16 Figure 2.11.17

Figure 2.11.18 Figure 2.11.19

Evade a lunge punch by dropping beneath it. Punch your opponent two times, and then launch a kneeling-up side kick to his ribs. Follow up with another punch to the face, and finish the fight with a spin-back back kick.

2.12 The Drop Side Kick

General

For this kick you drop down on your hands and knees and side kick your opponent from below. Here again, such a kick is important only because of its unexpectedness. It is useful only on an attacking opponent who is opening himself during his attack: you disappear from view and let him impale himself onto your side kick. However, this is a powerful kick, thanks to the strong base formed by the hands and the knee.

Description

The kick can be executed from three footwork patterns: (a) On the spot, just going down onto the rear leg and placing the hands on the floor; (b)Stepping back with the front leg in front of the rear leg. (c) The third possibility is stepping forward with the rear leg behind the front leg, but it is much less practical, as the kick does not lend itself easily to an attack mode. We explain only the most common stepping-back options.

You are trying to time an attack by your opponent, and therefore, as soon as you discern the attack, turn your back slightly and step back with your front leg in front of your already bending rear leg (Figure 2.12.2). Alternatively, "fall" directly in place. In both cases, place both your hands on the floor, as your rear knee touches the floor, and keep your eyes on your opponent (Figure 2.12.3). Start developing the side kick, pushing with the hips and hands at impact (Figure 2.12.4). Chamber back and lower your kicking foot, while you are already coming up on your other leg, back to fighting stance (Figure 2.12.5).

Figure 2.12.1 Figure 2.12.2 Figure 2.12.3

Figure 2.12.4

Figure 2.12.5

These illustrations depict a side view of the drop side kick.

Figures 2.12.6 through 2.12.8 show a flawless application of the kick as a stop kick against a high kicker, attacking with a high roundhouse in this case.

Figure 2.12.6 Figure 2.12.7 Figure 2.12.8
These images show the execution of the drop side kick.

Key Points

- The success of the kick is highly dependant on timing and how fast you can get down into the chambered position.
- The hips must be used, just like in a regular side kick.

Typical Application

Although this is also an excellent "timing" stop-kick against a full-momentum punch, we present the preferred application against a high kicker. Your opponent is a high kicker and closes the distance with a lunge punch or backfist (Figure 2.12.9). You prepare your drop, while he starts his hop for a front leg high side kick (Figure 2.12.10). Drop while he develops his kick and hit him in the groin when he is fully open (Figure 2.12.11).

Figure 2.12.9 Figure 2.12.10 Figure 2.12.11
Slip under your opponent's high kick and launch your own drop side kick to his groin.

Specific Training

- Practice the drop to chambered position first, before working on the bag for power.
- Practice dropping down at different distances, marked on the floor: slightly forward, slightly backward.
- Practice the drop with a partner swinging a stick at solar plexus level.

Self-defense

Here again, we present the drop side kick against a kicking attack. Your assailant lunges with a jab to close the distance and launches a full rear leg roundhouse (Figure 2.12.12). You step back and drop down (Figure 2.12.13) to catch him with your side kick in the groin at full extension (Figure 2.12.14). Immediately drop the kicking leg down behind you and use your hand to lift the body and extend the knee you have been standing on in such a way that your foot hooks his standing ankle (Figure 2.12.15). In this position, you drop on the floor while side kicking behind the knee of his hooked standing leg (Figure 2.12.16).

Figure 2.12.12

Figure 2.12.13

Figure 2.12.14

Figure 2.12.15

Figure 2.12.16
Slip under your opponent's lunge and roundhouse kick and launch your own drop side kick to his groin. Then hook his ankle and take your opponent to the ground.

Figure 2.12.17
A drop side kick.

More Advanced Side Kicks

What follows is a brief review of some more advanced kicks. They are not presented in detail here, as they are beyond the scope of this book.

The Ground Side Kick

Very much like the drop side kick, but are already on the floor. No doubt the best kick to be used from the ground.

The Sacrifice Drop Side Kick

This is the drop side kick, but performed when you do not have time to go down orderly to the floor, as in Section 12 of this chapter. So you just let yourself fall while kicking, receiving yourself on the hands. It is very effective to time stop an attack.

The Knee Drop Side Kick

This is a difficult kick practiced in some Korean styles.

The Flying Side Kick
The popular flying side kick is the typical example of the flying kick.

The Double Flying Side Kick
This one is even more spectacular. A flying kick where you hit your opponent with both legs simultaneously.

The Low Flying Side Kick
This is a very special kick, typical of Vietnamese arts. You jump high to side kick your opponent knee.

The High Roundhouse Feint to Side Kick
This is a classic feint kick, natural and effective, where you gradually turn a roundhouse kick into a side kick.

Comparative Tables

Table 1 — Comparative table of main different possible chambers for side kicks.

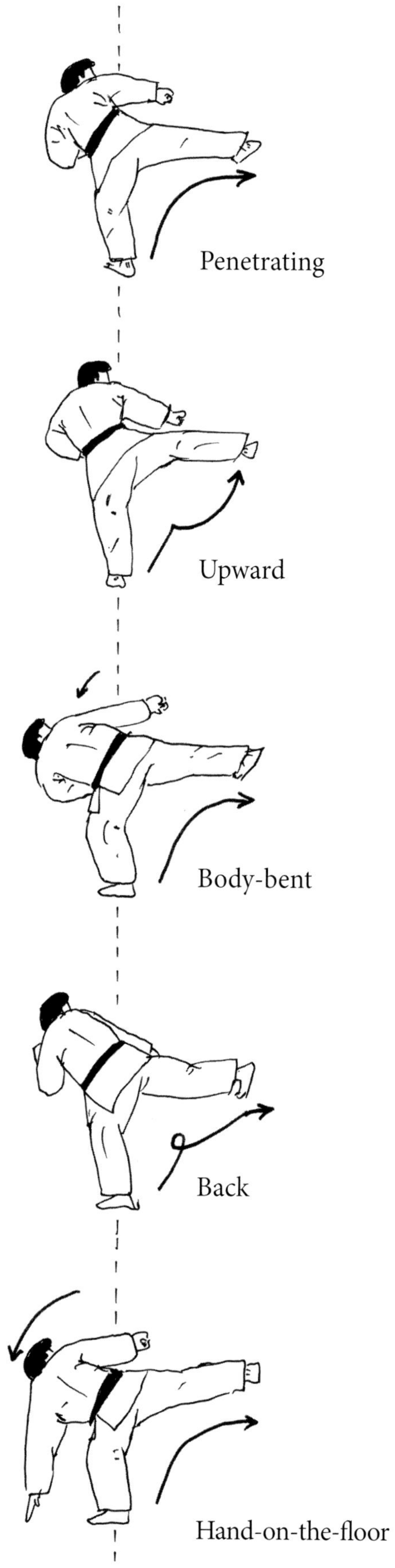

Penetrating

Upward

Body-bent

Back

Hand-on-the-floor

Table 2 — Comparative table of trajectory and body position for main side kicks.

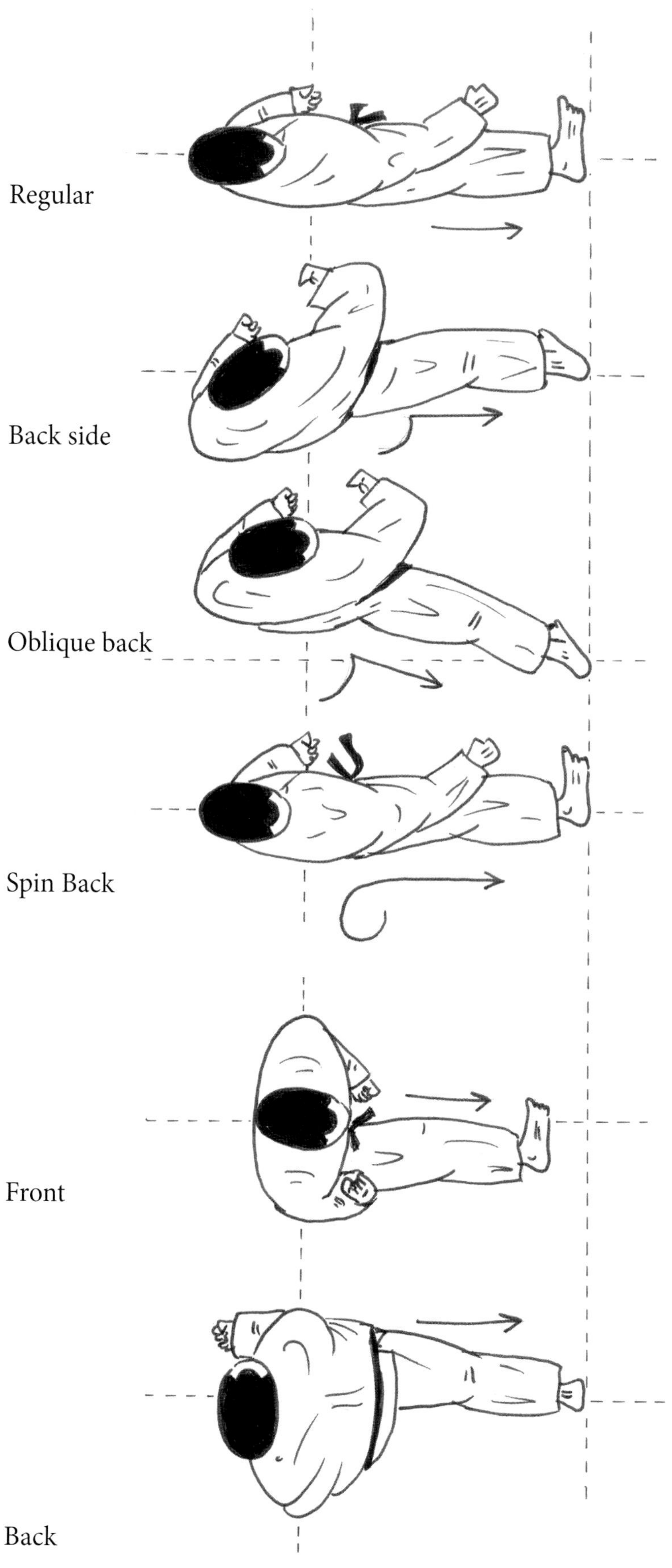

Regular

Back side

Oblique back

Spin Back

Front

Back

Table 3 — Comparative overhead view of trajectory and body position of main side kicks.

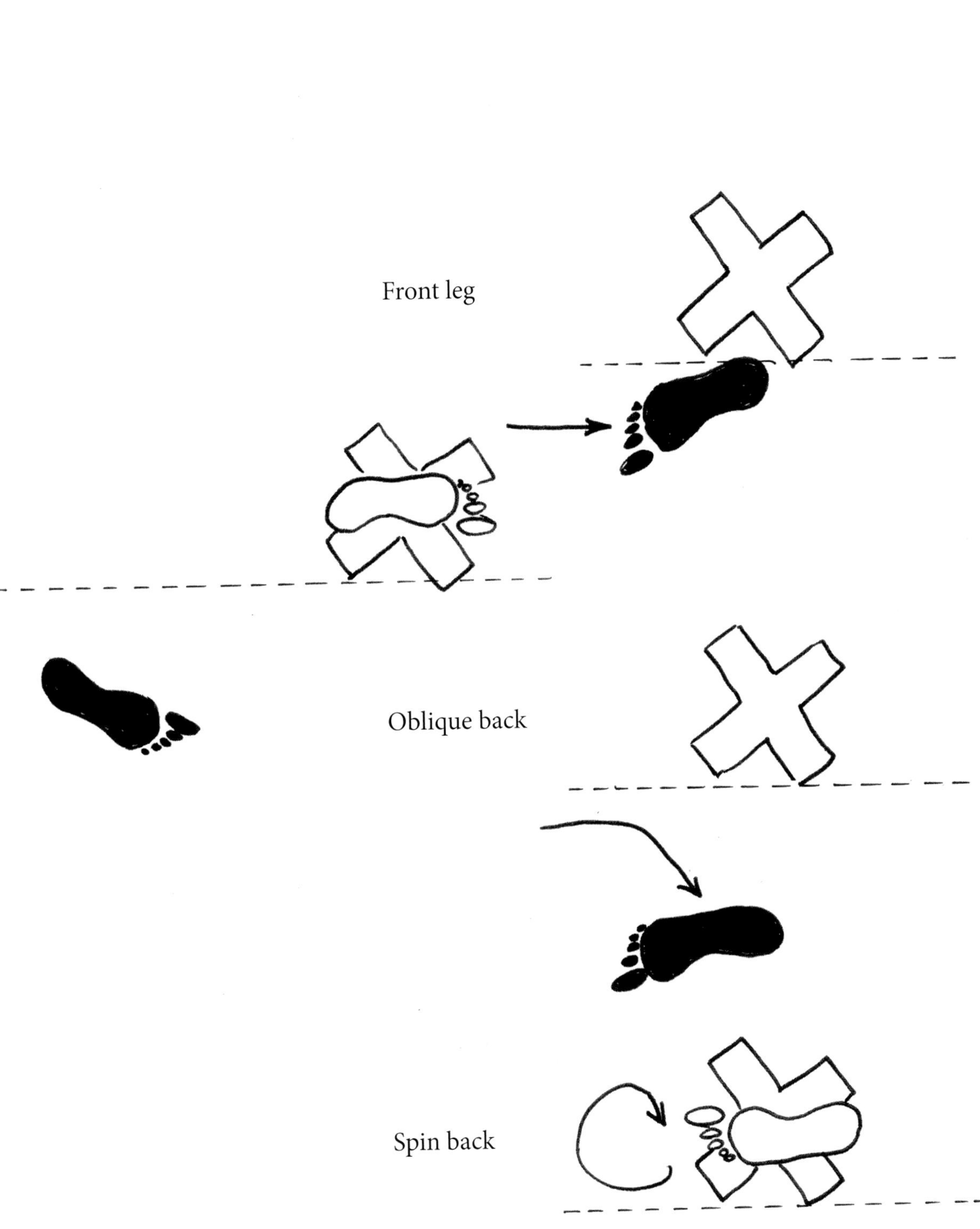

Table 4 — Comparative footwork for main side kick variations.

CHAPTER THREE

Roundhouse Kicks

Straight leg roundhouse kick. (M. De Bremaeker)

Roundhouse kicks are a rather modern phenomenon. Most traditional styles of kung fu and karate sport very few roundhouse kicks in their classic forms. The emergence of the sporting side of martial arts has spurred their development and roundhouse kicks are certainly the most widely used kicks in sporting events of all types, from MMA to traditional non-contact karate, through, of course, taekwondo tournaments. These kicks, attacking the sides of the opponent facing you, are very different in feeling and execution than the previous straight kicks. They require flexibility, speed, and a lot of training. Once these kicks are mastered, they become a very powerful weapon, suitable for nearly every possible situation, including self-defense.

In the sections that follow we present all the basic variations of the kick from the fast classic version to the lethal straight-leg low kick of the "hard" arts, and include exotic kicks like the spinning-back and downward roundhouse kicks.

3.1 The Full Roundhouse Kick

O mawashi geri (karate), *Tohllyu cha tzirugi / Dol lyeu cha gi* (taekwondo), *Hao the / Yuan jiao / Pai lie tui* (kung fu), *Martelo em pé* (capoeira), *Hoanh phong cuoc / Hoanh cuoc* (viet vo dao), *Fouetté* (savate-boxe française), Hook kick (jeet kune do)

General

The roundhouse kick is the workhorse of tournament fighting, and hence of fighting in general. Not only is it a powerful kick in itself as an attack, a counterattack or a "timing" stop, it is also very useful, when done without full commitment, as a check and gauge of your opponent's reactions and footwork. The roundhouse allows you to attack the unprotected side of your opponent. It is not as powerful as the "straight" kicks, like the front or the side kick, because you can't push with the hips into the kick. It does not have the centrifugal force of the spinning kicks either. The kick derives its power from the pivot of the hips and its "whipping" action: getting a few inches into the target and being pulled back like a whip. The name of the kick in savate is *fouetté* (whipped kick). It is interesting that in no traditional kata of the Shotokan style, and most of the "oldest" styles, does the roundhouse kick appear, with the exception of a sequence of two drop roundhouse kicks (Chapter 3, Section 14) in the *Unsu* kata.

The target is to be hit with the ball of the foot, or, especially in tournament fighting, with the upper side of the foot and the front of the ankle joint (In Japanese: *Haisoku*, *Kasokutei*, *Asi no ko*, or *Sokko*).

Description

From the fighting position (Figures 3.1.1 and 3.1.6), lift the rear leg, bent at the knee, on your side, parallel to the ground. This first stage looks like, and basically is, a circular knee strike at hip level (Figures 3.1.2 and 3.1.7). You then pivot on your standing foot, turning your hips strongly, while you extend the leg in a circular motion parallel to the ground. When you hit the target, the kicking leg is fully extended, the hips are perpendicular to your opponent, your standing foot is pointing nearly opposite from your opponent, and your body is slightly bent backward (Figures 3.1.3 and 3.1.8). As soon as you connect a few inches into the target, with the ball or the upper side of the foot (Figure 3.1.9), you retract the leg forcefully into bent chambered position (Figure 3.1.4). Lower the kicking leg forward (Figure 3.1.5) or backward. It is useful, especially at the beginning of practice, to throw the extended arm of the kicking leg backward, to counterbalance the hip movement. With practice, you do not need this arm move to control your balance and the kick delivery with the same "whipping" feeling.

Figure 3.1.1 Figure 3.1.2 Figure 3.1.3 Figure 3.1.4 Figure 3.1.5
Side view of the full roundhouse kick.

Figure 3.1.6 Figure 3.1.7 Figure 3.1.8
Front view of the full roundhouse kick.

Figure 3.1.9
The parts of the foot that make contact during the roundhouse kick.

Figures 3.1.10 through 3.1.12 show a clear front view of the delivery of the full roundhouse kick.

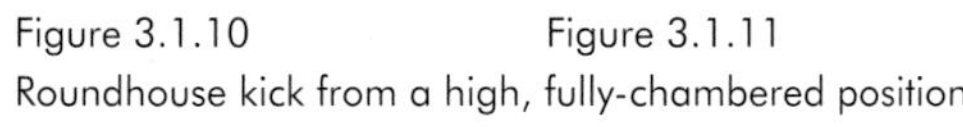

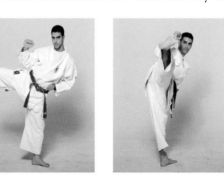

Figure 3.1.10 Figure 3.1.11 Figure 3.1.12
Roundhouse kick from a high, fully-chambered position.

Key Points

- The pivot on the standing foot is crucial. Do not lift the heel.
- This is the full version of the roundhouse: this is a powerful kick that needs the full swing of the hips, simultaneously with the leg-whipping extension.
- As already mentioned, the leg retraction is key to the kick's effectiveness.
- During the first knee-lifting move, the upper body stays straight. Only during the rest of the kick do you bend backward and sideways (up to 45 degrees).

Targets

The kick is in range of all targets, and effective all over. Being a whipping kick however, softer targets are preferred: the head, the groin and the knee first. Targets of secondary preference include: the solar plexus, the kidneys, the lower ribs, both sides of the thigh. The kick is also a great harassment kick to be used against the guarding hands and elbows.

Typical Application

Figures 3.1.13 and 3.1.14 illustrate a roundhouse kick application that brought this author many tournament points. The kick's success is based on the mistaken feeling that, in a side fighting stance, one's back is not vulnerable. There is a very common misconception that a kick toward your back, when you stand in a side fighting stance, can be easily blocked and controlled with the front hand. Wrong! The key to the success of this move is not telegraphing it! Stand in the same stance as your opponent, keeping your body away in spite of the fact that you shift your body weight to the front leg. The upper body is relaxed and does not move, and the head stays at constant level (Figure 3.1.13). With minimal upper body movement, throw a fully committed back leg roundhouse, directly into the lower back of your opponent, at belt level (Figure 3.1.14). This is a very difficult move to block because of the position of your opponent's body and elbow. Once the kick is on its way, bend your body 45 degrees backward, while you keep the standing leg bent, and extend your hips to gain range. Retract the leg immediately after contact.

Figure 3.1.13 Figure 3.1.14
These images illustrate a full roundhouse to the lower back of a side-stanced opponent.

Specific Training

- Lift the knee over a chair on your side, and kick (See Figures 3.1.15 through 3.1.17).

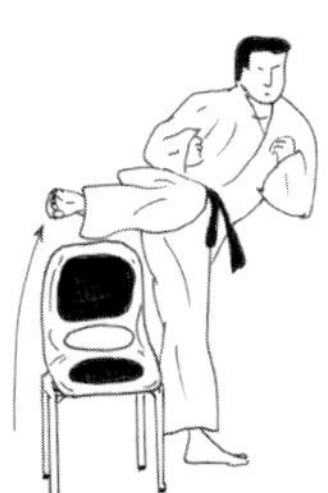

Figure 3.1.15 Figure 3.1.16 Figure 3.1.17
The chair forces the practitioner to lift the leg and chamber fully.

- Work on your hip socket flexibility with stretches like the hurdle stretch (Figure 3.1.18).

Figure 3.1.18
Hurdle stretch for roundhouse flexibility.

- As it is the power version of the roundhouse kick, it is important to practice on the heavy bag.
- Have a partner helping you correct and stretch the chambered position (See Figure 3.1.19).

Figure 3.1.19
Lifting the chambered leg for roundhouse flexibility.

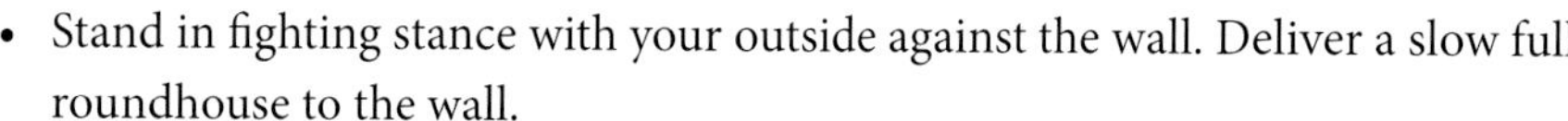

- Stand in fighting stance with your outside against the wall. Deliver a slow full roundhouse to the wall.

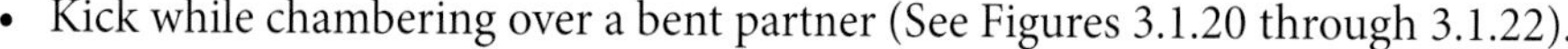

- Kick while chambering over a bent partner (See Figures 3.1.20 through 3.1.22).

Figure 3.1.20 Figure 3.1.21 Figure 3.1.22
Use a partner to force a full chamber and kick delivery parallel to the floor.

- Kick slowly and chamber back in "Runner stretch" position (See Figures 3.1.23 through 3.1.25) while seated on the floor.
- Use a dancing bar to balance yourself while kicking very slowly with perfect form.

Figure 3.1.23 Figure 3.1.24 Figure 3.1.25
Slow kicking while sitting on the floor will strengthen your kicking muscles.

Self-defense

An assailant seizes your right wrist with his right hand (Figure 3.1.26). Immediately step to the left, with your left foot, in order to get away from any left punch or kick he could be planning. Simultaneously lift your (and his) right arm (Figure 3.1.27) in an encircling move and roundhouse kick him in his open abdomen (Figure 3.1.28). If possible, complete the circling move and take hold of his right wrist. You can then repeat the kick, and then launch a crescent kick (Chapter 6, Section 1) to the head with your other leg (Figure 3.1.29).

Figure 3.1.26 Figure 3.1.27 Figure 3.1.28 Figure 3.1.29
A roundhouse kick used against a wrist-hold.

3.2 The Small Roundhouse Kick

Ko mawashi geri (karate), *Pahn tohllyu chagi* (taekwondo), *Sepak bulat* (pencak silat), Groin kick (jeet kune do)

General

The "small" version of the roundhouse kick is basically the same kick but delivered from a front kick chamber, with the knee in front of you, perpendicular to the ground (Figure 3.2.3). In fact, this is an extreme version, and there are countless variations in between the full roundhouse (chamber parallel to the ground, Figure 3.2.1) and the small roundhouse (front kick chamber, Figure 3.2.3). Generally, the roundhouse kick in most styles is the middle version in between these two extremes: the leg is chambered at 45 degrees (See Figure 3.2.2). As all variations are possible, we present the extremes only.

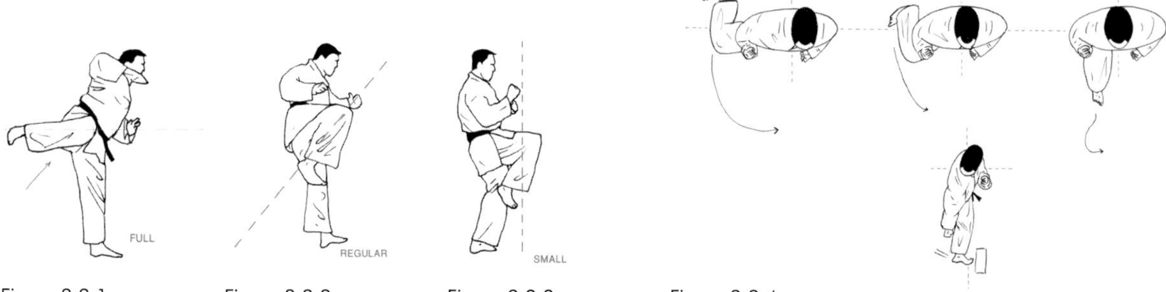

Figure 3.2.1 Figure 3.2.2 Figure 3.2.3
Side view of the different chambering positions for the roundhouse kick.

Figure 3.2.4
Overhead view of the different chambering positions for the roundhouse kick: full, regular, and small, respectively.

The small roundhouse is much less powerful than the full roundhouse presented earlier, but it has the advantage of being quicker, with less forewarning to the opponent, and offers some protection of the body during the early stages of delivery. It is an excellent kick to gauge your opponent's reactions and footwork, and a great first combination attack to be followed by more powerful kicks.

Description

See Figures 3.2.5 through 3.2.9. The kick can also be delivered with the front leg, but we describe here the rear leg version. Lift the knee of the rear leg into a front kick chamber (Figure 3.2.6). You then simultaneously extend the leg and pivot the hips into roundhouse kick position (Figure 3.2.8). When you hit the target, again with the ball or the upper part of the foot, the leg is parallel to the floor and the body is in the same position as the final position of the full roundhouse kick. Do not forget the immediate recoil of the leg. Lower the leg in front of you or backward as the circumstances dictate.

Figure 3.2.5 Figure 3.2.6 Figure 3.2.7 Figure 3.2.8 Figure 3.2.9
Side view of the small roundhouse kick, clearly showing the front kick chamber.

Figures 3.2.10 to 3.2.13 show the front view of the different stages of the development of the kick. Compare chambered position to the traditional full roundhouse kick, as in Figure 3.1.11, shown previously.

Figure 3.2.10 Figure 3.2.11 Figure 3.2.12 Figure 3.2.13
Front view of the small roundhouse kick, clearly showing the front kick chamber.

Key Points

- Lift the knee high—do not get tempted to deliver the kick diagonally.
- Turn the hips fully, just like the full roundhouse—do not make this kick an inward-tilted front kick (Chapter 1, Section 10).

Targets

If the kick is not a feint, a distance-closer or a gauge for your opponent's reactions, it must be target-specific. As it lacks power, it must be directed to soft targets, and/or those susceptible to the whipping effect of the recoil: the groin, the solar plexus (precisely), the kidneys, the throat and the face.

The legs (thighs and knees) are good targets to prepare for a follow-up. See Figures 3.2.14 through 3.2.17 for the use of the kick as a "softener" for an outer reap takedown (*O soto gari*—judo) coupled with an unbalancing elbow strike.

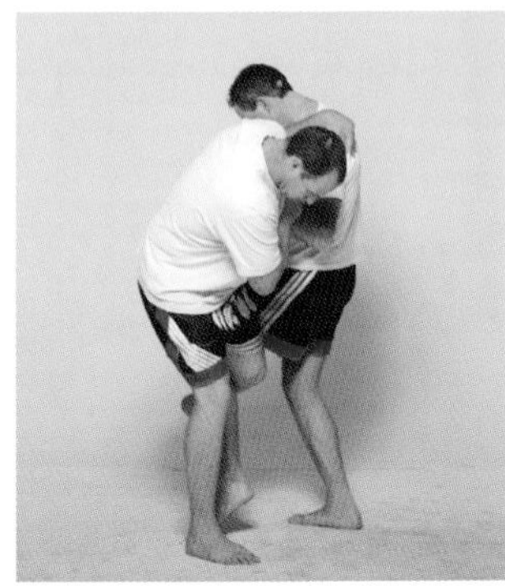

Figure 3.2.14 Figure 3.2.15 Figure 3.2.16 Figure 3.2.17
Front-leg small roundhouse to thigh and elbow strike combination will soften the opponent and set him up for a takedown.

Typical Application

Use the small roundhouse as a set-up. Attack your opponent's lower back with a rear leg, fast small roundhouse (Figures 3.2.18 and 3.2.19). It is a difficult kick to block, and it hurts the kidneys, even though it is not a very powerful kick. Even if the kick has been blocked, keep going as it was only a fast opening move (for which the full roundhouse is not suitable). As you retract the leg in a whipping effect, you backfist your opponent's face with the redressing of your upper body. In fact, this is a typical movement in which you make use of the recoil of the leg to power up your trunk coming back to erect, and even leaning toward your opponent, while delivering a one-legged backfist. You then lower your kicking leg forward, as your opponent is stepping back. Throw a second backfist toward your opponent's face (Figure 3.2.20) while crossing your rear leg forward, behind your front leg, in a forward cross step. You then launch a hook kick (with the same kicking leg, Chapter 5, Section 3) to your opponent's head, hooking around his raised hand (Figure 3.2.21).

If possible, you should try to get a hold of your opponent's wrist, as in Figure 3.2.22, if and when he blocks your second backfist.

Figure 3.2.18 Figure 3.2.19 Figure 3.2.20 Figure 3.2.21 Figure 3.2.22
A fast small roundhouse will allow for closing the distance or setting up an opponent for a coming combination.

Specific Training

- Speed and precision training: hit dangling tennis balls (Figure 3.2.23), and kick in increasing and decreasing order into the gaps of a ladder in front of you (see Figure 3.2.24).
- Over a chair in front of you, but close to a wall to force the (high) front chamber (Figures 3.2.25 and 3.2.26).

Figure 3.2.23 Figure 3.2.24
Training for speed and accuracy of the small roundhouse kick.

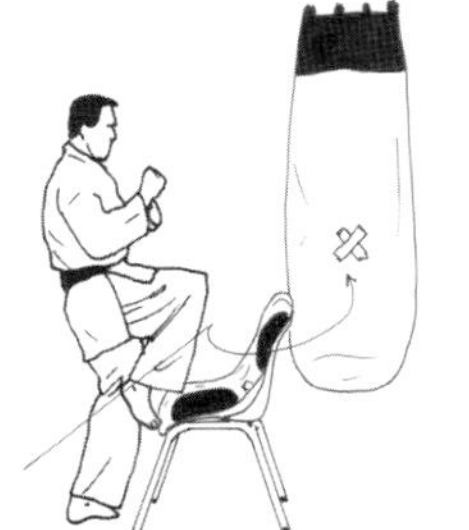

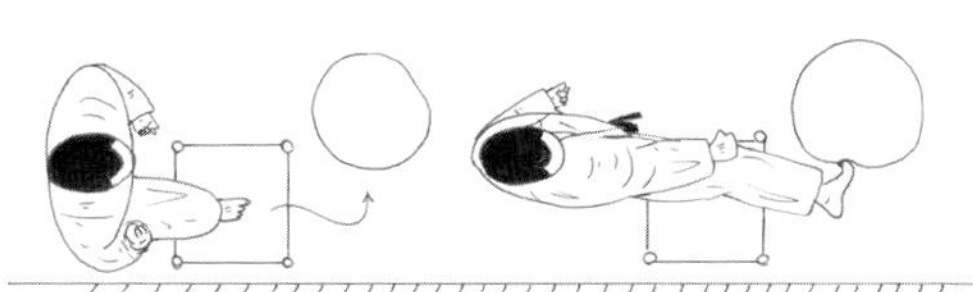

Figure 3.2.25 Figure 3.2.26
The wall will force you to twist the hips at the last minute and the chair will ensure a high chamber.

Self-defense

An assailant grabs your collar from behind (Figure 3.2.27). You immediately grab your lapels, to catch his fingers inside your collar, and then bend forward and step forward. Reverse your momentum suddenly and start turning toward your opponent while passing your head under his arm, still caught in your collar. His fingers are painfully locked (Figure 3.2.28). In order to keep his fingers locked, keep big shifts to a minimum and chamber your coming roundhouse as a front kick (Figure 3.2.29). Deliver the small roundhouse to his groin while releasing your lapels. Keep kicking! For example, use your other leg for a full-powered straight leg roundhouse (Chapter 3, Section 7) to the side of the knee (Figure 3.2.30).

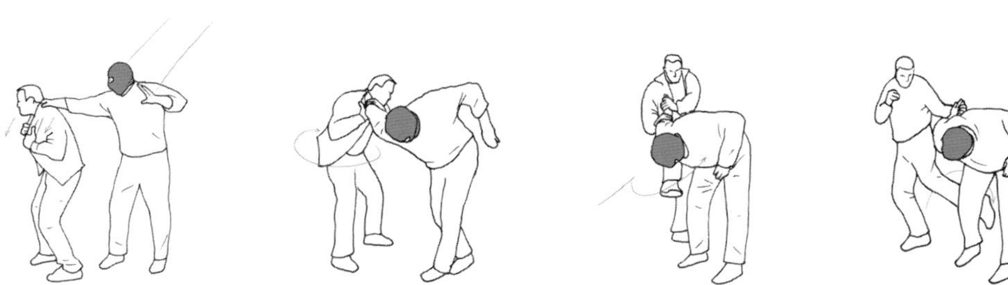

Figure 3.2.27 Figure 3.2.28 Figure 3.2.29 Figure 3.2.30
The small roundhouse is perfectly adequate for self-defense maneuvers like a back collar grip-release.

3.3 The Front Leg Roundhouse Kick

Kizami geri / Mae ashi mawashi geri (karate)

General

This is the most used version of the roundhouse kick: it is fast and allows for relative protection during the preparatory phases. The front leg roundhouse kick can be delivered in all its variations (small to full roundhouse), and with or without footwork. The front leg kick with no footwork, being nearly exclusively a "timing" kick, should be described as an advanced stop kick. However, it can be used as an attack when used as a low kick, as in the combination described in Figures 3.3.1 through 3.3.3—a roundhouse to the inside of your opponent's leg will open his guard, make him retreat, and allow for a "shoot" takedown for example.

Figure 3.3.1
These images show a set-up for takedown.

Figure 3.3.2

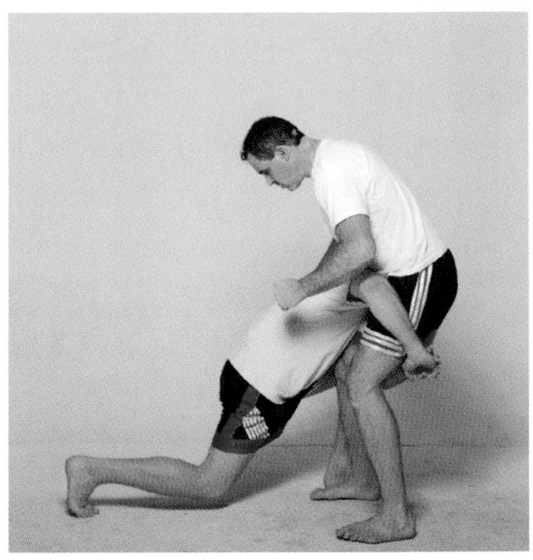

Figure 3.3.3

The footwork for advancing with a front leg roundhouse can be one of the following: cross the rear leg in front of the kicking leg, or hop and the rear leg takes the place of the kicking front foot. Those will be described here.

The third possibility, more in use with a side stance, is bringing the rear foot close and parallel to the front foot, and then chamber. This option will be presented, more appropriately, with the universal chamber roundhouse kick (Section 4 of this chapter).

Description

See delivery from starting position in Figure 3.3.4. Either cross your rear leg in front of your front foot while turning the hips (Figures 3.3.5 through 3.3.7), or hop with the rear foot taking the place of the raising front foot (Figures 3.3.8 through 3.3.10). Lift the knee directly into chambered position with the hips already turned. Extend the leg in parallel to the floor and recoil. Lower the leg in front.

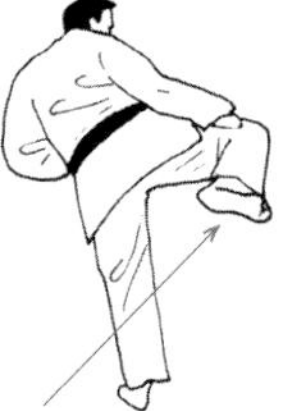

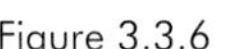

Figure 3.3.4 Figure 3.3.5 Figure 3.3.6 Figure 3.3.7
Front leg roundhouse delivered with a step.

Figure 3.3.8 Figure 3.3.9 Figure 3.3.10
Front leg roundhouse delivered with a hop.

Figures 3.3.11 and 3.3.12 show the application of a fast front leg roundhouse kick, aiming just above the belt in competitive fighting (in order to make spotting and blocking difficult, speed is of the essence here).

Figure 3.3.11
Attack to the back from inverted stances.

Figure 3.3.12
Attack to the lower abdomen from same stances.

Key Points

- In the chambered position, the body is already in place with the hips sideways and the standing foot pointing backward.
- Speed and recoil are key to the power of the kick: sink a few inches into the target and pull back!

Typical Application

See Figures 3.3.13 through 3.3.19. You are in fighting stance with slightly more weight on the back leg. This is the typical stance for direct front kicking, as there is less weight on the front leg. Your opponent punches you and you avoid the punch by leaning backward, while lifting your front leg into roundhouse chamber (Figures 3.3.14 and 3.3.15). This is a 'timing' kick, reaching your opponent's head at full extension of his punch. Your stunned opponent retreats and you follow him by crossing your rear leg in front of your front leg, while feinting with a low jab toward his lower abdomen. Chamber and release your front leg roundhouse kick toward his head, again. You can follow up by again using a roundhouse kick from the same leg, but this time to the groin, as the previous kick caused your opponent to lift his hands. For this last kick, the leg can start directly from the chambered back position without touching the ground, or you can have your foot "rebound" off the floor (Figure 3.3.19).

Figure 3.3.13 Figure 3.3.14 Figure 3.3.15 Figure 3.3.16

Figure 3.3.17 Figure 3.3.18 Figure 3.3.19
Triple front-leg roundhouse kick combination.

Targets

All the typical targets are available, from the knee up to the face.

Specific Training

- Work on the footwork alone.
- Then kick the heavy bag from farther and farther away.
- Then repeat, but place a chair in front of the bag to make sure you start the kicking from chamber with the leg up.

Self-defense

See Figures 3.3.20 through 3.3.24. In self-defense especially, the simplest things are safer. And it is always better to take the initiative. Close the distance to your assailant, with a lunge punch toward his groin. This will make your approach safer, as everyone tends to protect their groin instinctively, and it will help to lure him into believing the punch was a feint and the real attack will be higher. You then, indeed, attack his eyes with the same (open) hand, as soon as he lowers his hands. This is not the real attack, but another feint to allow you to close the distance with your rear leg, while having him lifting his hands back up. And you front leg roundhouse him in the groin or lower abdomen (Figure 3.3.23).
As he will definitely lower his hands, backfist him forcefully while lowering your kicking leg.

Figure 3.3.20

Figure 3.3.21

Figure 3.3.22

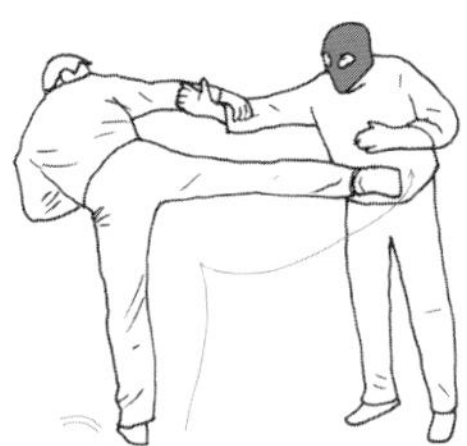

Figure 3.3.23

Figure 3.3.24

Typical progressive indirect attack leading to a mid-level roundhouse.

Body bent roundhouse to lower back. (R. Faige)

3.4 The Universal Chamber Roundhouse Kick

General

This is simply a roundhouse kick, usually front leg, delivered from the already described universal chamber position popularized by Bill Wallace. From this protected position (Figure 3.4.1), the opponent does not know if he should expect a roundhouse, a side or a hook kick.

Figure 3.4.1
This image illustrates the versatile universal chamber.

Description

Figures 3.4.2 through 3.4.4 illustrate the front leg version, where the rear foot is brought close and parallel to the front foot, before the leg is chambered.

Figure 3.4.2 Figure 3.4.3 Figure 3.4.4
The universal chamber position makes it difficult for the opponent to discern which kick is coming.

Figures 3.4.5 and 3.4.6 show a high roundhouse delivered from the universal chamber.

Figure 3.4.5 Figure 3.4.6
A side kick or a hook kick could be thrown from this same chamber.

As mentioned before, there are many nuances for each movement, emphasizing different aspects and angles. For example, you could deliver a roundhouse kick from a chambered position more suitable to a side kick: it wouldn't constitute a full universal chamber, but close, and with the same principle in mind.

Key Points

- The body is inclined 45 degrees to the side and to the back.
- The chambered leg protects both the groin and the lower trunk.
- There are some differences between the three kicks in the movement of the hips: make sure to keep them at a minimum and to move the hips at the last moment during the kicking, so as not to reveal your intentions.

Targets

The universal chamber is generally not used for low kicks. Therefore, all vital points from the groin up!

Typical Application

See Figures 3.4.7 through 3.4.12. The best way to use the universal chamber kicks is to alternate kicks when your opponent expects more of the same. Again, remember: the simplest things work best! Attack your opponent with a universal chamber front leg hook kick (Chapter 5, Section 5) to the face. Whether your kick scores or not (Figure 3.4.9), keep going and lower the leg into fighting stance to immediately repeat your forward movement (Figure 3.4.11) and universal chambering. Your opponent will instinctively expect the same kick and lift his hands for protection, but you will be delivering this time, from the same chambering position, a roundhouse kick to the other, unprotected, side—the back of his head.

Figure 3.4.7 Figure 3.4.8 Figure 3.4.9 Figure 3.4.10

Figure 3.4.11 Figure 3.4.12

Two different kicks launched in succession from the same chambering position.

Specific Training

The key to success is mastering the chambered position. Therefore you'll have to practice in front of the mirror and throw the three kicks from this position. Do it with the lowering of the leg, and with no lowering in between the kicks. Practice slow and fast kicks.

Self-defense

Hop forward into universal chamber (3.4.14), and deliver a high roundhouse to your opponent's head. Chamber back to universal chamber position (3.4.16) and deliver, this time, a low side kick to his lower belly. This time you change kicks, but also change levels. Backfist as you lower your kicking leg (3.4.18), and then can follow up with a reverse punch. Kicking at different heights and angles from the same chamber can be very confusing to your opponent!

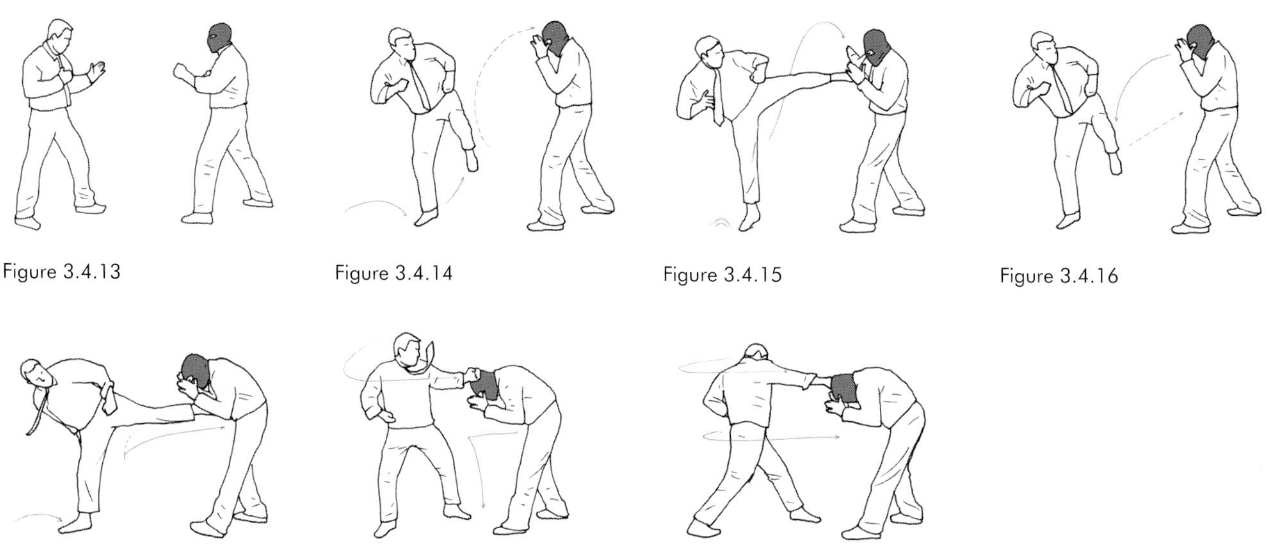

Figure 3.4.13 Figure 3.4.14 Figure 3.4.15 Figure 3.4.16

Figure 3.4.17 Figure 3.4.18 Figure 3.4.19

Two kicks from different angles and to different levels, but both from the same inscrutable chamber.

3.5 The Hopping Roundhouse Kick

Surikonde mawashi geri (karate)

General

As with the previously described hopping front and side kick, the hopping roundhouse is delivered with a forward hop in the chambered position to allow for greater range. The kick can be delivered in this way in all its forms: full, small or universal chamber, and can be executed with the front or the rear leg. The arduous practice of these hopping kicks is part of the mastery of being able to kick from any position and any distance.

Description

Figures 3.5.1 through 3.5.4 illustrate the classic rear leg roundhouse in its "hopping" form. Chamber as usual and hop forward while extending the leg and pivoting with the hips. The hop is as close to the ground as possible, in a full forward movement, and when completed, finds you with the foot pointing backward, as per delivery of the kick in a regular fashion.

Figure 3.5.1

Figure 3.5.2

Figure 3.5.3

Figure 3.5.4

The hopping roundhouse allows you to cover a long distance while kicking.

Figures 3.5.5 through 3.5.7 show the application of the "hopping" principle to a front-leg, hand-on-floor roundhouse kick.

Figure 3.5.5

Figure 3.5.6

Figure 3.5.7

These images clearly show the hop in chambered position.

Figures 3.5.8 through 3.5.10 detail the different stages of a classical hopping roundhouse kick.

Figure 3.5.8

Figure 3.5.9

Figure 3.5.10

Hopping while delivering the roundhouse allows you to close the gap unexpectedly.

Key Points

- The hop is forward, not upwards, and should be done with as little upper body movement as possible.
- Make sure you do not bob up with your head, and so telegraph your intentions.
- Your kicking foot should connect just as your standing foot "lands."

Targets

All of the body is fair game as a target, just as with the corresponding roundhouse kick that you are "hopping."

Typical Application

The following images illustrate a front leg hopping roundhouse with no first step. You just lift the leg and hop-kick (3.5.11 and 3.5.12). This is a very fast kick, extremely effective against an opponent who is not retreating (waiting in place to counter you or to "time" your attack). Preferably as he feints forward or initiates an attack as a response to a body movement of yours, you just lift the front leg and push forward from the standing foot. You deliver the hopping roundhouse at belt level. As you lower your kicking leg, keep your forward and circular momentum, and spin in place to deliver a spinning side or hook kick to your opponent's face or throat (Figure 3.5.14). This is a typical low/ high combination. You can follow up by using the circular momentum to deliver a circular ridge hand strike to your opponent's face while lowering the leg (Figure 3.5.15).

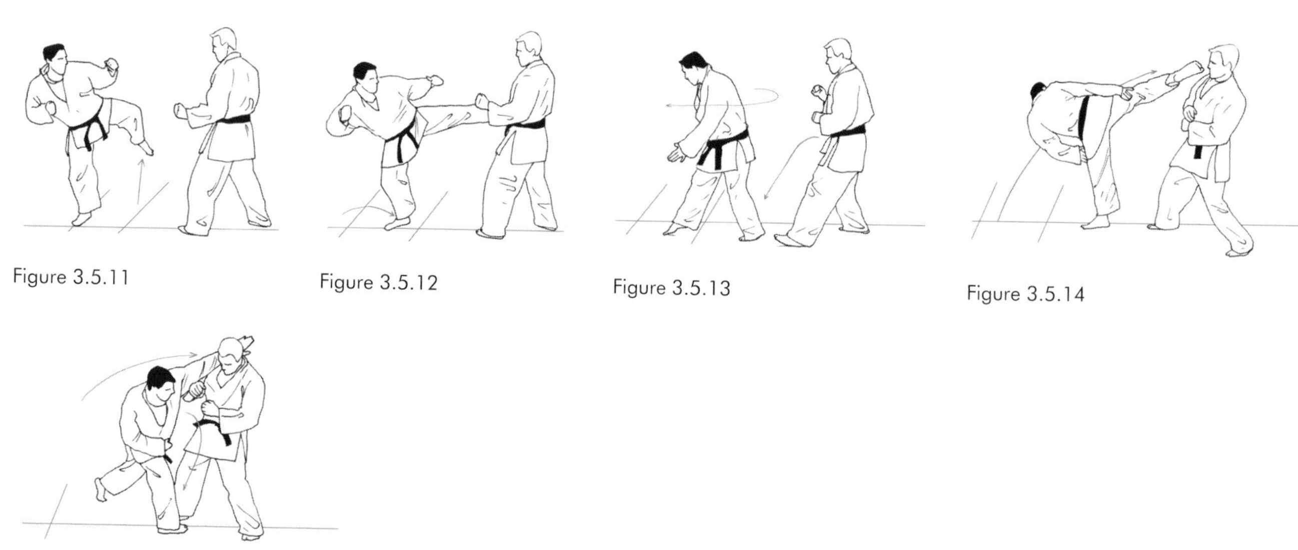

Figure 3.5.11

Figure 3.5.12

Figure 3.5.13

Figure 3.5.14

Figure 3.5.15
The front-leg hopping roundhouse is a great kick to use to close the gap at the start of a combination.

Specific Training

- Strengthen your calves by long sessions of rope jumping.
- Kick in front of the mirror and check for telegraphing moves.
- Work the heavy bag from farther and farther away (mark the floor).

Self-defense

You confront a menacing assailant, and without the hesitation he expects, deliver a hopping front leg roundhouse to the groin (Figure 3.5.18). Make sure you do not hop upwards and do not telegraph your move. Whether you have scored the hit or not, aggressively backfist your opponent in the side of the head (as his hands must be down from the hit or the threat) while lowering your leg forward (Figure 3.5.19). Follow up with a straight leg low roundhouse to the knee or the side of the thigh (Figure 3.5.20). Low inside / High outside / Low outside!

Figure 3.5.16 Figure 3.5.17 Figure 3.5.18 Figure 3.5.19 Figure 3.5.20
When an assailant lifts a stick, you can kick fast to his open groin while closing the gap.

3.6 The Oblique Roundhouse Kick

General

This is simply a roundhouse kick delivered to a target situated not in front of you but on your outside. You simply accentuate your pivot and keep kicking for more than the 180 degrees necessary to reach an opponent in front of you. This kick is more powerful on one side, as you have the distance to accumulate more centrifugal energy, but on the other side takes longer to reach the target. But it is a surprising kick—it is out of view of your opponent during its first stages, and it usually comes from a blind angle. It's a perfect kick to attack an opponent whom you have overtaken on either side, preferably his blindside. It is a kick important to master and to strenuously practice, as it will allow you to catch an evading opponent and surprise him as you are able to overreach and follow him in his side-stepping.

Description

What follows is a description of a way to practice the kick as a classic rear leg roundhouse to an opponent who is 45 degrees on your outside. The kick can also be practiced as a front leg kick, and should be developed until it reaches an opponent totally on your outside (90 degrees). Lift the rear leg and chamber as usual (Figure 3.6.2). Kick with an exaggerated pivot on the standing foot and turn the hips for another 45 degrees while extending the leg and consciously gathering centrifugal energy (Figure 3.6.4). Do not forget to recoil just after penetrating impact—this is still a whipping kick!

Figure 3.6.1 Figure 3.6.2 Figure 3.6.3 Figure 3.6.4 Figure 3.6.5
Kicking through up to 3/4 of a circle and gathering speed and power.

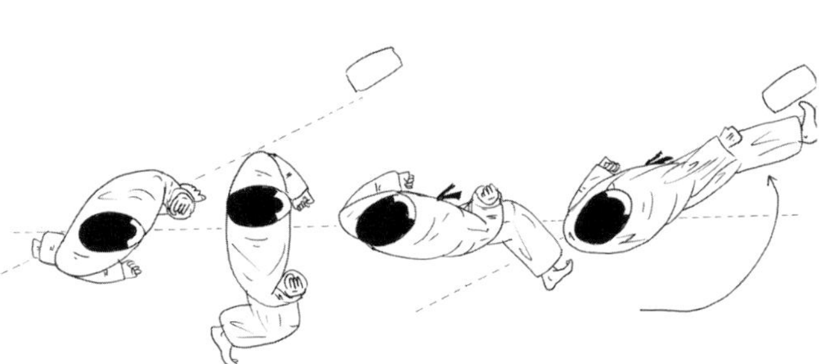

Figure 3.6.6
Overhead view of the kick.

Figures 3.6.7 to 3.6.9 show how, by evading a lunge punch with a step forward and outside evasion, you can roundhouse kick with the rear leg! This is shorter but based on the same principle. Note, again, the punching hand control while kicking, this time alternating hands. This limits your opponent's options, and keeps him focused unnecessarily on the caught hand.

Figure 3.6.7
A fast roundhouse kick under an incoming punch.

Figure 3.6.8

Figure 3.6.9

Key Points

- Keep the first stages of the kick similar to a regular kick, so as not to alert your opponent.
- To pivot on the standing foot is key and it is now 225 degrees, instead of 180.
- Keep your guard up during the kick, as it takes longer to reach target.

Targets

This kick is more powerful than a regular roundhouse, and all targets come into account, from knee to head.

Typical Application

What follows is a description of a front leg version of the oblique kick, easier to perform than the rear leg version. Therefore, practice the rear leg version often, so you have an easy and natural front leg version. The described application is a very good kick to be performed on an opposite guard opponent, as your oblique lunge gets you on his blind side and allows for a powerful roundhouse to the back of the head. See Figures 3.6.10 through 3.6.14. You stand in opposite guard to your opponent, and step to his outside while he lunges or jabs at you. Evade him while going forward and preferably with an oblique jab of yours from his blind side (Figure 3.6.11). In the same movement you hop with the back leg and chamber front leg, in a classical front leg roundhouse. But this time you have to pivot another 45 degrees on your standing foot to catch your target (Figure 3.6.13). A classic follow-up would be the lowering of the recoiling leg directly into an outside foot sweep: you sweep his leg forward while pulling his front shoulder backward and down (Figure 3.6.14).

Figure 3.6.10 Figure 3.6.11 Figure 3.6.12 Figure 3.6.13 Figure 3.6.14
Always try to get on your opponent's blind side. Then kick!

Specific Training

The training illustrated in Figures 3.6.15 through 3.6.17 is very important to help you master the art of being able to kick from all positions, situations, and ranges.

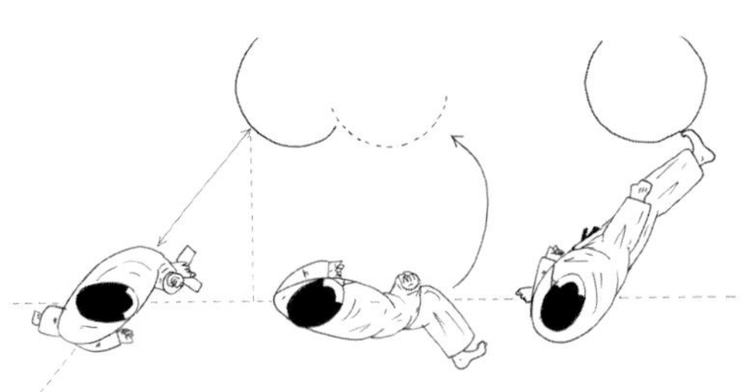

Figure 3.6.15
Kick the heavy bag from a static fighting stance totally on your blind-side.

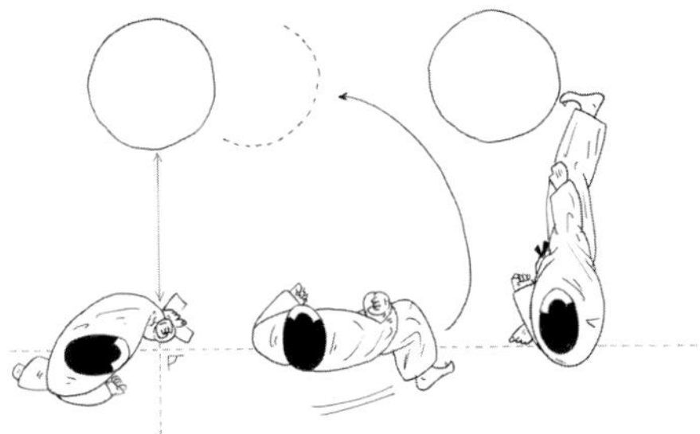

Figure 3.6.16
Kick the heavy bag from a static fighting stance 45 degrees to your outside.

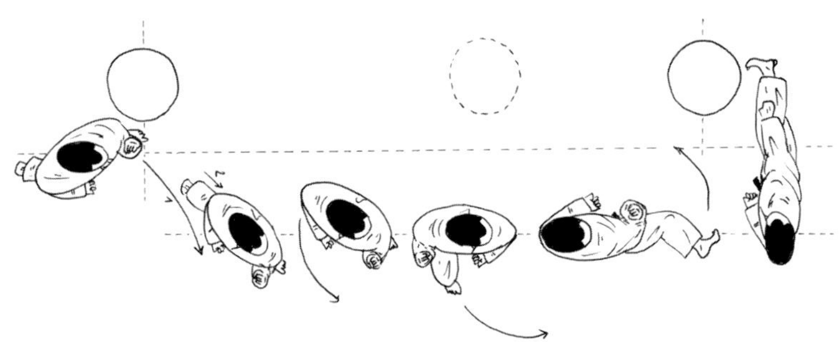

Figure 3.6.17
Repeat with a side step bringing you to this position.

Self-defense

In opposite stance, your assailant launches a front leg side kick toward your ribs, which you evade by retreating on his inside, while controlling (and pulling if possible) with your front hand (Figure 3.6.20). You are now on his inside, out of the centerline. Immediately start launching a full rear leg oblique roundhouse to his head, while keeping your guard high. The kick should connect as his kicking leg reaches the floor (Figure 3.6.22). You can follow up with a circular ridge hand strike (*Haito uchi*—karate), toward which is his momentum anyway (Figure 3.6.23).

Figure 3.6.18

Figure 3.6.19

Figure 3.6.20

Figure 3.6.21

Figure 3.6.22

Figure 3.6.23
Evading a side kick to its inside gives a perfect set-up for the oblique roundhouse.

3.7 The Straight Leg Roundhouse Kick

Te lam toa / Te tad glang—to the body, *Te sung / Te karn koa*—to the head (muay thai)

General

This is the extremely powerful roundhouse as delivered in the hardest of martial arts styles, like Kyokushinkai karate or muay thai kickboxing. The kick is no longer a whipping kick, but a powerful "momentum" kick into which you put your entire body. Although usually seen delivered at lower levels, like the thigh and the ribs, the kick can be delivered to the head as an extremely punishing move.

Description

See Figures 3.7.1 through 3.7.4. The kick is generally not delivered from the front leg, as it necessitates momentum generated by the whole body. In this kick, it is the upper body and the hips that pull the straight rear leg directly into the target. The feeling is reminiscent of the spinning kicks where you start by pivoting the head and the shoulders to "pull" the leg, but this time in the other direction. The shoulders and arms pivot and pull the hips into a pivot, while the legs are under tension, like an elastic band waiting to be released. When the leg is released in full force, the arms, shoulders and upper body come back from their pivot to counterbalance the kick. In some schools, the leg is slightly bent and locks straight at impact to add a little snap, but the authors think it unnecessary. The impact is with the shin (in Japanese: *ashibo*) and/or the top of the foot (*haisoku*).

Figure 3.7.1

Figure 3.7.2

Figure 3.7.3

The most powerful straight-leg roundhouse, often called "low kick."

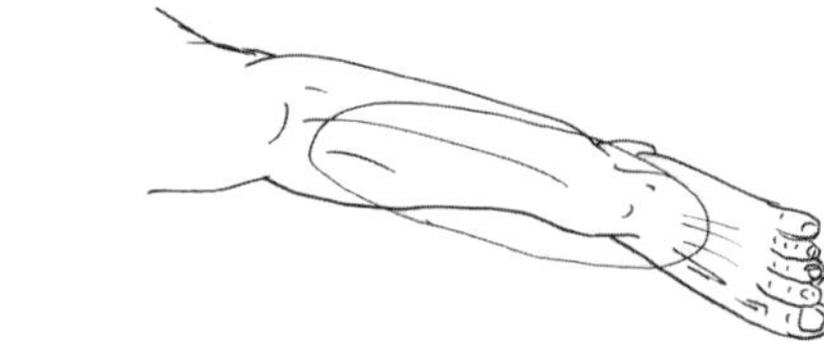

Figure 3.7.4

The area used to strike with in the straight-leg roundhouse.

Figures 3.7.5 through 3.7.8 show a classic and devastating use of the straight leg roundhouse. It is a low kick in this instance, but the principles stay the same. In these photos, a committed front kick is blocked on the outside while stepping back (*Gedan barai*—karate), and if possible the block tries to "extend" the forward move of the lowering leg. A rear leg, full power straight-leg roundhouse is then launched into the knee of the kicking leg as it reaches the floor.

Figure 3.7.5

A devastating counter to a front kick.

Figure 3.7.6

Figure 3.7.7

Figure 3.7.8

Key Points

- This is a full commitment kick: kick with no afterthought.
- Keep your guard high during the kick.

Targets

As the shin is usually used, only big targets should be sought:

- The knee, inner and outer thighs, as will be described in the low kicks.
- The ribs and kidneys. See Figures 3.7.9 and 3.7.10.

Figure 3.7.9

Figure 3.7.10

Simple and effective High/Low combination, targeting the kidneys.

- The head (See Figures 3.7.11 through 3.7.13) and neck (Figure 3.7.14).

Figure 3.7.11

Figure 3.7.12

Figure 3.7.13

The powerful high straight-leg roundhouse to the head. Notice the hip twist.

Typical Application

This is an example of a "trap" move, and very similar to that shown in Figures 3.7.5 through 3.7.8. You purposely open your guard and "invite" your opponent to kick you in the ribs (Figure 3.7.15). As he does so, you block and control his kicking leg, preferably by hooking under it (Figure 3.7.16). Deflect the kick and pull the leg to your outside, in order to bring your opponent off-balance and with his back turned toward you (Figure 3.7.17). As he is close enough, swing your shoulders and arms to launch a punishing straight leg roundhouse, with your shin, in your opponent's exposed lower back (Figure 3.7.18). You can follow up with a high straight leg or regular roundhouse from the other leg (Figure 3.7.19). Low outside / high inside!

Figure 3.7.14
Targeting the neck.

Figure 3.7.15

Figure 3.7.16

Figure 3.7.17

Figure 3.7.18

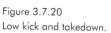

Figure 3.7.19
"Invite" the opponent's kick for a devastating counter-attack.

Figures 3.7.20 through 3.7.23 show an excellent follow-up for self-defense or MMA. After the kick to the outside of the opponent's knee, you lower the leg behind him and crouch for a double leg lift takedown from behind.

Figure 3.7.20
Low kick and takedown.

Figure 3.7.21

Figure 3.7.22

Figure 3.7.23

Specific Training

- The feeling of the kick cannot be understood without heavy bag training.
- Also practice with a partner holding target pads at all levels.

Figure 3.7.24
Target at low- to medium-level. Notice the hip twist.

Figure 3.7.25

Figure 3.7.26
Target at medium- to high-level.

- Practice the kick in combinations. Figures 3.7.27 through 3.7.31 show the classic pre-kick combination—jab and cross, and the classic follow-up—knee strike to the abdomen.

Figure 3.7.27

Figure 3.7.28

Figure 3.7.29

Figure 3.7.30
The classic combination.

Figure 3.7.31

Another classic combination to work on is illustrated in Figures 3.7.32 through 3.7.36. Jab, front leg roundhouse to front inside leg, rear leg straight-leg roundhouse to inside rear leg, knee strike.

Figure 3.7.32

Figure 3.7.33

Figure 3.7.34

Figure 3.7.35
Punch, double kick, knee strike.

Figure 3.7.36

Self-defense

This is a perfect kick for self-defense: very punishing, usable in close combat, and easy to deliver at low levels. Remember that the simplest things work best. Confront your assailant and immediately launch a high reverse punch to get him to lift his guard (Figure 3.7.38). Use the turn of the hips and shoulders to release your rear leg into a straight-leg roundhouse to the exposed lower abdomen (Figure 3.7.39). Even if your opponent reacts or still has an arm to protect his body, the kick is extremely punishing and will, at least partly, hurt the kidneys. The natural follow up, as practiced in muay thai, would be a knee strike of the other leg while controlling his outside shoulder (Figure 3.7.40). You can then deliver a full-hipped circular (and downward) elbow strike to the back of his neck (Figure 3.7.41).

Figure 3.7.37

Figure 3.7.38

Figure 3.7.39

Figure 3.7.40

Figure 3.7.41

These images show a punishing offensive combination.

Anyone who has watched MMA tournaments is aware of the importance of the straight leg roundhouse. Another example of their versatile use is presented here. As an attack to the standing leg of a kicking opponent, whether the kicking leg has been "caught" (Figures 3.7.42 through 3.7.44), or whether the kick is still ongoing (Figures 3.7.45 through 3.7.47).

Figure 3.7.42

Catch the kicking leg and kick the standing leg.

Figure 3.7.43

Figure 3.7.44

Figure 3.7.45

Evade the kick and kick the standing leg.

Figure 3.7.46

Figure 3.7.47

3.8 The Downward Roundhouse Kick

Chapéu de couro (capoeira)

General

This variation of the roundhouse kick is the second best preferred technique (*tokui-waza*) of this author, and together with the bent-body hook kick, has brought me the bulk of my tournament points! No wonder, as nobody really expects a kick to come from above. As can be expected from an exotic and sneaky kick, a variation of it is used and practiced in the art of capoeira. In karate circles, the kick is sometimes referred to as the "Brazilian" kick.

There are many possible nuances in the execution of this kick, which go from a slightly angled roundhouse up to the totally vertical kick. We will describe here, as usual, the extreme version, and the experienced reader will practice, research and choose the variation most suitable to his flexibility, his temperament or the situation.

The downward roundhouse is simply a full roundhouse kick, in which you keep turning the hips when chambered, in such a way that you are nearly with your back to your opponent when the foot connects, which makes it connect from above. The more flexible you are, the more you can turn your leg and the less back you have to "give" the opponent while kicking. The kick is extremely surprising, very difficult to block, and deceptively powerful because of the innate weight of the leg. But it needs a lot of work to perfect! It can be executed with both the front and rear leg.

Description

We present the technique as a rear leg kick (Figures 3.8.1 through 3.8.5). Chamber your rear leg just as you would a high full roundhouse kick. Lift the knee as high as possible, and keep pivoting on your standing foot and turning your hips while you start developing the kick. Time the development of the kick in such a way that it connects as you complete the turning of your hips, and your back is toward your opponent. The kick has come from above (See also Figure 3.8.6). You chamber immediately as you turn back your hips into the opposite direction for a regular chamber.

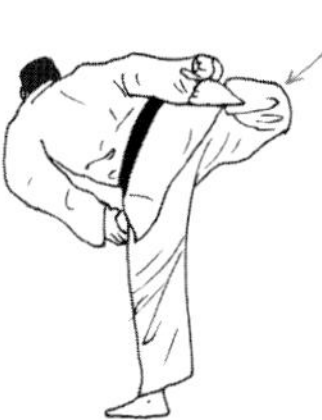

Figure 3.8.1
The roundhouse coming downward.

Figure 3.8.2

Figure 3.8.3

Figure 3.8.4

Figure 3.8.5

Figure 3.8.6
The trajectory is easier to understand when kicking a standing bag.

Figures 3.8.7 through 3.8.9 show an application of a less pronounced version of the kick, a favorite technique of Sensei Roy Faige attacking the hip joint. Although the kick is delivered low, the principles of delivery are the same: high chamber and twist of the hips, although less emphasized, to allow for the downward movement. Figure 3.8.7 shows the outside evasion and control of the punching arm. Figure 3.8.8 shows clearly the high chamber, already directed downward, with the foot higher than the high knee. And Figure 3.8.9 shows the impact with the shin into the hip joint.

Figure 3.8.7
Attacking the hip joint from above.

Figure 3.8.8

Figure 3.8.9

Figures 3.8.10 through 3.8.13 show the delivery of the kick as a rear leg high kick. Note that in this example, the chambering of the leg intentionally suggests a side kick or a hook kick coming to the inside. With the pivot of the hips, the kick switches to an oblique kick coming from above and to the outside.

Figure 3.8.10

Figure 3.8.11
Note the beginning of the kick as a virtual feint.

Figure 3.8.12

Figure 3.8.13

Key Points

- The development of the kick comes as late as possible, so as to make it come vertically downwards.
- Pivot on your standing foot as much as needed to allow the full turn of the hips.
- The kick works only if you chamber as high as possible.

Targets

Typical targets include the head, the clavicle, and the back of the neck if your opponent is bent-over, or has his back to you. Of course, if your kick is not a full downward roundhouse and you come down diagonally, you also can target the sides of the head.

Typical Application

This is our favorite set-up for the kick, performed as a front leg kick. Fast, and excellent for competition, although the unexpectedness of the hit often causes knock-downs, which make it very good for self-defense as well. The set-up is a clear hook kick preparation: a high punching feint, the turning of the body and hips, the step up behind the front leg (Figure 3.8.15). It works even better, if you have taught him that a hook kick will follow these steps. This author used to touch the outside of the lower front leg of my opponent, as in Figure 3.8.16, although it is not imperative. It just misdirects his concentration for a second. You keep lifting the leg as a hook kick coming to his outside for as long as possible, according to your degree of proficiency and flexibility. At the last moment, you turn the hips and chamber the leg as high as possible with most of your back toward the opponent. You develop the kick to make it come diagonally downwards to the inside of your opponent's head (Figure 3.8.17). Once the kick has connected, chamber and lower the leg. If necessary, you are in a perfect position for a back kick, from either leg, to his midsection (Figure 3.8.19).

Figure 3.8.14 Figure 3.8.15 Figure 3.8.16 Figure 3.8.17

Figure 3.8.18 Figure 3.8.19

The perfect combination: feint high punch then low hook. Follow up with a high and downward angled roundhouse, and finish up.

Specific Training

- The kick requires flexibility: a lot of flexibility work is required.
- Work the chamber only, as many reps as possible in front of the heavy bag (See Figure 3.8.20).
- Work on the standing bag to ensure downward trajectory (See Figure 3.8.6, shown previously).
- Work with a partner holding the striking pad facing upward lower level. Kick through!

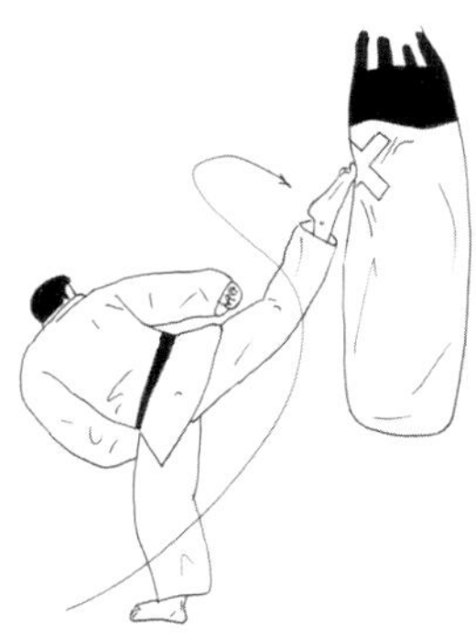

Figure 3.8.20
Drill fast chambers just touching the bag lightly.

Figure 3.8.21
Drilling at high level.

Figure 3.8.22
Drilling at low level.

Figure 3.8.23

Figure 3.8.24

Figure 3.8.25

Self-defense

Here, we present as an illustration the capoeira-like version of the kick, delivered with the rear leg. Your assailant is chain-punching you to the head, and you retreat to get out of range while lowering the body onto bent legs, for a "spring" effect (Figure 3.8.27). You spring back with the rear leg that just retreated, directly into a very high chambered knee position, while bending the body and turning the hips for a nearly full turn (Figure 3.8.28). Keep turning while hitting your assailant's head diagonally from above (Figure 3.8.29). This is not a snap kick, but a full penetrating kick. Complete the leg trajectory until the foot lands, and you find yourself with your back to the opponent. Finish him off with the logical back kick with the other leg (Figure 3.8.31). An interesting follow-up would be landing very low on his outside, pivoting into kneeling position and throwing him off by lifting his knee and pulling down his shoulder (Figure 3.8.33).

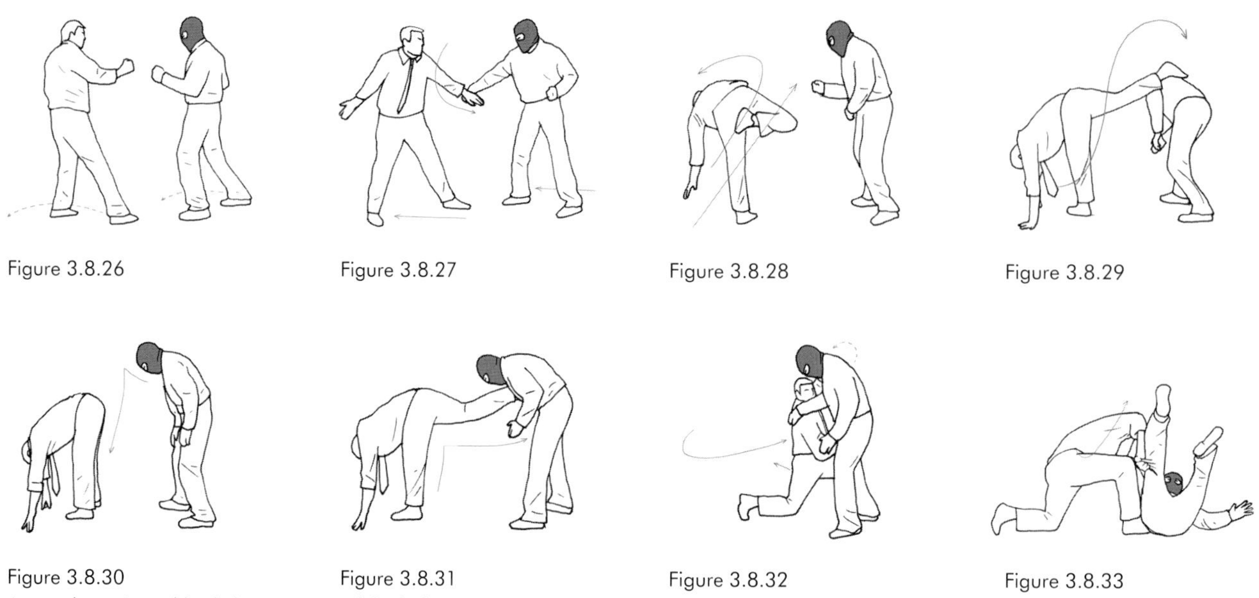

Figure 3.8.26 Figure 3.8.27 Figure 3.8.28 Figure 3.8.29

Figure 3.8.30 Figure 3.8.31 Figure 3.8.32 Figure 3.8.33

A very dynamic and body-bent version of the kick.

3.9 The Bent-body Long Roundhouse Kick

General

The idea behind this variation of the roundhouse kick is to keep the body away from your opponent as much as possible. The reasons could be various: your opponent is a counter-puncher, your assailant is armed with a club or a stick, you need to be further away for a specific follow-up, you are checking your opponent's reactions, and so on.

In order to keep your body away, you bend backward during the kick to the point of having your body parallel to the floor, and extend your hips while bending your standing leg. Although we have not presented it as a separate variation, you can bend the body up to the point where you put your hand on the floor, for support and/or for the preparation of the follow-up kicks; that would be typical of capoeira for example (*Martelo preso*), but not exclusively.

There is an interesting variation of this kick taught in Shorinji kempo under the name *Ryusui geri*. It is a roundhouse kick to the body delivered while evading a punch to the outside by bending sideways. See Figures 3.9.1 through 3.9.5.

Figure 3.9.1

Figure 3.9.2

Figure 3.9.3

Figure 3.9.4 Figure 3.9.5
Kicking while stepping and leaning away: effective and economical.

Description

See Figures 3.9.6 through 3.9.9. The kick can be executed with both front and back leg, but is more logical with the front leg, as you want to keep your body away. However, the rear leg version is presented as the more classic and didactic one. Once mastered, the front leg version is faster and easier to deliver. Lift the rear leg in a regular chamber. As you are doing so, you're already bending your body away from him. Bend the leg you are standing on while developing the kick and bending even more. Bend as much as necessary for the specific application. While you develop the kick, turn your hips in such a way that you can extend the hip joint a little more. You can also place a hand on the floor, if relevant to the situation (See Figure 3.9.9). Chamber back immediately after the hit, with your leg between you and your opponent.

Figure 3.9.6 Figure 3.9.7 Figure 3.9.8 Figure 3.9.9
Lean away while kicking, with or without your hand touching the floor.

Figure 3.9.10
This photo shows the primary advantage of the kick: The body is far from the opponent's reach.

This kick is, by definition, very useful from close range, as you lean away. Figures 3.9.11 and 3.9.12 show the delivery, up to hand-on-the-floor, from a very close range, after a small forward hop and front hand hooking jab. You'll note that this specific delivery is also a hybrid of the downward roundhouse kick.

Figure 3.9.11 Figure 3.9.12
Step in with a jab and lean away with a kick. This is a front leg delivery.

Key Points

- For a long kick, you need to fully turn the hips, and therefore the standing foot.
- Align your hips and body to allow the slight overextension of the hip joint.

Targets

The long kicks with which you want to keep your distance usually target the mid body, therefore, typical targets include: the ribs, the groin and the kidneys. Also, the thighs and knees in low kicks are suitable targets.

Typical Application

See Figures 3.9.13 to 3.9.18. Close the distance with a jab, get his guard up with a reverse punch that also helps you to turn your hips and prepare your rear leg kick (Figure 3.9.14). Try to reverse punch slightly to his inside, to cause him to overblock (Figure 3.9.15). Roundhouse kick his lower back at belt level, while bending your body and standing leg, and extending your hip (Figure 3.9.16). The kick is very difficult to block, longer than expected from a roundhouse, and difficult to jam or time, as your upper body is out of the range of his hands. Backfist his face while lowering the leg and redressing the body (Figure 3.9.17). You can follow up with an outer reap throw (*O soto gari*—judo), using the momentum generated from the twisting of your hips and hitting him with the forearm (Figure 3.9.18).

Figure 3.9.13 Figure 3.9.14 Figure 3.9.15 Figure 3.9.16

Figure 3.9.17 Figure 3.9.18

These images illustrate a very simple but effective combination.

Specific Training

- Practice the kick on the heavy bag (mid-body height) from a given distance marked on the floor. Gradually move the mark farther away.
- Practice the kick with and without the hand on the floor.

Self-defense

See Figures 3.9.19 through 3.9.23. Here, we give the opposite example. It will be a preventive front-leg bent-body roundhouse to the inside. You attack a menacing opponent who is holding a stick or knife before he is able to attack. Hop forward for a front leg roundhouse, but deliver the kick in the long, bent-body way, in order to stay out of the range of his weapon as much as possible. Kick in a committed way, with no hesitation, toward his groin (Figure 3.9.21). Kick again with the same leg, if possible without lowering the foot, with a bent-body side kick to his front knee (Figure 3.9.22). As soon as you have connected and he lowers his hands in pain, spring up and forward with your upper body, while you are still chambering the leg, for a backhand punch to the face, in a body move sometimes called "jack knifing" (Figure 3.9.23).

Figure 3.9.19 Figure 3.9.20 Figure 3.9.21 Figure 3.9.22 Figure 3.9.23
Kicking while keeping the body away is useful against an armed assailant.

3.10 The Spin-back Roundhouse Kick

General

Again a kick in which the value lies in its surprising effect! It could have been classified as a feint kick. The confusion of the opponent on the receiving end of the kick comes from the way that, when the kick finally comes, it comes from the opposite direction than the spin of the body. That is all there is to it. The idea is simple, but the kick is quite complex and requires a lot of training for a fast delivery. Once mastered, it's hard to believe how efficient the kick actually is.

Description

See Figures 3.10.1 to 3.10.10. You pivot on your front leg, just as for any spin-back kick. The head and shoulders go first, then the hips, finally releasing the leg. But, this time, the spin stops when your side is facing forward. Instead of using the twist to continue the circular spinning movement, use it to chamber the formerly back leg into a regular roundhouse chamber, preferably universal (Section 4 of this chapter). This stops the spin, and you develop the kick like a regular roundhouse. The opponent expects a spinning kick or punch, but gets a kick from the other side!

Figure 3.10.1 Figure 3.10.2 Figure 3.10.3 Figure 3.10.4 Figure 3.10.5
Side view of the spin-back roundhouse.

Figure 3.10.6 Figure 3.10.7 Figure 3.10.8 Figure 3.10.9 Figure 3.10.10
Front view of the spin-back roundhouse.

Figures 3.10.11 through 3.10.14 show the delivery of the kick into a striking pad held facing the side opposite to the direction of the spin.

Figure 3.10.11 Figure 3.10.12 Figure 3.10.13 Figure 3.10.14
These images clearly suggest the unexpected trajectory of the kick.

Key Points

- As it is partly a feint kick, it aids training to consider this a spinning back kick until the last possible moment.
- The spin must be fully committed.

Targets

This is not a powerful kick, but a fast kick designed to surprise. Only soft targets are valid: the groin and head.

Typical Application

See Figures 3.10.15 through 3.10.20. Use this technique as a feint spin-back back kick turning into a roundhouse.
On a "blocking and counterattacking" opponent, start a spin-back back kick, and keep it looking like that for as long as possible, with a high chambered knee looking ready to straighten up. Then change momentum into a roundhouse to the head. Surprise! After connecting with his head, you lower the leg and can "rebound" into a back kick to the abdomen.

Figure 3.10.15 Figure 3.10.16 Figure 3.10.17 Figure 3.10.18

Figure 3.10.19 Figure 3.10.20
Note the hand feint at the beginning of the spin, and the blocking reaction on the wrong side!

Specific Training

- Work the heavy bag from a close stance, touching the bag with the front hand (Figures 3.10.21 through 3.10.24).
- Work the heavy bag while alternating between this kick and the spinning back side kick.

Figure 3.10.21 Figure 3.10.22 Figure 3.10.23 Figure 3.10.24
Drilling in front of the heavy bag forces you to complete the spin before kicking.

- Work on a striking pad held by a moving partner (Figures 3.10.25 through 3.10.27).

Figure 3.10.25
There is no substitute for partner training.

Figure 3.10.26

Figure 3.10.27

See Figures 3.10.28 through 3.10.33. Lunge and then spin back. Your opponent may think you have decided to retreat or flee. As you switch your weight back onto your front leg, you are getting back into range, and able to deliver a full spin-back roundhouse kick. Your assailant will expect a kick from the side of the spin, not a roundhouse from the other direction. You can follow up with a palm strike to the face while landing and a groin knee strike while controlling his shoulder.

Figure 3.10.28

Figure 3.10.29

Figure 3.10.30

Figure 3.10.31

Figure 3.10.32

The spin-back roundhouse kick is part of a great combination based on misdirection.

3.11 The 360 Spin-back Roundhouse Kick

General

This kick, unlike the previous spin-back roundhouse, is a very powerful kick, building on the power of centrifugal force. It is basically a full roundhouse with some fancy footwork. Again, its importance is in the surprising effect, and it allows for "catching" opponents who retreat on a regular spin-back kick, but do not expect an additional step. The spin back can be done with a bent upper body to evade an attack or a danger, or to give the impression to your opponent that you are fleeing away. This kick is often referred to by practitioners as the "tornado" kick, especially in its jumping or hopping form. The kick is powerful enough to squash the guard of the opponent, and basically cause him to hit himself with his upper limbs.

Description

See Figures 3.11.1 through 3.11.6. You basically spin back, just as for any spin-back kick. Turn the head first, then the shoulders, then the hips, and then you release the leg. When you start your spin-back, move away from your opponent; when you complete it, move back toward him. Instead of kicking, the leg is released into a step, while you keep the momentum of your spinning. You put your weight on your now front leg (which was your rear leg at the beginning) and kick with the rear leg into a full roundhouse that has all the momentum of a full turn.

Figure 3.11.1

Figure 3.11.2

Figure 3.11.3

Figure 3.11.4

Figure 3.11.5

Figure 3.11.6

The spinning movement packs a lot of power into this kick.

Figures 3.11.7 through 3.11.11 show the delivery of the kick to the opponent's head. Note that the power of the kick makes it difficult to block: should your opponent lift his arms to block, the kick would crash them into the target.

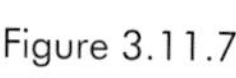

Figure 3.11.7

Figure 3.11.8

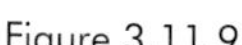

Figure 3.11.9

Figure 3.11.10

Figure 3.11.11

These images clearly show the delivery of the kick, powerful enough to be used against a heavier opponent.

If your kick is offensive, you can gain some distance by doing the step first: do a full cross step (rear leg behind front leg) toward your opponent and do the spin back from this position and then release the now back leg into a full momentum roundhouse. You have, in fact, done the step first and the spin back second, instead of the classic spin-back first, then step!

Key Points

- Develop the step just as you would a kick.
- Do not break the momentum of the spinning when you step.
- Keep your guard up when you move forward again.

Targets

This is a powerful kick: all targets count from knee to head. You can even kick "through" the guard.

Typical Application

Although this kick can be used in many situations, it is our feeling that its best use is as a backward evasion flowing naturally forward again. Therefore, we'll present such an application against a roundhouse kick (Figures 3.11.12 through 3.11.19). Evade your opponent's roundhouse by shifting your weight on to the rear leg and starting to pivot. You can bend the upper body if needed. You come back forward with the full force of the circular movement of the hips, while your opponent is chambering back and lowering his leg. There, you are catching him with the full power of the kick. If you have evaded the kick at the last moment, as it should be, you have probably caused him to overextend himself, even slightly, therefore catching him at least slightly off-balance.

A natural follow-up would be a rebounding back kick from the kicking leg (Figure 3.11.19).

Figure 3.11.12 Figure 3.11.13 Figure 3.11.14 Figure 3.11.15

Figure 3.11.16 Figure 3.11.17 Figure 3.11.18 Figure 3.11.19

These images illustrate a very powerful counter after evading a kick.

Specific Training

- Heavy bag kicking, as powerfully as possible.
- Train the step only, for speed and range (mark on the floor). Work the step fast and fully, as if it was a kick.
- Drill all possible variants on the striking pad held by a moving partner. See Figures 3.11.20 through 3.11.29.

Figure 3.11.20

Figure 3.11.21

Figure 3.11.22

Figure 3.11.23

Figure 3.11.24

These photos show the delivery of the kick from a static position, connecting with the top of the foot.

Figure 3.11.25

Figure 3.11.26

Figure 3.11.27

Figure 3.11.28

Figure 3.11.29

These photos show the delivery of the kick after a short step back, and connecting with the ball of the foot.

Self-defense

This is again an evasion that is luring your opponent into a safe feeling of you being away. When assailed with a downward stick attack, retreat with a full step turning away from him, while bending your head and upper body (Figure 3.11.32). While your attacker is still off-balance from his momentum, surge back forward with the most powerful of roundhouses (Figure 3.11.35). If he is close enough, you should use a straight- or near straight-leg roundhouse kick. Keep your guard up all the time. Kick through his guard or stick if necessary, and follow-up with a reverse punch or palm while getting in control of his armed hand (Figure 3.11.36).

Figure 3.11.30 Figure 3.11.31 Figure 3.11.32 Figure 3.11.33

Figure 3.11.34 Figure 3.11.35 Figure 3.11.36

The 360 spin back roundhouse kick allows you to evade a stick attack and come right back on the offense.

3.12 The Switch Roundhouse Kick

General

This is again a simple variation of the roundhouse kick, just like the switch front and side kick we have already presented. The "switch" footwork allows you to: trick your opponent into a false estimation of range, use your strongest leg for a kick even if it is in front, totally adjust your distance when kicking an opponent coming forward, standing in place, or waiting to time your attack. The switch can be executed on all types of roundhouse kicks, but as it is generally a stop kick, it needs to be powerful. Therefore, regular roundhouse, full roundhouse and straight leg roundhouse kicks are the more suitable techniques.

Description

See Figures 3.12.1 through 3.12.4. Hop and switch legs in the air, as close to the floor as possible. While switching, adjust your distance as needed: in place, slightly forward or slightly backward. As soon as the (now) rear leg touches the floor, it rebounds into chambering and developing the kick, using the momentum to negate any inertia. Chamber back.

Figure 3.12.1 Figure 3.12.2 Figure 3.12.3 Figure 3.12.4

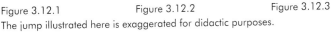

The jump illustrated here is exaggerated for didactic purposes.

Figure 3.12.5

Figure 3.12.6

Figure 3.12.7

These photos show the static delivery of the kick, with an exaggerated hop.

Figures 3.12.8 through 3.12.14 show the kick used in a great combination, but in its more straight-leg form, and attacking the front leg of the opponent. From close range, jab, cross, switch roundhouse the inside front leg of the opponent and use the momentum to spin-back and kick him in the abdomen.

Figure 3.12.8

Figure 3.12.9

Figure 3.12.10

Figure 3.12.11

Figure 3.12.12

Figure 3.12.13

Figure 3.12.14

The switch allows for a powerful rear-leg roundhouse to the inside knee of the opponent.

Key Points

- There is no stopping during the move: make sure your foot rebounds off the floor.
- Do not hop up, and keep your head height constant.

Targets

All body targets are appropriate, from knee to head.

Typical Application

See Figures 3.12.15 through 3.12.20. This kind of technique as an attack is to be used on a standing or "waiting" opponent. You are in an opposite stance. Switch legs on the spot to confuse him, and let your back leg rebound up into a full roundhouse to the head. Lower the leg directly into a lower hook sweep of the outside of his front leg. If possible, catch his front arm while lowering, in order to be able to use it to control him and accentuate his loss of balance. As he lands on the floor, lift your same leg high for a downward heel (axe) kick.

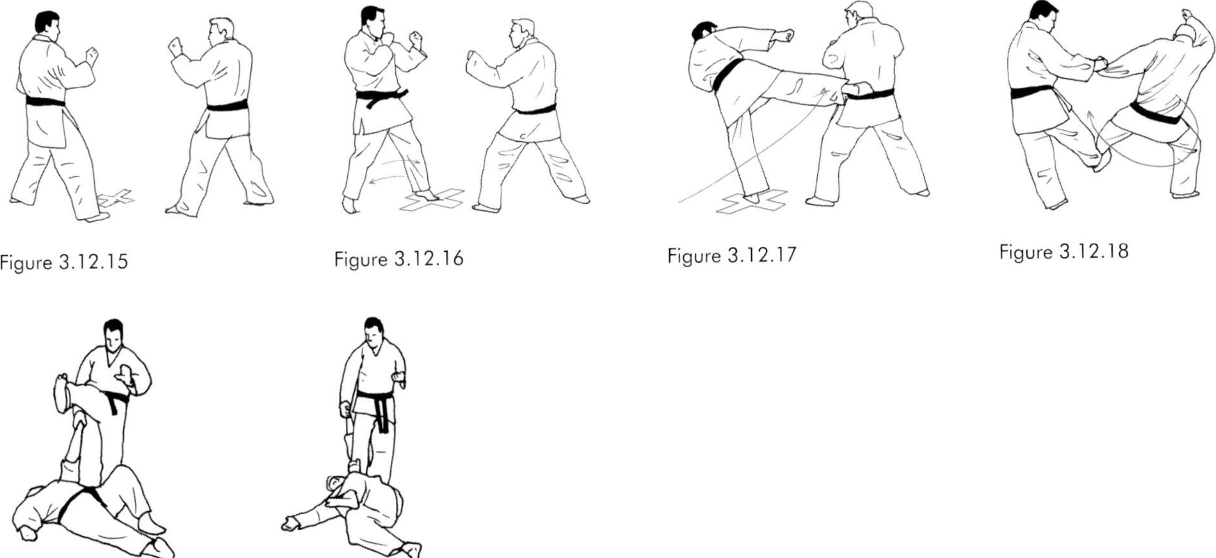

Figure 3.12.15 Figure 3.12.16 Figure 3.12.17 Figure 3.12.18

Figure 3.12.19 Figure 3.12.20

Switch legs to confuse a "waiting" or counterattacking opponent.

Specific Training

Hit the heavy bag from various distances (marked on the floor).

Self-defense

See Figure 3.12.21 through 3.12.26. This example is more of a stop-kick. You retreat out of range of your assailant's front kick with the switching-legs hop of a high switch roundhouse kick. Lower your kicking leg directly into a hooking sweep of his front leg, and pull his shoulder to take him down. For safety, keep your hand in front of his face during the lowering of the leg.

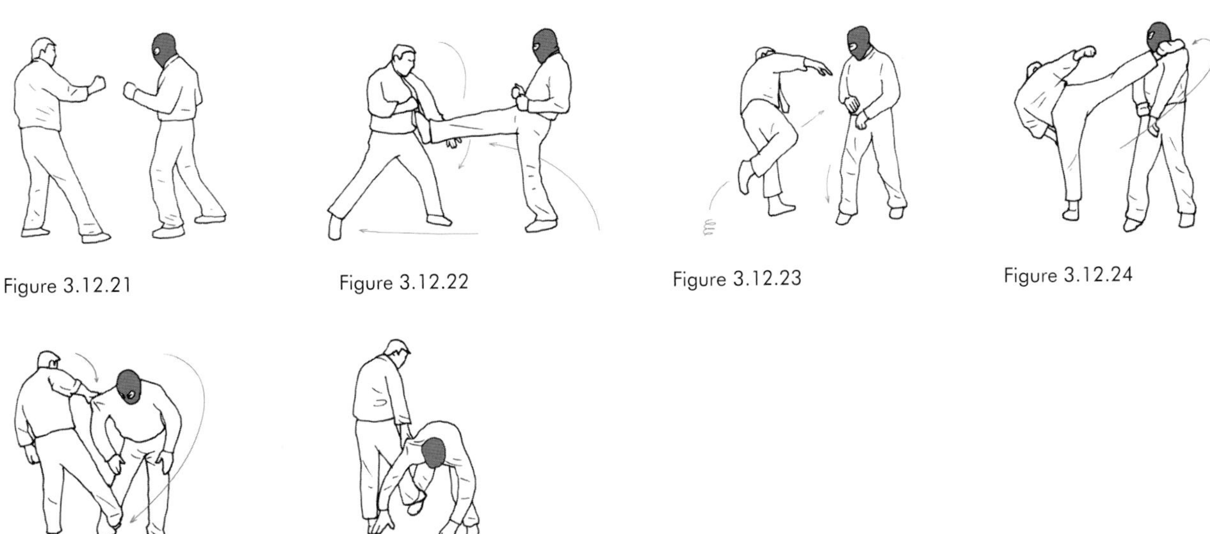

Figure 3.12.21 Figure 3.12.22 Figure 3.12.23 Figure 3.12.24

Figure 3.12.25 Figure 3.12.26

These illustrations show an example of an individual countering a kicking attack and finishing with a takedown.

3.13 The Heel Roundhouse Kick

General

This is, very simply, a roundhouse kick delivered with the foot flexed to its maximum, in such a way that it connects with the heel instead of the ball of the foot. This kick is, in many styles, a scraping kick going through the target, and we present such a kick in *Applications* for the sake of completeness. Its classical form is still a roundhouse with some penetrating effect. In fact, just before impact, the leg is still slightly bent, and straightens at impact with a small push of the hips as for a penetrating side kick. It could be considered to be a hybrid with a lot of roundhouse and a little bit of side-penetrating finish. It is an interesting kick, which can be used in special set-ups, but quite exotic and, being shorter than its regular counterpart, not very practical. It also requires a lot of training to master.

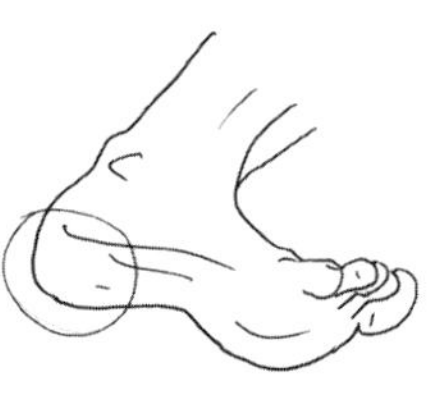

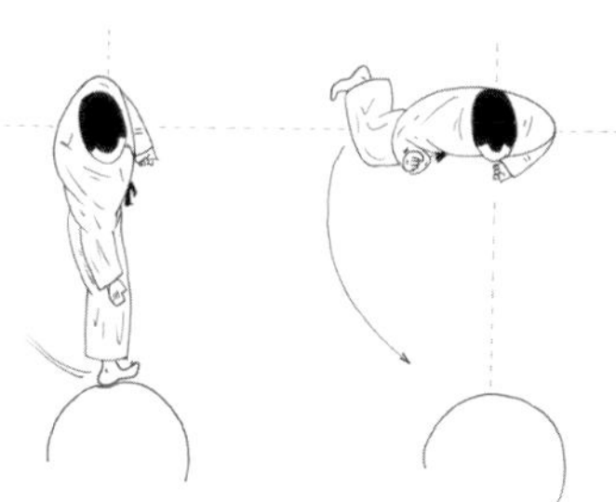

Figure 3.13.1 Figure 3.13.2
A roundhouse kick connecting with the bottom of the heel.

Figure 3.13.3

Figure 3.13.4

Description

See Figures 3.13.1 through 3.13.4 above. You chamber as you would for a regular roundhouse or full roundhouse, flex the foot to its maximum and straighten on impact with a small push of the hips. The contact is with the lower side of the heel.

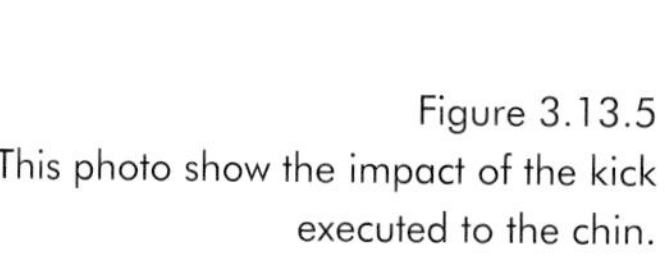

Figure 3.13.5
This photo show the impact of the kick executed to the chin.

Figure 3.13.6 Figure 3.13.7 Figure 3.13.8
These photos show the delivery and impact of the kick from another angle. The small extension of the leg at impact is clearly noticeable.

Key Points

Full leg extension at impact only, with a hip push.

Targets

Being a scraping kick, it is limited in practice to hitting the face or the shin.

Typical Application

I recommend using this kick on a standing opponent, or an opponent who likes to stay close, after pushing him away. This is just based on personal preference, and you may decide to use it in different ways that better suit you. In this example, you deal with an opponent with a high guard and who stays close as he waits to stop you by timing you out. Feint up with a jab to his inside and crescent kick (Chapter 6, Section 1) his guard from the outside (Figure 3.13.10). This is a kick to the arm, not a shove, and it should be painful. As your kick connects, push your hips forward and extend the leg while pushing your heel downward and into his upper body (Figure 3.13.11). You are pushing him away. As soon as your leg is extended, chamber back and lower the foot (Figure 3.13.12). Immediately as the foot touches the floor, the rear legs jumps up into chambering for a roundhouse heel kick to your off-balance opponent's chin (Figure 3.13.14).

Figure 3.13.9

Figure 3.13.10

Figure 3.13.11

Figure 3.13.12

Figure 3.13.13
Push and scrape the chin.

Figure 3.13.14

Specific Training

- The feeling of the kick can only be understood by kicking the heavy bag (see Figure 3.13.4, shown previously).
- Alternate with the regular roundhouse (ball of the foot).

Self-defense

See Figures 3.13.15 through 3.13.18. An assailant takes hold of your right wrist with his right hand. Step aside while using your whole body to roll around his own wrist, before he can continue his attack. Circle his wrist from the outside in a classical release, and as soon as his wrist is bent and yours is over it, push his arm away with both of your hands, putting your body into the push, and pushing through him. While he is pushed away off-balance, heel roundhouse kick him in the chin with the rear leg.

Figure 3.13.15

Figure 3.13.16

Figure 3.13.17

Figure 3.13.18

Aggressive wrist-hold release: push and kick.

3.14 The Drop Roundhouse Kick

So tung toy (kung fu)

General

The drop roundhouse kick is, in our opinion, the most useful of the drop kicks: it is fast, relatively easy, and usually can accurately hit your opponent's groin. It is also an easier kick to get back up from. The kick described here could be called the front leg drop roundhouse, to differentiate it from the next kick we'll describe, which is more powerful and performed with the rear leg. The front leg drop roundhouse is a defensive kick with efficiency that is dependent on its surprising effect and the speed and accuracy of its delivery. The kick is present, in one form or another, in most styles of Asian martial arts.

Description

See Figures 3.14.1 through 3.14.7. You bend down backward on your rear knee, whether it was your starting stance or you got there by retreating in a back step. Your knee and both of your hands get to the floor simultaneously, while you keep watching your opponent and chamber your leg for a roundhouse movement. Develop your leg in a snapping movement. Your kicks gets a few inches into the target at full speed and recoils back as fast, in a whipping movement! From your chambered position you either keep moving on the floor, or lower the kicking foot onto the floor while standing up from your bent knee.

Figure 3.14.1 Figure 3.14.2 Figure 3.14.3 Figure 3.14.4 Figure 3.14.5 Figure 3.14.6 Figure 3.14.7
Drop down, kick fast and stand back up!

Figure 3.14.8 Figure 3.14.9 Figure 3.14.10 Figure 3.14.11
These photos show a very painful timing counter against a high roundhouse.

Key Points

- Put your hips into the kick, just as for a standing roundhouse.
- Drop down in one move.
- Snap the kick.

Targets

Only soft targets are applicable: the knee or the groin.

Figure 3.14.12
The front view of the groin impact.

Typical Application

See Figures 3.14.13 through 3.14.16. The typical application for the kick is of course against a high kick, as shown before. Your opponent is in opposite guard and throws you a full high roundhouse from the rear leg. You drop backward and throw your roundhouse, trying to connect with his exposed groin at full kick extension. No more is needed, but you can keep kicking from the floor, ground side kick to the back of the knee, for example (Fig 3.14.16), or stand up away from him, ready for more.

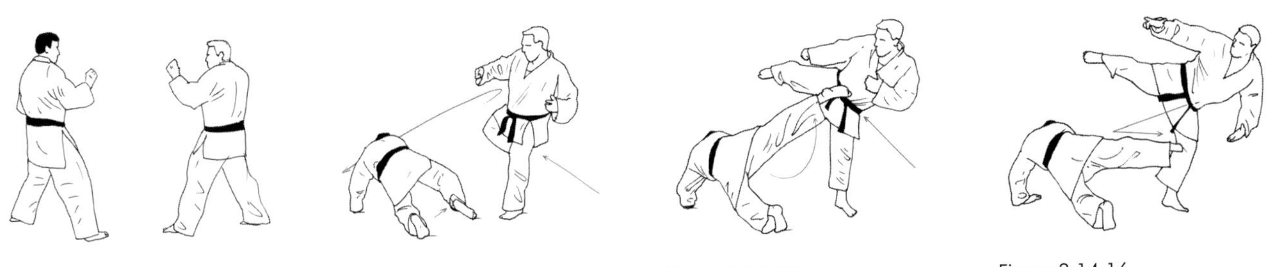

Figure 3.14.13 Figure 3.14.14 Figure 3.14.15 Figure 3.14.16
After the groin kick, you can keep kicking from the floor.

Specific Training

- Train the drop-down for speed. Alone, and the with a partner swinging a stick at waist level.
- Heavy bag kicking, but only accurately at a mark on the bag at groin level.

Self-defense

See Figures 3.14.17 through 3.14.21. You want to keep your distance from an opponent rushing toward you with a weapon. Drop down suddenly to evade and apply a roundhouse kick to his groin. You can follow up with a twin ground back kick. Keep kicking his knees and shins from the floor or joint-kick him down until he loses his weapon or decides to leave you alone. Contrary to common belief, it is safer to be (actively) on the ground, especially if your opponent is armed with a stick or a knife. From his standing position, his targets are few and he needs to unsafely bend to get to you.

Figure 3.14.17 Figure 3.14.18 Figure 3.14.19 Figure 3.14.20 Figure 3.14.21
Avoid a rushing, wide stick attack and counter.

3.15 The Drop Twin Roundhouse Kick

General

This is a more acrobatic drop kick, where you kick your opponent with both legs in a circular path. It is an interesting kick as it is very powerful: you use the momentum of the whole body to kick. The kick is powerful enough not to have to be accurate. If you hit only the general area of the groin or the kidneys, the reverberation of the shock wave will be enough to inflict a lot of pain. On the other hand, you have to be totally committed to execute this kick, and we could have classified it as a "suicide kick." The kick is to be used on an advancing opponent, preferably hitting high on a strong forward momentum. Like all drop kicks, this is a great kick against a high-kicking opponent. This kick is even better (though we will not illustrate this here) against high jump kicks, which are sometimes overpowering. You disappear down and wait for gravity to bring him back to the ground where your twin roundhouse clears his legs from under him while inflicting severe damage to his knees and shins!

Description

See Figures 3.15.1 through 3.15.4. You crouch and put your hands on the floor. Immediately throw both bent legs around, using your hands both as a support and a pivot. Put your whole body into the kick and use the centrifugal force to gather power. Extend the legs in a double kick while "flying" toward your target in such a way that you reach full extension as you connect. You should land on the balls of your feet, in a push up-like stance. Immediately roll or jump away from your opponent.

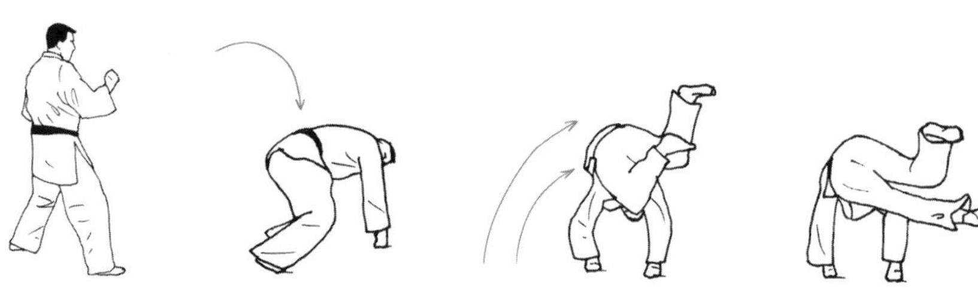

Figure 3.15.1 Figure 3.15.2 Figure 3.15.3 Figure 3.15.4
Drop down and twin kick with the whole body.

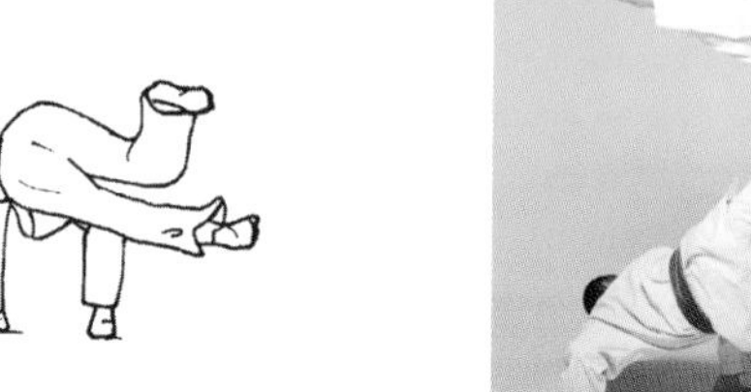

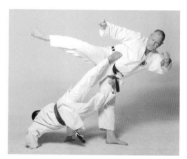

Figure 3.15.5
The photo shows the kick at impact, connecting simultaneously with the groin and thigh.

Key Points

- For this kick to work, you need to be fully committed.
- Get away from opponent as soon as you have kicked.

Targets

Typical targets include the knees, groin, kidneys, and lower abdomen.

Typical Application

See Figures 3.15.6 through 3.15.8, which illustrate this kick against a rear leg high roundhouse, although the beauty of the move is that it could counter any other high kick. Catch him at full extension.

Figure 3.15.6 Figure 3.15.7 Figure 3.15.8
Evade the high kick and counter at the same time: drop and kick.

Specific Training

This is a powerful kick. Train on the heavy bag, and always work both sides.

Self-defense

See Figures 3.15.9 through 3.15.12. Use this against an assailant who is threatening you with a knife. Drop down and away as swiftly as possible and catch him in his forward momentum. Give all the power of your body momentum and try to catch him both on the knee and the groin for maximum damage. If needed, keep kicking from the floor, always keeping your legs between you and him.

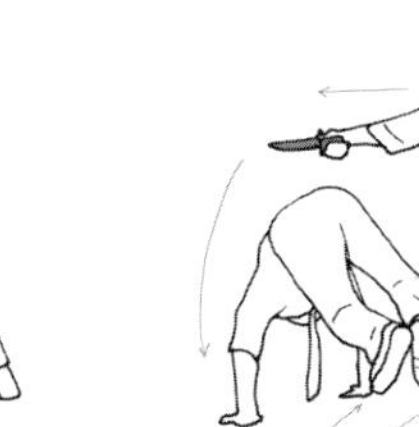

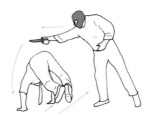

Figure 3.15.9 Figure 3.15.10 Figure 3.15.11 Figure 3.15.12

Evade a knife attack by dropping and kicking.

3.16 The Rear Leg Drop Roundhouse Kick

General

This is the more powerful version of the drop roundhouse, as it is executed with the rear leg. This kick is also more offensive as there is more forward momentum, but it still is a kick to be performed on an advancing opponent. Besides the obvious groin kicking on a high kicking opponent, those drop kicks are useful simply as surprise kicks, especially for experts in ground kicking, or kicks to handle overpowering forward rushing opponents, or to use against armed opponents, in order to keep as far away as possible from the weapon. The kick will be described in its more classical form, where you stand on your hands and knee, but it can be delivered lying on the floor where you have let yourself drop for faster delivery. An example of this is highly typical of the *Unsu* kata of Shotokan-ryu karate, which is probably the only traditional Shotokan kata where a roundhouse kick is found. The illustrated sequence of the kata is presented in Figures 3.16.1 through 3.16.5. It is a double rear leg drop roundhouse kick.

Figure 3.16.1 Figure 3.16.2 Figure 3.16.3 Figure 3.16.4 Figure 3.16.5

This kata excerpt shows how Shotokan-ryu karate's Unsu kata incorporates a double rear leg drop roundhouse kick.

Description

See Figures 3.16.6 through 3.16.9. From a relatively high stance, bend forward and pivot while going down to your hands and *front* knee. Keep your eyes on your opponent. Chamber your rear leg with the knee high and throw a roundhouse, in a similar way to a standing one.

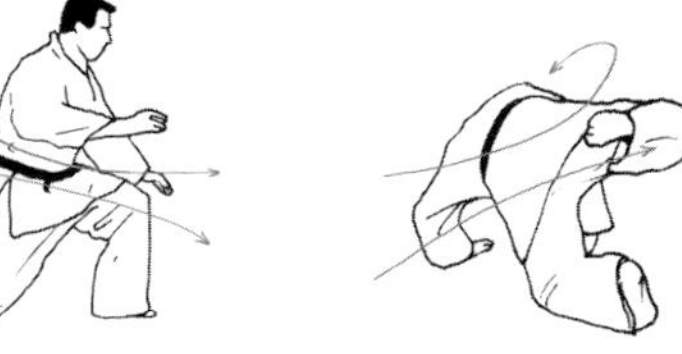

Figure 3.16.6 Figure 3.16.7 Figure 3.16.8 Figure 3.16.9

Going down forward and kicking with the rear leg.

Alternatively, you can first squat straight down while pivoting slightly back and then start your pivot forward close to the floor (See Figures 3.16.10 through 3.16.14).

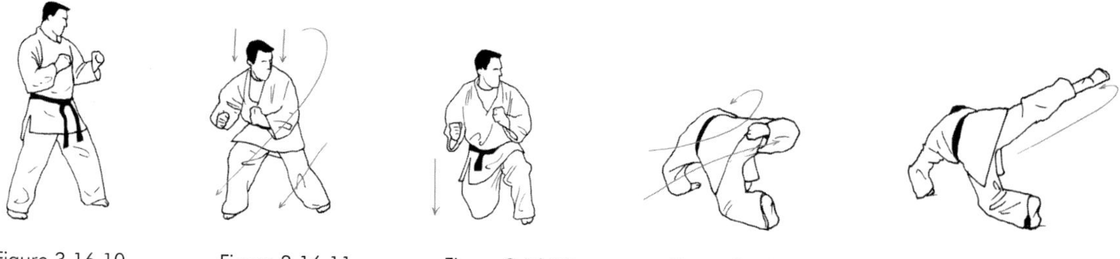

Figure 3.16.10 Figure 3.16.11 Figure 3.16.12 Figure 3.16.13 Figure 3.16.14
Moving down, then forward.

Key Points

- Keep your eyes on your opponent when dropping down.
- The entire process of dropping down and kicking must be delivered in one continuous movement—there is no pause during the execution, as time is of the essence and the power comes from the uninterrupted circular move.

Targets

Appropriate targets include the knee, groin, and kidneys.

Typical Application

See Figures 3.16.15 through 3.16.20. Your opponent is a high kicker. When you see a committed high roundhouse coming, you crouch back, keeping your guard up, and drop swiftly forward to the floor on your side and hands, close to him. Time your roundhouse to catch his groin at full extension. As he lowers his kicking leg, open your legs inside his legs, hook-kicking both his ankles and causing him to fall down with open legs. Keep kicking (his groin is open), and create some distance before standing up.

Figure 3.16.15 Figure 3.16.16 Figure 3.16.17 Figure 3.16.18

Figure 3.16.19 Figure 3.16.20
Evading a kick by kicking and delivering a great finish.

Specific Training

- Work the drop movement, alone and with a partner swinging a stick at waist level.
- Alternate on the heavy bag: a standing roundhouse, a rear leg drop roundhouse.
- Practice the whole *Unsu* kata, or the sequence described previously in Figure sequence 3.16.1 through 3.16.5.

Self-defense

See Figures 3.16.21 through 3.16.27. In this scenario, an assailant, who is pointing a knife at your belly, suddenly attacks you. You have just enough time to drop to the floor, on your and his side, directly into kicking position. You must drop with commitment—you do not have the time to just let yourself fall. kick his groin with full power, while he's still in mid-movement. As soon as you have connected a few inches into the target, keep using your momentum to roll on yourself and pass your kicking leg behind his front leg. Keep rolling forcefully on yourself and kick his abdomen in a crescent kick-like move, while "scissoring" his leg. This is not a shove, but a real kick, using the centrifugal force of your roll as powerfully as possible. Your assailant falls backward and you immediately (back) hook kick your heel between his legs, again, before you take your distance to stand up.

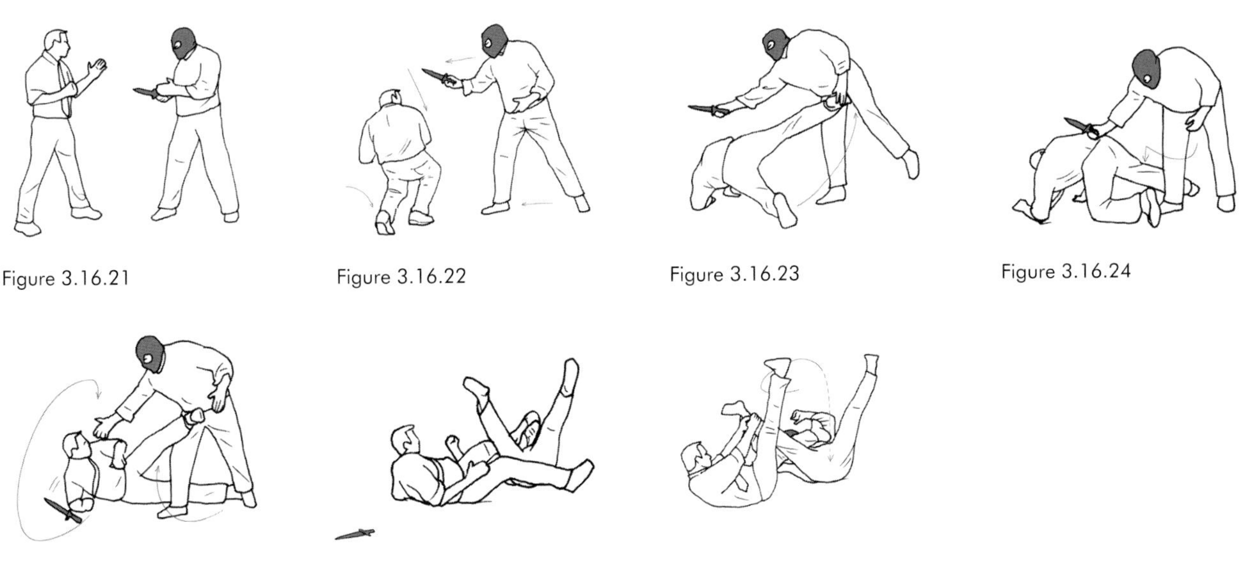

Figure 3.16.21 Figure 3.16.22 Figure 3.16.23 Figure 3.16.24

Figure 3.16.25 Figure 3.16.26 Figure 3.16.27

The images above illustrate a difficult but effective defense against a knife attack.

3.17 The Kneeling Up Roundhouse Kick

Sien fung tie (kung fu)

General

Just like the kneeling-up side kick, the kneeling up roundhouse is a surprising kick because of the popping down/up. But the kneeling up roundhouse has the added advantage of using the twisting up motion for a more powerful roundhouse. In order to roundhouse kick from the low crossed leg position, you have to pivot into a full 180 circle which adds to the centrifugal force of the kick. In fact, in some styles of kung fu, this kick is called the "whirlwind" kick. Always use it to surprise your opponent, however, as it is difficult to perform from a static position. Crouch down suddenly and pop back up powerfully and with full commitment. Even if this type of kick is not your cup of tea, and you do not feel it compatible with your style, do practice it a lot. It's a great way to build stamina, kicking proficiency, powerful muscles, and above all, it is one of those kicks that will get you on the road to being able to kick from any position or situation.

Description

There are several ways to get to the crossed leg crouching stance, you can just pivot down without moving the feet (see the kneeling up side kick—Chapter 2, Section 11), or you can step back and sit on your knee. Some footwork will be described later. In this example (see Figures 3.17.1 through 3.17.5), you step forward with your rear foot and go down to a crossed leg stance. You then pop up and chamber the rear leg, using the upward momentum and the pivot of the hips to kick.

Figure 3.17.1

Figure 3.17.2

Figure 3.17.3

Down, then up, pouring the power of the move into the kick.

Figure 3.17.4

Figure 3.17.5

Key Points

- The kick is one continuous move from the crouching down to the chambering back—no stopping.
- The kick has to go through the target before chambering back.

Targets

All roundhouse targets come into account, from thigh to head. The kick has no logical use below the knee. You don't have to go down, then up to kick down!

Typical Application

See Figures 3.17.6 through 3.17.10 for the "twist and down" application. Your opponent is a strong and overpowering puncher: he attacks you with a fully committed high jab. You pivot on yourself without moving your feet position and deliver a spin-back backfist (*Uraken uchi*—karate) or "hammer" punch (*Tettsui*—karate) to his head from his outside. This is a very surprising and extremely powerful punch, especially when delivered as a "timing" stop punch. As soon as you have connected, you sit down on your crossed legs and evade any punching reaction to your move. You can punch his groin from there. Your opponent starts to retreat and you forcefully pop up in chambered roundhouse position to catch him from his inside this time.

Figure 3.17.6

Figure 3.17.7

Figure 3.17.8

Figure 3.17.9

Figure 3.17.10

These images illustrate a disorienting technique: Twist and punch, disappear down, then kick back up.

Specific Training

- Vigorously practice the classical footwork around the low cross stance, with your hands on your hips. See Figures 3.17.11 through 3.17.24.

Figure 3.17.11

Figure 3.17.12

Figure 3.17.13

Figure 3.17.14

From standing position, twist down on one side without moving your footing. Stand up and repeat on the other side. Keep alternating.

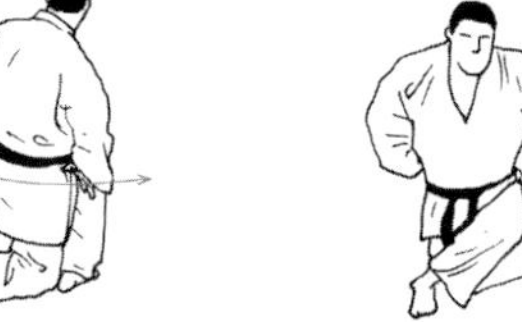

Figure 3.17.15

Figure 3.17.16

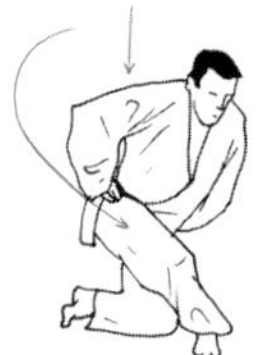

Figure 3.17.17

From crossed leg stance, stand up while lifting your rear leg up high and in front. Go down with this leg in front this time, back in crossed-leg stance, but on the other side. Repeat and advance this way.

Figure 3.17.18 Figure 3.17.19 Figure 3.17.20
Step forward with your front foot and twist down. Stand up and repeat. Keep advancing.

Figure 3.17.21 Figure 3.17.22 Figure 3.17.23 Figure 3.17.24
Step forward and outside with your front foot in an evasion step. Follow the body with the back leg, out of the mid-line, directly into a crossed-leg stance. Crouch down. Stand up and repeat. Keep advancing. Then switch legs and work on the other side.

- As mentioned, these are excellent and important overall kicking drills. Practice on both sides until your legs burn.
- This is a powerful kick: kick the heavy bag.
- The down/up move is key. Practice with a partner swinging a stick at shoulder level.

Self-defense

In this example, you just crouch down directly after a small retreating shuffle, with no footwork and just a little twist. You are attacked by a high kicker and step back to avoid and control a high rear leg roundhouse (Figure 3.17.26). Your overpowering opponent keeps turning for an obvious spin-back kick (Figure 3.17.27). As he is turning you slightly shuffle back, back leg first, then front leg and go down into low crossed leg stance with your guard up (Figure 3.17.28). As soon as his spin-back hook kick has passed over your head, you pop up forcefully in chambered position and roundhouse kick him while he is still off-balance (Figure 3.17.30).

Figure 3.17.25

Figure 3.17.26

Figure 3.17.27

Figure 3.17.28

Figure 3.17.29

Figure 3.17.30
An obvious use: crouching down below a high spin-back hook kick.

More Advanced Roundhouse Kicks

What follows is a brief review of some more advanced kicks. They are not presented in detail here, as they are beyond the scope of this book.

The Low Roundhouse Kick

A great kick for self-defense, fast, easy and punishing.

The Low Straight Leg Roundhouse Kick

There is no doubt that this is one of the most powerful kicks around, and the hallmark of the hardest and most aggressive styles. Versatile, and relatively easy to deliver, as it does not require great flexibility, it is the ideal kick for self-defense. It is the "low kick" par excellence, and even so-called in the kickboxing styles.

The Ground Roundhouse Kick

This kick is probably the most versatile of all ground kicks because it is fast and nimble. It is very close to the drop roundhouse.

The Kneeling Roundhouse Kick

The kneeling roundhouse kick is a roundhouse delivered while you are going down onto the knee of the standing leg. It is mentioned here for the sake of completeness, as this kick is practiced in some Korean styles and is a great drill for general kicking performance.

The Front Chamber Roundhouse Kick

This kick is the archetype of the feint kick. This is, rightfully, a very popular kick. You deliver a full front kick for as long as possible, before turning it into a roundhouse when your opponent is committed to his defense. This kick is not to be confused with the small roundhouse, which is not a feint kick.

The Hook Chamber Roundhouse Kick

Again a feint kick, the name says it all. A hook kick for as long as possible fades into a roundhouse coming, obviously, from the other direction.

The Front Kick to Hopping Roundhouse Combination

This is a popular and quite natural combination. It is a very offensive kick combination that allows for a long range, and is great to catch a "fleeing" opponent. The different angles of the two kicks in close succession give great odds of success.

The Flying Roundhouse Kick

The flying roundhouse kick is a flying kick first. It is an interesting kick because it combines the forward momentum of the flying, with the circular path of attack of the roundhouse.

The Double Flying Roundhouse Kick

This highly acrobatic kick has both legs kicking simultaneously while "flying." It may suit some martial artists, and, again, the importance of surprise and unpredictability should never be underestimated in fight.

The Double Roundhouse Kick

The double roundhouse is a typical "double kick." It is a very important kick for the striving kicking artist—a great drill, but also a very practical kick that could be considered a feint kick. It is, in a way, a bread and butter move for the kicking artist. You use the same leg to kick, chamber back and kick again from the chambered position. You can kick low/high, high/low, high/high, and low/low.

The Hook to Roundhouse Kick Combination

This classical and very natural combination follows the natural circular movement of the hook kick with a roundhouse on the same circle.

Comparative Tables

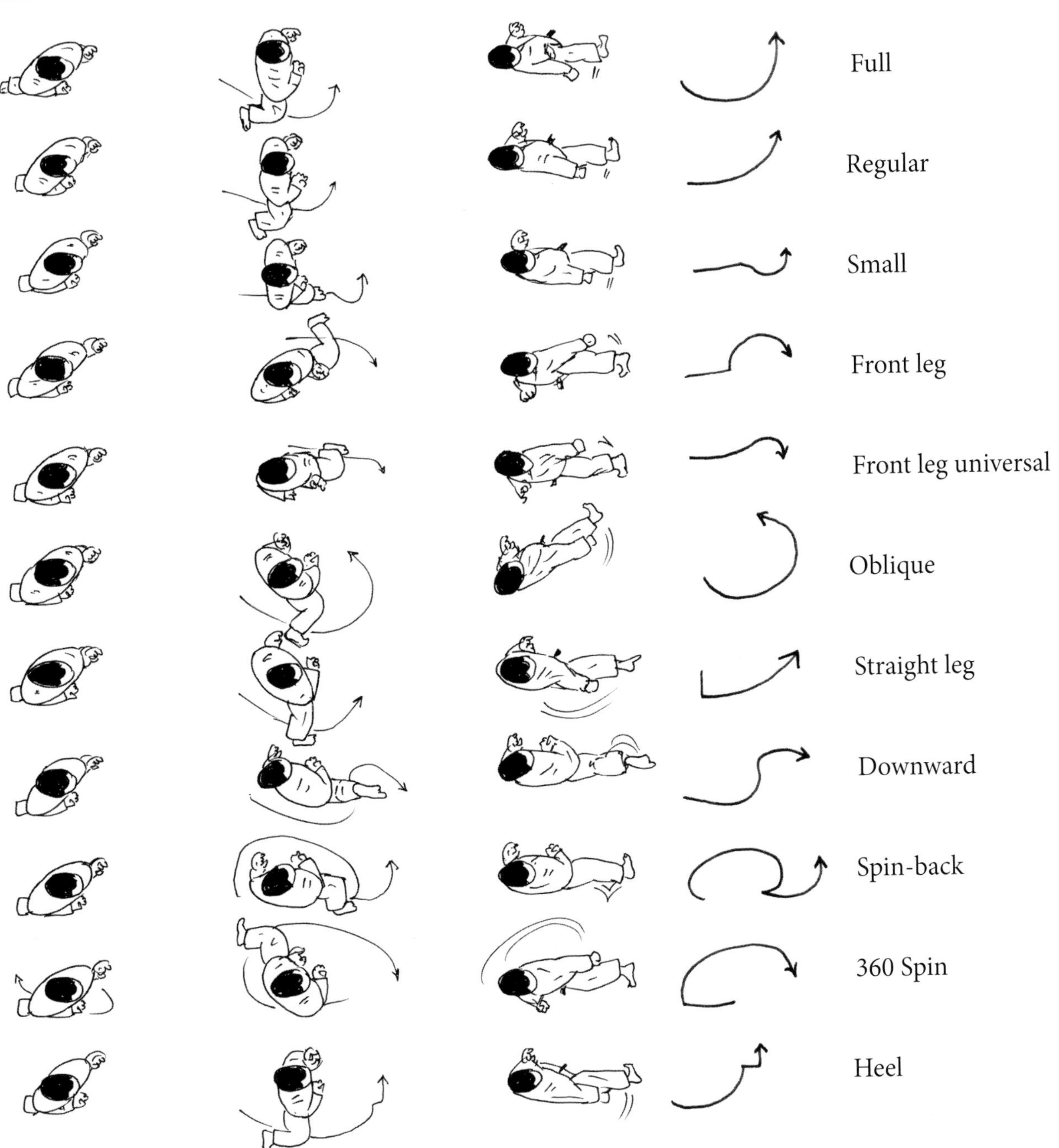

Table 1 — Comparative overhead view of chambering positions and trajectories for different roundhouse kicks.

Table 2 — Comparative table of chambering positions for the main roundhouse kicks.

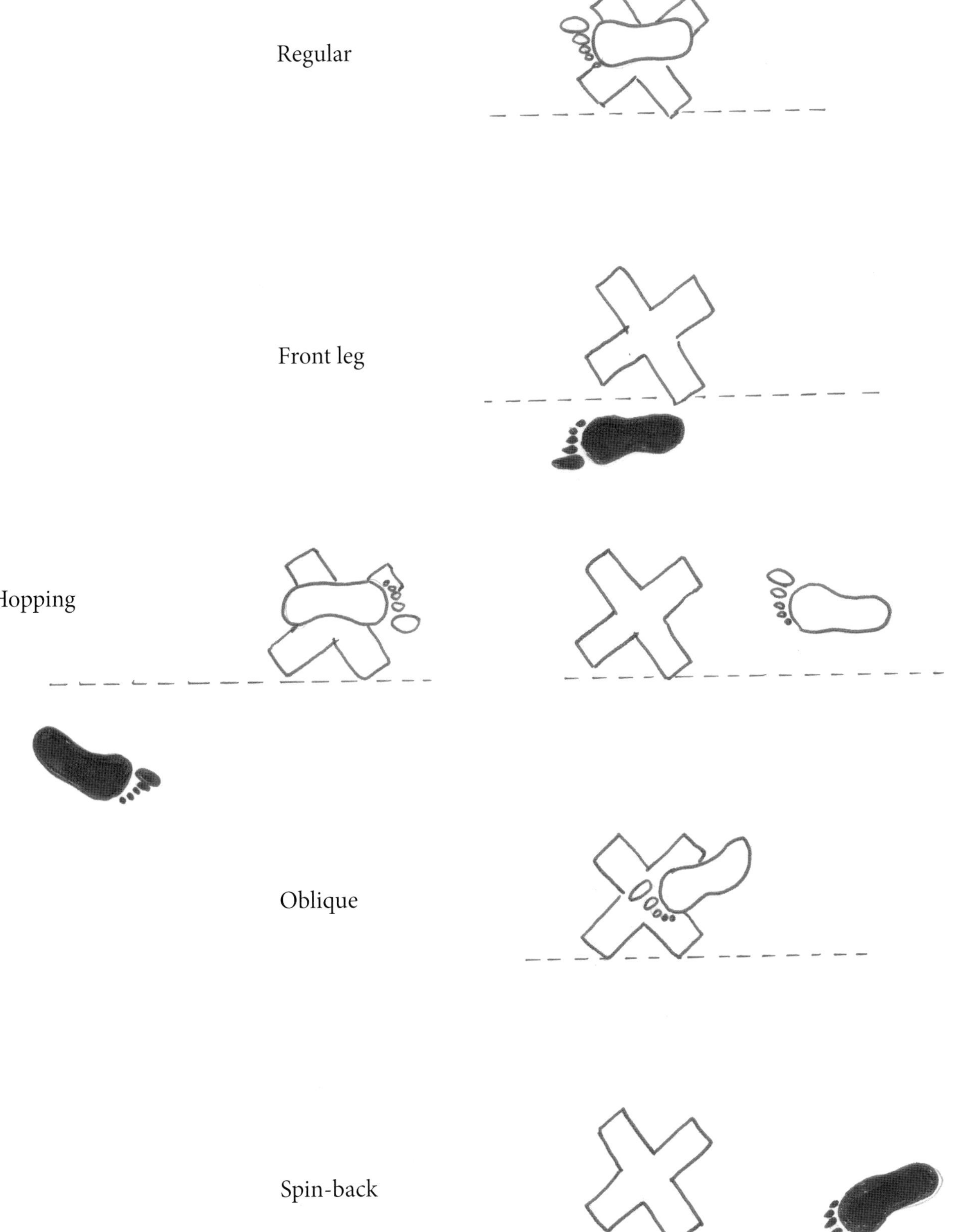

Table 3 — Comparative table of footwork patterns for the main roundhouse kicks.

CHAPTER 4

Back Kicks

Back kicks are, again, straight kicks, but delivered to the rear. This has obvious applications for real life self-defense against attacks from behind. Back kicks are very powerful kicks and are present in all martial arts, often with appropriate names like mule or donkey kicks.

They are not limited to use against assailants from the rear, however, and this chapter presents the many footwork variations that will allow their use against an opponent facing you, as well as several surprising executions.

4.1 The Penetrating Back Kick

Ushiro geri (Wado-ryu karate), *Dwit chagi* (taekwondo), *Hu jiao / Hao tshok tsha / Huwai tek* (kung fu), *Tendangan belakang* (pencak silat), *Ho vi cuoc* (viet vo dao)

General

Back kicks are even more powerful than side kicks, because of the use of the strong and large back and gluteus muscles. The kicks are also generally delivered with the upper body leaning away from the danger zone. The only problem with those kicks is the absence of eyes on the back of our heads—these kicks are delivered partially blindly. They still are very important kicks to master, not only for their power, but also because they are sometimes the only solution to certain situations. For example, in self-defense cases where you are attacked from the back, having to turn and look first would take too much time. These are also the perfect follow-up kicks when you find yourself led by your momentum to a partially back-giving position. For example, if carried away by a circular kick which momentum you won't be able to stop in time, you can exaggerate the pivot, lower you leg with your back toward your opponent, and back kick!
Also don't forget that deception and surprise are the best fighting tactics. By turning away, you can look like you are fleeing, causing your overconfident opponent to attack and impale himself on your back kick.

The penetrating back kick can be executed with a range of nuances to how much "back" versus "side" you are giving toward the opponent. Refer to the text about the previously described back-side kick (Chapter 2, Section 7). The kick described in this chapter is the back kick as performed in the Wado-ryu school of karate (*Ushiro geri*). This is mentioned, because the *Ushiro geri* of the Shotokan school is basically the back-side kick mentioned. The kick described here is, appropriately, a full back back-kick. It can be delivered from a standing stance, a fighting stance with both front and back leg, and, as presented later, after a spin back or a spin forward. We'll present the traditional way to practice it, with the rear leg from the fighting stance.

Description

See Figures 4.1.1 to 4.1.11. Lift your rear leg forward, just like for a front kick, while looking back. Extend the leg straight back while leaning forward. Connect with the heel, while pushing your hips into the kick. Retract the leg and lower it in front or back, while pivoting toward the danger zone.

Figure 4.1.1 Figure 4.1.2
Side view of the back kick delivery.

Figure 4.1.3

Figure 4.1.4

Figure 4.1.5
Back view of the back kick delivery.

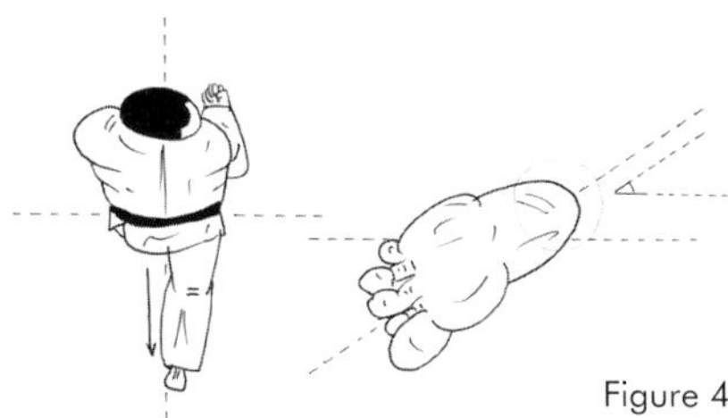

Figure 4.1.6
Overhead view of the back kick delivery and point of impact.

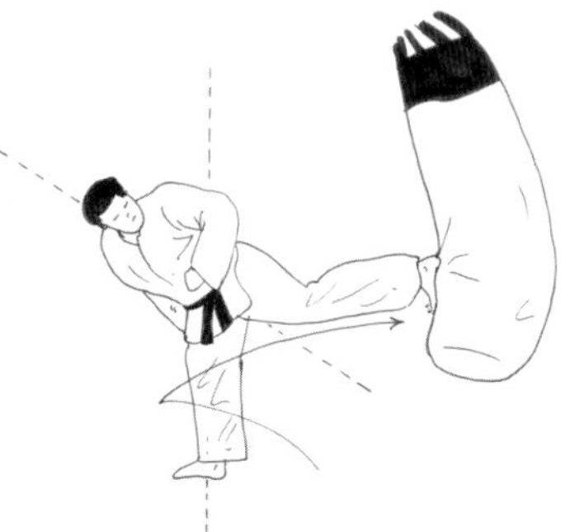

Figure 4.1.7
Trajectory of the back kick.

Figure 4.1.8 Figure 4.1.9
These photos show the classic execution of the kick.

Figure 4.1.10

Figure 4.1.11

Key Points

- Lean forward, but not lower than horizontal. Try to look *over* your shoulder, and not under.
- Do not try to look back first before kicking. In doing so, you lose time and endanger yourself. Practicing will make your kick straight, without having to look. During the kick, if your position and training allows, start turning the head and looking.
- At impact, your kicking foot is pointing anywhere between downward to a 45 degree angle, as comfort dictates.
- The kick lands in the centerline, as shown in Figure 4.1.12.

Targets

The kick is straight and coming somewhat from below. As it is extremely powerful, all targets are worthwhile. Even if you hit the arms he is protecting himself with, you will probably impact through and hurt him. Aim for the groin, the ribs, the lower abdomen, the sternum, the throat and the face.

Figure 4.1.12
This image clearly shows that the foot is aligned with the head.

Typical Application

See Figures 4.1.13 through 4.1.17. This is an example of using the back kick after lowering a kicking leg in such a way that your back is partially vulnerable. Jab on the inside of your opponent's face to force him to block inwards, while you close the distance for a front leg hook kick (Chapter 5, Section 3) to the outside of his head. Lower the kicking leg with your back facing partially toward your opponent. Spin back a little bit more and back kick with the other leg to the open midsection of your opponent. Lower the leg close to him while he is staggering back from the impact, and immediately deliver a second full-penetrating back kick with the other leg.

Figure 4.1.13 Figure 4.1.14 Figure 4.1.15 Figure 4.1.16 Figure 4.1.17
The powerful back kick is the kick of choice when you land a kicking leg sideways.

Specific Training

- It is important to master a straight trajectory for the kick. Practice kicking the heavy bag on a specific spot marked in the middle!
- Repeatedly hit the bag with a straight back kick, after first delivering a front kick forward over a stool (see Figures 4.1.18 through 4.1.20).

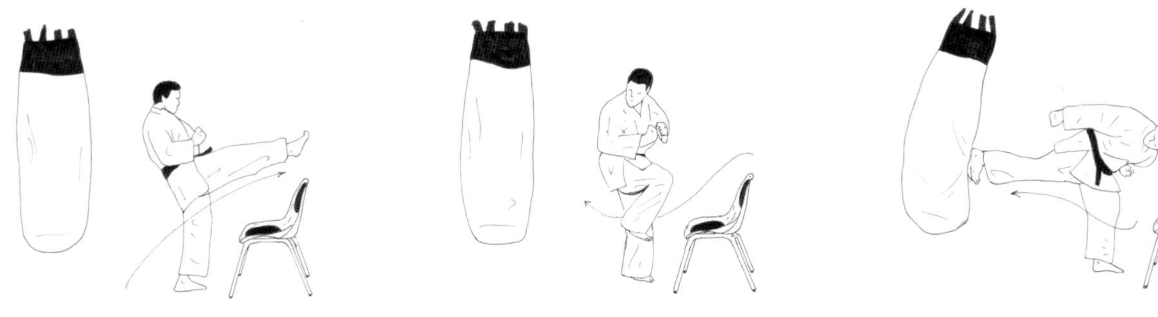

Figure 4.1.18 Figure 4.1.19 Figure 4.1.20
Drilling both kicks at the same time.

- Work with a partner holding a striking pad, as seen in Figures 4.1.21 through 4.1.23. It is very important to learn to kick straight into the target, and not "slip" on it.

Figure 4.1.21 Figure 4.1.22 Figure 4.1.23
Make sure you kick straight and a few inches "into" the pad.

- Blindfolded kicking to the heavy bag is very efficient training.

Self-defense

In a self-defense situation, when attacked from behind, always kick first and look after! The example illustrated in Figures 4.1.24 through 4.1.28 is a more complex situation—your assailant grabs your arm and tries to apply a straight arm armlock. Turn away from him, while leaning down and deliver a penetrating back kick to his groin area. As soon as he releases you, probably with his hands down toward the pain, you use the full pivot back of the hips to knife-hand him on the throat or the side of the neck. You can then keep on kicking him, for example with another rear leg upward front kick to the groin (low/high/low).

Figure 4.1.24
Defending against a standing arm-lock attempt.

Figure 4.1.25

Figure 4.1.26

Figure 4.1.27

Figure 4.1.28

Figure 4.1.29
The back kick is the kick of choice if attacked while getting into your car.

4.2 The Short Back Kick

General

The short back kick is the way to deliver a back kick when your adversary is close to you—too close for a full power penetrating back kick. The idea behind this variation is to start developing the kick directly from the chambering position, by lifting the knee and chambered leg parallel to the floor. The kick is not traveling directly in a straight line anymore, but, in its first phases, as an arc, and then straight but from the outside and in parallel to the floor. This is an important kick to practice, together with a few other "short" kicks, as it will give you the ability to instinctively kick even very close opponents. Of course, it must be stressed that all the nuances of the kick are possible, per the situation, your flexibility, and your preferences—It can go all the way from the (vertical) classical penetrating back kick to the short (horizontal) kick described here, going through all intermediate trajectories.

Description

See Figures 4.2.1 through 4.2.7. Just as with the full back kick, you chamber the rear leg in the front while looking back. Then lift the chambered knee to the side (as done for a full roundhouse kick) while starting to lean forward and slightly to the side. Simultaneously start to develop the kick, straight from this position.

Figure 4.2.1

Figure 4.2.2

Figure 4.2.3

Figure 4.2.4

Notice that the kick travels in an arc and in parallel to the floor.

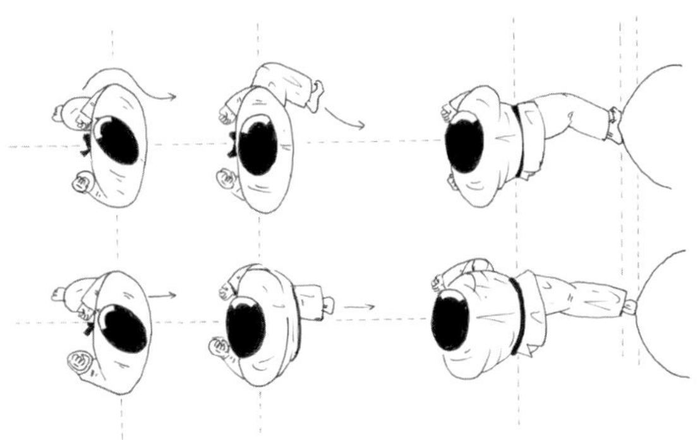

Figure 4.2.5
You can see the trajectories and ranges compared in this illustration. The short kick is shown above, and the regular kick is shown below.

Figure 4.2.6

Figure 4.2.7
As you can see, a short back kick allows you to get enough momentum for an effective kick very close to you. Going the classical way, your kick would be jammed long before gathering power.

Figure 4.2.8 illustrates the use of the kick at mid-distance. Compare leg position to previous Figure 4.1.11.

Figure 4.2.8
Close combat use.

Figure 4.2.9 shows how the kick can be used against an opponent standing very, very close behind you. The kick is not to be confused with another kick suitable for this very close starting position: the small heel back hook kick (Chapter 5, Section 17).

Figure 4.2.9
Very close combat use.

Key Points
- All steps described are performed nearly simultaneously, and the move is one smooth motion. Do not: look first, then chamber, then lift knee.
- Lean forward at impact to put some hips into the kick.

Targets
Although it is feasible to kick the head and throat if you are very flexible, this is basically a very powerful body kick. Typical targets include the groin, lower abdomen, ribs, solar plexus, and armpit.

Typical Application
This kick must be automatic if you find yourself with your back turned to a close assailant! A very useful example, in a spin-back version and successfully used in tournament fighting, is presented in Figures 4.2.10 through 4.2.14. You block a roundhouse to the body with a strong circular knee block with your front leg (*Ashibo kake uke*—karate). This leaves you with your back partly

turned toward your opponent, who gets close to you as he lowers his (hurt) kicking leg. Use your momentum to continue your pivot and deliver a spin-back short back kick to his lower abdomen. Finish with an elbow strike to the face.

Figure 4.2.10 Figure 4.2.11 Figure 4.2.12 Figure 4.2.13 Figure 4.2.14
This kick is recommended when spinning back close to the opponent.

Specific Training

- This is a very important kick to master, and needs a lot of practice.
- Stand in the fighting stance with your back *against* the heavy bag (See Figure 4.2.15). Kick with both front leg (Figure 4.2.16) and back leg, as powerfully as possible, without moving the body first. Repeat endlessly!
- Figures 4.2.17 and 4.2.18 show the drill of a lower version of the kick against a striking pad held by a partner. Work at different close ranges and heights. Strike hard.

Figure 4.2.15 Figure 4.2.16
Practice extremely close to the bag for better performance from all ranges.

Figure 4.2.17 Figure 4.2.18
There is no alternative to practice with a moving partner holding a focus pad.

Self-defense

This is a perfect kick for all self-defense situations. As mentioned, if someone gets close behind you, kick first, look later. The example presented in Figures 4.2.19 through 4.2.23 is a little more complex. An assailant attempts to grab your lapels or your neck from the front. React immediately by lifting your hands forcefully and then striking both his ears with your palms. Start pivoting while elbowing him on the side of the head. Keep turning away and back kick him as soon as possible. The short back kick to the body will both disable him and push him away to a safer distance.

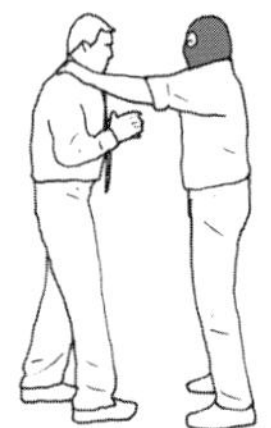
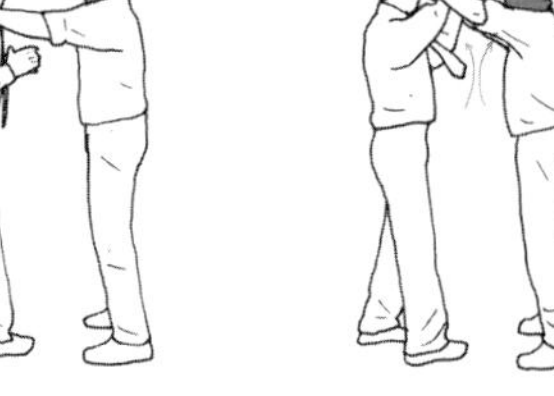

Figure 4.2.19 Figure 4.2.20 Figure 4.2.21 Figure 4.2.22 Figure 4.2.23
These images illustrate a technique to counter an attempted lapels grab.

4.3 The Spin-back Back Kick

Dora yop tshagy (taekwondo)

General

The spin-back back kick is the stop kick par excellence, because it adds the power of the spin to the intrinsic power of the kick, but we present its other uses here. The kick is basically a rear leg kick, where you spin back half a turn, until your back is toward the opponent and then kick. On top of the power of the kick itself and of the spin-back, you also have the momentum of the hips toward the opponent. This added energy makes it a kick that is nearly impossible to block—only avoidance will save you! If you add to it the surprise effect of the spin back (which is not followed by a circular move), you have a kick that is a must to master. The drawbacks: 1. Again, you don't have eyes in the back of your head; and 2. The combination of the straight kick with the circular spin move requires thorough training. This kick was the preferred technique (*Tokui-waza*) of one of this author's national teammates, and having many times been on the receiving end, I can assure you that the hard training is worth the results.

Description

See Figure 4.3.1 through 4.3.4. From the fighting stance, you spin back—half a turn, no more—before you stop the spin to switch to a straight back kick. You connect with the heel. The spin back can be executed with a slight forward or backward emphasis, depending on whether this is a defensive or offensive move. If this is a forward offensive move, you can also add a little hopping once the spin is over and the kicking leg is chambered.

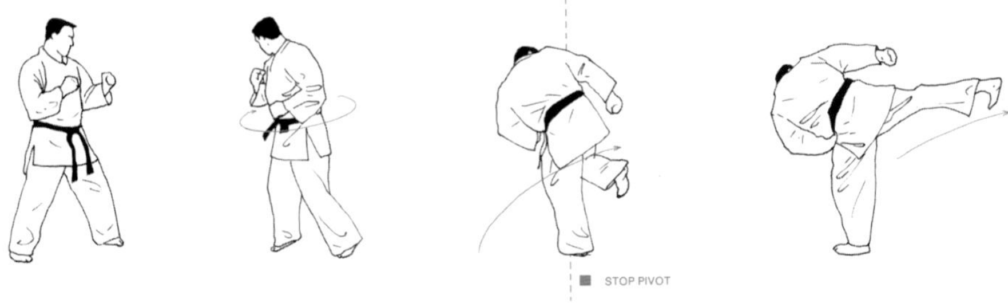

Figure 4.3.1 Figure 4.3.2 Figure 4.3.3 Figure 4.3.4
An important kick: Spin (circular) and back kick (straight).

Figures 4.3.6 through 4.3.9 show the classic execution of the kick.

Figure 4.3.5 Figure 4.3.6 Figure 4.3.7 Figure 4.3.8
Notice the transition from circular to straight movement.

Figures 4.3.9 through 4.3.15 show the "short" version of the kick in close combat, delivered while making use of the momentum of a hook (punch) to start the spinning motion. This is a classic combination: jab, cross, hook to the head and spin-back short back kick to the body.

Figure 4.3.9

Figure 4.3.10

Figure 4.3.11

Figure 4.3.12

Figure 4.3.13

Figure 4.3.14

Figure 4.3.15

These photographs depict a short back kick to the body following a classic boxing combination to the head.

Key Points

- The key point here is to *totally* stop the spinning motion, in its tracks, as soon as you have completed your half-turn. If you do not, the kick will not be straight but angled, and will probably miss its target.
- On the other hand, the transition between the spin and the straight motion must be smooth.
- Once the leg is chambered, start delivering the kick while pushing your hips toward your opponent and leaning forward.

Targets

The preferred targets are on the lower trunk, especially if it is a stop-kick. But, as it is probably the most powerful kick possible, everything goes, even if protected by a limb: thighs, groin, hips, ribs, belly, sternum, throat, face, and more.

Typical Application

Figures 4.3.16 through 4.3.22 present the simplest but so effective way to place an offensive spin-back back kick. Lunge high and to the inside of your opponent head to force him to lift his lead hand, and lift it to his inside. Spin back smoothly and back kick his uncovered side at belt level. The spin back and forward hip thrust make this kick surprisingly long! Once you have connected with his ribs, pivot in a continuation of the spin move, and lower your leg behind his front leg. Hit him in the face or throat, while sweeping his leg (*O soto gari*—judo) to throw him to the floor. If necessary, you can downward heel kick him (Figure 4.3.22).

Figure 4.3.16

Figure 4.3.17

Figure 4.3.18

Figure 4.3.19

Figure 4.3.20

Figure 4.3.21

Figure 4.3.22

A very effective combination: Moving to the inside of the centerline to close the distance.

Please note that the move illustrated is against an opposite guard opponent, but it is totally valid against an opponent standing in the same guard as you: feint high to his outside, spin-back back kick and lower the leg to his inside, hit the back of his neck while sweeping his lead leg from the inside (*Uchi mata*—judo).

Figure 4.3.23
Practice on the marked heavy bag.

Specific Training

- As mentioned, this kick requires a lot of training. The key point to master it is to stop the spin back movement as soon as half-a-turn is complete, to start with a clean straight kick. See Figures 4.3.23 through 4.3.25.
- Mark the heavy bag in its middle, and kick from an increasingly distant fighting stance. If you do not stop the spin movement, you will turn too much and miss the bag totally, or at least miss the mark in the middle!
- One of the best targets to practice this kick on is an old car tire, held by a partner or in a frame held in place on the wall. The tire is narrow and forces you to be precise in your execution, and it "gives" like hitting a partner. Kick hard, but with precision.
- Practice kicking a hanging ball, a tennis ball for example.
- For people who have difficulties kicking straight, the following practice is recommended at the beginning: spin back and, instead of chambering the leg, leave the kicking foot on the floor and slide it back in a straight line toward your target. Start lifting the foot to deliver the kick only after it has overtaken the standing leg. Doing so prevents over-spinning, and you can later lift the kicking leg slowly earlier and earlier in the kick.
- Kicking the heavy bag while blindfolded is an advanced form of training.

Figure 4.3.24
Practice on a much narrower tire.

Figure 4.3.25
This drill on an even smaller target will force you to become much more precise.

Self-defense

Figures 4.3.26 through 4.3.30 present a "short back kick" version of the spin-back back kick. Your assailant has caught you in a high outside wrist lock. Lean down and forward, and spin back immediately to relieve pain. As soon as you have your back toward him, back kick, if he is close, slightly from the outside (like a short back kick). As soon as you have connected and he releases you, lower the leg and deliver a second back kick with the other leg, this time with a full-penetrating back kick.

Figure 4.3.26

Figure 4.3.27

Figure 4.3.28

Figure 4.3.29

Figure 4.3.30

A great counter to an attempted standing wrist-lock. Spin to alleviate the pressure on the joint.

4.4 The Spin-forward Back Kick

General

The spin forward back kick is a classical way to practice the back kick. It is a great drill, and helps to establish the perception that kicking is possible with all kinds of footwork and body positions. In practice, we don't think it is a very important kick to use for other purposes. Basically, it is delivered very much like a classical rear leg penetrating side kick (Chapter 2, Section 1), but with a continuation of the pivot for another quarter of a turn. Therefore, in practice and in a given situation, you can satisfy your kicking needs with a side kick, or even a back-side kick (Chapter 2, Section 7). It is still a great kick, however, if the chambering of the leg is modified into a feint or a block, which leaves you naturally with your back facing toward your opponent.

Description

See Figures 4.4.1 through 4.4.4. Lift your rear knee to the front, as you would for a front kick, while pivoting on your standing leg. You'll find yourself knee-up with your side toward your opponent, just as for a penetrating side kick. But you keep pivoting until your back is toward your opponent, and then develop the back kick, and chamber back.

Figure 4.4.1 Figure 4.4.2 Figure 4.4.3 Figure 4.4.4
Make three quarters of a turn forward, and then kick.

Figures 4.4.5 through 4.4.8 show the execution of the kick.

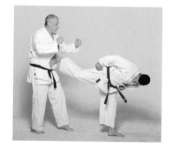

Figure 4.4.5 Figure 4.4.6
Note transition from circular forward to straight backward.

Figure 4.4.7

Figure 4.4.8

Key Points

- Though it is easier to manage than it is in the spin-back version, the key point here is also to avoid mixing the circular and straight movements which compose the kick.
- As you pivot in front and toward your opponent, keep your guard up and use your raised knee as protection for the body.

Targets

Like all back kicks, it is powerful enough for all possible targets: from knee to head.

Typical Application

See Figures 4.4.9 through 4.4.15. This is the kick based on a crescent kick feint. You lunge with a high jab, followed by a rear crescent kick to his blocking arm, in order to get him used to the *high outside* crescent kick attack. Lower the leg and repeat a high crescent kick with the same leg, but this time, use the momentum to pivot with your back toward him, leg chambered. You then deliver a long back kick, *to the body and from the inside.* Follow up with a full-powered backfist to the face while lowering the leg.

Figure 4.4.9 Figure 4.4.10 Figure 4.4.11 Figure 4.4.12

Figure 4.4.13 Figure 4.4.14 Figure 4.4.15

After conditioning your opponent to expect a crescent kick attack, surprise him with the spin-forward back kick.

Specific Training

- Even if you do not "feel" the kick, practice it as a drill!
- Just as with the spin-back, practice the kick from different ranges, on the heavy bag, tires, and hanging balls!
- Figures 4.4.16 through 4.4.19 show the practice of the kick on a moving partner holding a target pad.

Figure 4.4.16

Figure 4.4.17

Figure 4.4.18

Figure 4.4.19

Perfect form and kicking a few inches into the target.

Self-defense

Although the kick can also be delivered from a circular leg block, we have chosen to present another crescent kick application in Figures 4.4.20 through 4.4.26. Your assailant holds a stick or tries to hit you with one. You determinedly crescent kick (Chapter 6, Section 1) his armed arm, aiming for the joint if possible. Keep your forward and circular momentum to get into chambered position with your back toward him. Back kick while leaning forward, aiming for the groin or ribs. Lower the kicking leg behind his front leg and hit him in the neck with a hammer fist strike (*Tettsui uchi*—karate). Then you get a hold of his throat, chin, or shoulder, and upward hook back kick (Chapter 4, Section 7) him between the legs, before you sweep his leg out from under him (*O soto gari*—judo).

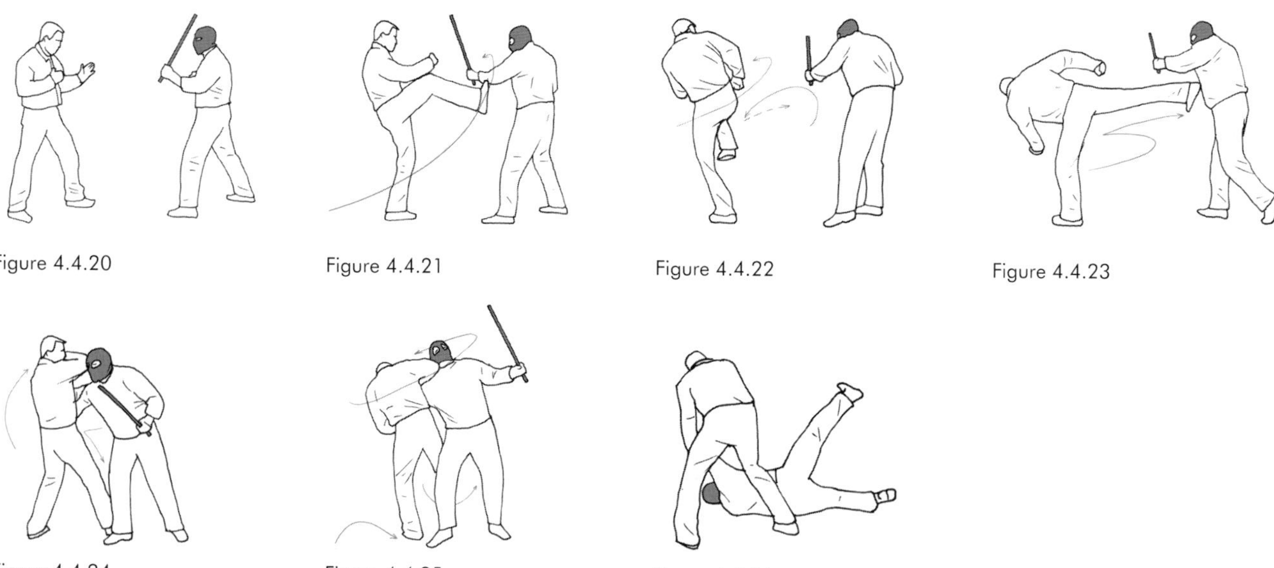

Figure 4.4.20 Figure 4.4.21 Figure 4.4.22 Figure 4.4.23

Figure 4.4.24 Figure 4.4.25 Figure 4.4.26

Take the offensive against a stick-wielding assailant.

4.5 The Low Back Kick

The low back kick is basically any kick you deliver behind you at knee or lower level.

4.6 The Uppercut Back Kick

Ushiro geri keage (karate), *Sepak ayam* (pencak silat)

General

We could also have named this kick the "upward back kick," but "uppercut" hints at its shorter range. This is simply a short kick going upward behind you, from the classic back kick chambering position. It is still a very powerful kick, because of the use of the muscles of the back and the posterior, but limited to targets accessible from down under: the groin or the chin, and the head of a bent-over opponent. Although it seems simple, the kick requires serious training to achieve smoothness and power.

Description

See Figures 4.6.1 through 4.6.3. You chamber just as for a regular back kick, but you do not straighten the leg. Hit back and upward while leaning forward, and hit the target (a heavy bag is illustrated in Figure 4.6.8) from downward with the heel or the sole of the foot, then chamber back.

Figure 4.6.1 Figure 4.6.2 Figure 4.6.3

A circular kick upward, just like an uppercut.

Figure 4.6.4 shows the delivery of the kick toward the groin.

Figure 4.6.4

The groin will always be the preferred target for this kick.

Key Points

- You need to lean forward with the kick in order to achieve power.
- Kick straight in a vertical plane. Make sure you do not open the leg outward as is done for a short back kick (Section 2 of this chapter).

Targets

- As mentioned, the preferred targets are the groin and the chin. Also, but more difficult: the armpit.
- The face and the head present worthwhile targets in general, if your opponent is bent forward.

Typical Application

This is, of course, a great kick to use against the groin of a kicking opponent. Figures 4.6.5 through 4.6.7 illustrate a "timing" *spin-back* version of the kick. When your opponent starts his front leg high roundhouse, spin back away from the developing kick, giving the impression of fleeing. At the end of your spin back, start your uppercut back kick to catch your opponent's groin at the apex of his own kick. Natural follow-ups include circular strikes to the head making use of the spinning momentum, like a backfist strike.

Figure 4.6.5

Figure 4.6.6

Figure 4.6.7

Spin and bend away from the kick and kick up into the exposed groin.

Specific Training

Only heavy bag training will allow you to train for power in this kick (see Figure 4.6.8). Hang the bag with bottom at different heights to train for kicking groin and chin.

Figure 4.6.8
Practice this kick on the heavy bag to develop power.

Self-defense

Figures 4.6.9 through 4.6.13 give an example of the use of the kick to hit the chin. Confront your assailant in opposite guard, and lower his guard with a jab toward his groin. This is one of our favorite openers, as no man alive can keep his hands up when his groin is threatened. In an uninterrupted smooth movement, your low jab becomes a powerful high hook (*Mawashi tsuki*—karate) to the side of his head, given with all your might. Let yourself go with your twisting motion and spin back until you have your back toward your opponent. Uppercut back kick his chin.

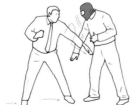

Figure 4.6.9

Figure 4.6.10

Figure 4.6.11

Figure 4.6.12

Figure 4.6.13

A devastating combination: The hook leads into positioning for the kick.

4.7 The Upward Hook Back Kick

Ushiro kake geri (karate)

General

This kick is very similar to the previous uppercut back kick, but derives its power from a whipping movement at the end of the kick. The kick is much less powerful than the uppercut kick and is almost exclusively for groin attack. Its uniqueness and importance comes from the hooking movement at the end of the kick: the kick overtakes the groin from under and then comes back up and forward, hooking into the groin. This is a typical self-defense kick against an assailant close behind you, and is practiced a lot in the classical karate styles (See Figure 4.7.1).

Figure 4.7.1
Classical "hooking" back kick into the groin against a rear bear hug attack.

Description

See Figures 4.7.2 through 4.7.4. From the regular back kick chambering position, kick back and upward, in such a way that you catch your target with the heel *from behind*. You then hook up with the heel in a circular forward movement, back toward the *high* chambering position.

Figure 4.7.2 Figure 4.7.3 Figure 4.7.4
Make sure your kick travels behind the target, then back forward.

Figures 4.7.5 through 4.7.8 show the classic application of the kick against a rear bear hug attack.

Figure 4.7.5 Figure 4.7.6 Figure 4.7.7 Figure 4.7.8
These photographs depict the classic use of the kick. Make sure you start the kick as soon as caught, to avoid letting your assailant close his legs.

Key Points

- This a smooth, uninterrupted circular movement—not a kick, then a hook.
- Hook *up* and forward, up *into* the target.

Targets

- The groin, from the front or the back.
- Eventually the head of a bent-over opponent.

Typical Application

See Figures 4.7.9 through 4.7.12 for an application the other way around. Evade an opponent in opposite guard by cross-stepping forward and on his outside while backfisting him in the face. Immediately pivot to hit him on the other side of his head with a *spinning* backfist using your other hand. Position your back to him and to his back, and upward hook back kick him between the legs.

Figure 4.7.9 Figure 4.7.10 Figure 4.7.11 Figure 4.7.12
This is a fantastic offensive combination, and a good use of the kick when you are behind the opponent.

Specific Training

- Practice on the heavy bag, but not for power.
- Practice the "hooking" movement forward on a hanging tennis ball (see Figures 4.7.13 and 4.7.14).

Figure 4.7.13 Figure 4.7.14
Drill for speed, accuracy, and the perfection of the "hooking" movement.

Self-defense

Although it is not the preferred target, we have chosen to illustrate the use of the kick with the face as the target. Step forward toward a punching assailant while blocking or controlling his punch from the inside (*Soto uke*—karate). See Figure 4.7.16. Keep your aggressive forward momentum, while turning your inside block into a downward knife-hand or forearm attack to the side of his neck (Figure 4.7.17). This is a "heavy" strike, turning into pushing his head down and around. Encourage him to bend forward by kneeing his groin with your front leg (Figure 4.7.18). As soon as he bends forward, use the same leg to back hook kick him in the face, while you continue pressing down on his head with your hand (Figure 4.7.20).

Figure 4.7.15 Figure 4.7.16 Figure 4.7.17 Figure 4.7.18 Figure 4.7.19 Figure 4.7.20
These images illustrate a very effective and naturally-flowing combination.

4.8 The Spin-forward Hook Back Kick

General

This kick is essentially the same as the previous one, but executed with the front leg, after a small step or hop forward. We've decided to present it separately, because it is the preferred offensive version of the kick, and slightly different because of its dynamic nature. This is a very effective kick, especially at close range and in self-defense applications, as the kick is fast and difficult to see coming. Again, its nature limits the possible targets to the groin, and eventually the head if your opponent bends down.

Description

See Figures 4.8.1 through 4.8.4.
You step forward by crossing your rear foot *behind* your front while starting to pivot. Keep turning the body while lifting the leg directly toward the target, without chambering in front. As with the regular upward hook back kick, you connect up and behind the target, in order to hook up and back forward.

Figure 4.8.1

Figure 4.8.2

Figure 4.8.3

Figure 4.8.4

This is a very fast kick: hop forward while pivoting.

Figures 4.8.5 through 4.8.8 show a classic application of the kick in close combat, following an outside block of a jab. The blocking hand hits the back of the neck of the attacker and pushes it forward to meet the raising heel of the front leg.

Figure 4.8.5

Figure 4.8.6

Figure 4.8.7

Figure 4.8.8

Not only the groin, but also the head can be a worthy target for this fast kick.

Key Points

- The difference with the previous kick is the step forward: practice just like you would for a front leg side kick (Chapter 2, Section 3), and just keep pivoting while kicking.
- Do not chamber: lift the heel directly just behind the target. Make use of the extra momentum of the forward hop!

Targets

- Groin.
- Head, if opponent bends down.

Typical Application

Figures 4.8.9 through 4.8.12 show a typical "trap" tactic against an opponent you know likes to counterattack with a reverse punch and kick. You goad him into his "timing" or counterattack move, by explosively leaning forward with a feint punch. Your feint must be committed, realistic and as long as possible. Evade his reverse punch by leaning back on the rear leg, and then retreating half a step with the front leg while pivoting and showing him your back. You look like you are fleeing—no reason for him not to keep his momentum and kick you. But you hop back forward again and upward hook back kick him in the groin while he still is developing a kick for a retreating opponent.

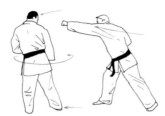

Figure 4.8.9 Figure 4.8.10 Figure 4.8.11 Figure 4.8.12
Draw your opponent into a committed kick and then stop-kick him.

Specific Training

Practice as you would for the regular upward hook back kick: on the heavy bag for distance and on a hanging ball for perfecting the "hooking" effect. But this time practice faster and faster from a marked distance on the floor, with the forward step/hop.

Self-defense

This is a great move against a punching assailant getting too close for full range kicking. Figures 4.8.13 through 4.8.16 show how to aggressively block a punch on the inside while keeping a closed guard up. Step in with no hesitation while starting to spin back, and use your blocking hand to catch him roughly behind the neck. This will distract/immobilize him long enough for your upward hook back kick to connect.

Figure 4.8.13 Figure 4.8.14 Figure 4.8.15 Figure 4.8.16
Get inside your assailant's guard, keep his attention up and hook kick his groin.

4.9 The Downward Back Kick

Escorpião, coice de mula (capoeira)

General

This is a strange kick, but we like it very much, as it is sneaky and deceptive. It is basically a "hook" back kick, but delivered when you are upside down, with one hand on the floor. And it is not delivered straight, but from the outside inwards. The kick looks simple enough, but requires serious drilling before it is powerful and easily executed. You have to practice a lot to get the "feel" of it, and then work on power. This is one of those kicks for close combat—you kick an opponent who you are basically already touching from very close.

Description

See Figures 4.9.1 through 4.9.3. From your fighting stance, lean forward and place the hand on the floor, one to two feet in front of your lead foot. As soon as the hand gets on the floor, switch your weight onto the front leg and hand and lift the rear leg in a straight arc above you and inwards, hitting your imaginary opponent from the front.

Figure 4.9.1 Figure 4.9.2 Figure 4.9.3
Bend forward and kick overhead. It's a very surprising kick when well-timed.

The kick will be easier to understand when shown being delivered to a partner. See Figures 4.9.4 through 4.9.10.

Figure 4.9.4

Figure 4.9.5

Figure 4.9.6

These photos show the delivery of the kick when overtaking a standing opponent from his outside.

Figure 4.9.7

Figure 4.9.8

These photos show the delivery of the kick from a different angle.

Figure 4.9.9

Figure 4.9.10

These photos show the delivery of the kick from yet another angle.

Key Points

- The leaning and kicking is executed in one uninterrupted move.
- Make sure you do not overkick and get unbalanced by your momentum. Aim for a few inches into the target (Your opponent's face), not more, and stop the kick there. Just as for any other kick, if your opponent evades or backs away, do not pursue him with the kick itself, as this puts you totally off-balance.

Targets

When mastered, this kick is very powerful, but the realistic targets are limited by the nature of the move itself: the face, the clavicle, and the higher sternum.

Typical Application

See Figures 4.9.11 through 4.9.13. The most typical application would be on a front kicking opponent, carried away forward by his momentum. This is a common and easy-to-perform outside downward block (*Gedan barai*—karate), preferably with a slight outward evasion. It is even better if you can get a hold of his kicking ankle and pull it forward to accentuate his loss of balance. As soon as you have performed the block, you lean forward and forcefully execute the downward back kick to his face. This also illustrates that the kick cannot be straight, but travels back into the line of attack. Note also that leaning forward puts you out of range of a follow-up punch.

Figure 4.9.11 Figure 4.9.12 Figure 4.9.13
Use the forward momentum of your kicking opponent to your advantage.

Specific Training

This kick requires a lot of training, on the heavy bag (See Figures 4.9.14 and 4.9.15), and with a partner protecting his head.

- First work on the feel of the kick, slowly, then faster, but without emphasizing power.
- Only when mastered, work on power.
- Then work on precision: mark the bag. (Work with a partner protecting his head with both arms).
- Then work from a little farther away and make sure you kick with power but do not go further than a few inches into the bag.

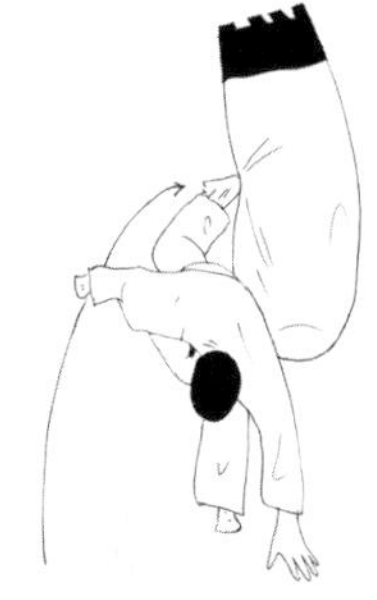

Figure 4.9.14 Figure 4.9.15
Work this kick from very close to the bag.

Self-defense

There are not too many fancy variations of the move, but Figures 4.9.16 through 4.9.19 show an offensive application, although on a just-about-to-attack opponent. One of the great moves emphasized in Wado-ryu karate, are the forward evading punches, where you "time-punch" a punching opponent by going forward and evading while punching. It works wonders, as an attacking opponent generally expects you to retreat and develops his punch accordingly. One of those moves, illustrated here, is a backfist executed while you lunge forward and to your inside. Your lunge takes you *just* out of the line of attack and close to your assailant, still developing his punch. As soon as your backfist connects, use your momentum to lean forward, place the hand on the floor and downward back kick him in the head, from a direction he does not expect.

Figure 4.9.16 Figure 4.9.17 Figure 4.9.18 Figure 4.9.19
As soon as you "feel" the opponent about to attack, get in sideways then disappear down and kick!

4.10 The Back Ghost Lift Kick

General

This is a very deceptive kick, in the spirit of the front "lift kick" (Chapter 1, Section 15), outstanding for use in self-defense. This is exclusively a groin kick, as it totally lacks power. You simply lift your front foot directly up into your opponent's groin, while you are pivoting back and away on your rear foot. It looks like you are fleeing, when in fact you are sending up an undetectable kick. It is, of course, very effective, as it unexpectedly hits the groin. Although the kick seems simple and easy to perform, it requires quite a lot of training, as the joint movements involved are not natural.

Description

See Figures 4.10.1 through 4.10.5. From a relatively high and nimble fighting stance, start spinning back and away by pivoting on your rear foot. *Simultaneously*, lift your front leg directly into your opponent's groin, *with no chambering or telegraphing* of the move, while you lean with your upper body. Connect with the side of the foot or the plant of the foot, depending on how much you have pivoted at impact.

Figure 4.10.1

Figure 4.10.2

The side view of the kick. Don't telegraph!

Figure 4.10.3

Figure 4.10.4

Figure 4.10.5

The front view of the kick. Make sure you kick without any tell-tale motions.

Key Points

- This is one uninterrupted move, with no preparations.
- The front foot goes straight to the target.
- The success of this kick is wholly based on its surprise effect: make sure you do not telegraph your intentions!

Targets

The groin—only.

Typical Application

See Figures 4.10.6 through 4.10.8 for an offensive variation of the move. You attack with a typical medium height front kick/high punch combination, and make sure you land your kicking foot inside his legs. As you land and he prepares to counterattack, you simply lift your front leg while turning away.

Figure 4.10.6

Figure 4.10.7

Figure 4.10.8

A sneaky combination: the high punch draws his attention away from the real attack.

Specific Training

- This kick requires training, despite its simple appearance. It is best to practice on a heavy bag hanging with its bottom at groin level (See Figure 4.10.9). The heavy bag practice is not for power, but just to have a target. Practice with both legs, making sure you kick smoothly, with no preparatory movements. Try to vary the distance from where you kick and check which part of the foot connects from the different ranges.
- Practice in front of a mirror.

Figure 4.10.9
Drill on the heavy bag, but always with relaxed movements for speed and distance, never for power.

Self-defense

As mentioned, this is a great kick for self-defense. Figures 4.10.10 through 4.10.12 show a typical use on an incoming assailant, in this case a stick-wielding one. Spin back as if retreating, and ghost lift kick him while he keeps coming toward you. As soon as you connect, lower the leg while completing your spin, and elbow him in the head.

Figure 4.10.10 Figure 4.10.11 Figure 4.10.12
A great move against any rushing attack.

4.11 The Drop Back Kick

Chapa de costas (capoeira), Mule kick (common name)

General

We have mentioned, for this kick, its capoeira name, as it is very much in use in this art. This is, of course, natural, as capoeira specializes in fighting while hovering close to the ground. This kick is also very typical of the ground fighting styles of kung fu and the deception-based styles like the Monkey and Drunken styles. This kick is very close to the drop side kick (Chapter 2, Section 12), but giving more back, and therefore, more powerful, but also more "blind." You deliver this kick directly to the back, or after turning. You can deliver the kick going forward or backward. You can execute the kick while using either your knee (low) or your foot (high) as support.

Description

See Figures 4.11.1 through 4.11.4. This is the classical way to practice the kick, directly to your rear, and resting on your knee. Look back to see your opponent to your rear, step back with your front foot toward him while leaning and kneeling on your previously front knee. Place your hands on the floor, and rest on the knee and hands while lifting the front leg into chambered position. Kick while pushing your hips into the kick.

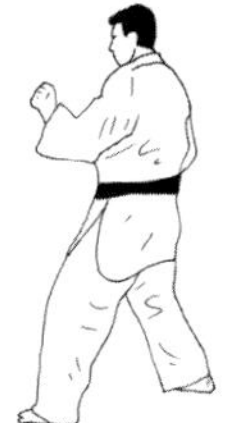

Figure 4.11.1 Figure 4.11.2 Figure 4.11.3 Figure 4.11.4
Drop and kick back.

Figures 4.11.5 through 4.11.7 show an application of the classic kick against a punching aggressor from behind.

Figure 4.11.5 Figure 4.11.6 Figure 4.11.7
Drop below the punch and kick.

Key Points

- You have to thrust your hips into the kick, by pushing onto your supporting tripod: hands and knee, or hands and foot.
- Always chamber back, so as not to get your leg caught.

Targets

This is a penetrating kick: typical targets include the knee, groin and lower abdomen.

Typical Application

Figures 4.11.8 through 4.11.11 show a more capoeira-like version of the kick. Just spin back, put your hands on the floor, and kick back. This is a great way to handle an aggressive puncher, coming at you overpoweringly with a salvo of high punches. You crouch, spin back, and kick to the groin or lower belly.

Figure 4.11.8 Figure 4.11.9 Figure 4.11.10 Figure 4.11.11
This is a great move against a rushing opponent.

Specific Training

The kick is not difficult to perform, but training is necessary to correctly learn to gauge distance. Practice kicking the heavy bag, with both legs:

- Kick directly back, knee on the floor, after stepping back.
- Kick directly back, knee on the floor, after stepping forward.
- Kick directly back, on foot and hands, after stepping back.
- Kick directly back, on foot and hands, after stepping forward.
- Spin back, knee on ground, kick.
- Spin forward, knee on ground, kick.
- Spin back, hands on floor, kick.
- Spin forward, hands on floor, kick.

Self-defense

Figures 4.11.12 through 4.11.15 show a very interesting application of this kick. It is a special use, obviously requiring some specific training, but a great illustration of how cunning is important in fighting. Your assailant succeeds in hitting you with a tilted heel low front kick to the front knee. Give in to the kick, before it becomes a stomp, turn and bend the knee, while going down. You find yourself with an immobilized knee on the floor, but a surprised opponent who has not yet taken advantage of his scoring kick. You lean and place your hands on the floor, for a powerful penetrating back kick to his groin area.

Figure 4.11.12 Figure 4.11.13 Figure 4.11.14 Figure 4.11.15
When hit, do not resist but go in the direction of the attack. In this case, turn it around to your advantage.

4.12 The Drop Hooking Back Kick

General

This kick is presented separately, because, although it is very similar to the drop back kick, the trajectory is different to allow for the hooking movement. Similar to the difference seen between the regular back kick (Section 1 of this chapter) and the upward hook back kick (Section 7 of this chapter), the way the kick is delivered is much less powerful: you do not push the hips into the kick. You try to quickly get *behind* your opponent's groin and then hook up and *forward.*
The preparatory movements to get into kicking position are the same as for the previous drop back kick: you can kick with your knee on the floor, or just bent while staying on the foot. Kick directly behind you, or spin back, or spin forward.

Description

See Figures 4.12.1 through 4.12.4. You spin back (on your back leg), bend, and put your hands on the floor with your back toward your opponent. Lift your previously front leg directly behind the target, then hook up and forward.

Figure 4.12.1

Figure 4.12. 2

Figure 4.12. 3

Figure 4.12.4

This kick represents a combination of both the drop back kick and the hook back kick.

Key Points

- No need to power the kick until you pull up and back forward: the first part of the kick must be fast, nimble and sneaky.
- Put your weight forward on your hands when you hook back forward.

Targets

The groin, exclusively, from the front or the back.

Typical Application

Figures 4.12.5 through 4.12.8 show you the technique delivered from behind your opponent: this is an extremely painful and unexpected move. The technique is also an example of a "trap" tactic in which you try to provoke your opponent into an attack you will turn to your advantage. Your opponent uses easily penetrating front kicks. You will stand in opposite guard with your side purposely open and uncovered. As he front kicks you as expected, you evade the kick by going *forward* and to his outside, while controlling the kick and, if possible, "pulling" it forward to put your opponent off-balance. Complete your step forward behind him, while bending forward to avoid being hit by a natural follow-up punch. You place your hands on the floor and use your front leg to back kick him between the legs and hook him in the groin from his front.

Figure 4.12.5

Figure 4.12.6

Figure 4.12.7

Figure 4.12.8

An extremely effective technique: hook his groin from behind.

Specific Training

The kick is different from the regular drop back kick and needs to be practiced from all possible footwork positions. You can use the heavy bag, but not for power, just for targeting. Much better is kicking a hanging ball to check the hooking movement.

Self-defense

Figures 4.12.9 through 4.12.12 describe an example of a direct kick, with no footwork, and with the knee on the floor. This is not a classic move, as only one hand is on the floor, with some additional support from the head and/or the shoulder. Your assailant has caught you in a bent arm arm-lock behind the back, while trying to control your shoulder to prevent you from pivoting. Bend forward to alleviate the pain and go down on your free hand and opposite knee. Try to use your shoulder and head for additional support. As it would be difficult to achieve power from this position, you hook back kick in the groin.

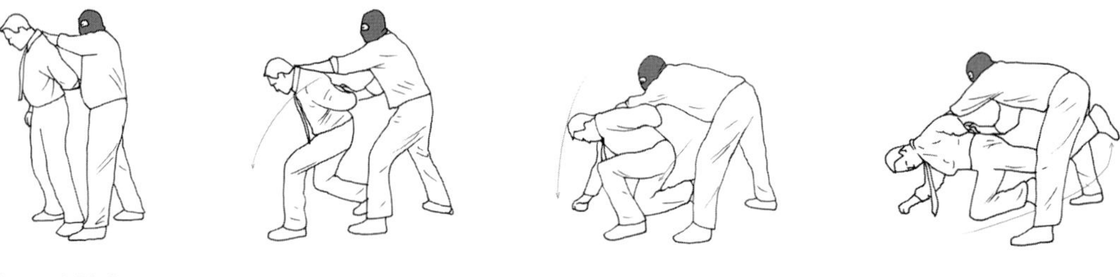

Figure 4.12.9 Figure 4.12.10 Figure 4.12.11 Figure 4.12.12
The kick as a counter to a classic behind-the-back armlock: Do not resist, go with the attack.

4.13 The Drop Overhead Back Kick

Rabo de arraia (capoeira angola)

General

This quite an acrobatic kick, typical of the Angola style of capoeira, but easier to perform than it looks. It takes a lot of practice to pack power into the kick, but its key advantage is surprise. One could argue against the unnecessary flourish and the danger of the kicking position, but, again, do so only after having faced an experienced *capoeirista* and their sneaky and totally unexpected moves.

Description

See Figures 4.13.1 through 4.13.4. You step forward and *suddenly* bend forward to place both your hands on the floor in front of you. Put your weight on the hands and lift the legs in a handstand. Kick into your opponent's face with one foot, while counterbalancing with the other leg. You then fall back to the starting position. You can also double kick, switching legs before falling back. You can even kick through and fall on your opponent!

Figure 4.13.1 Figure 4.13.2 Figure 4.13.3 Figure 4.13.4
Acrobatic, but always unexpected!

Figures 4.13.5 through 4.13.9 show the delivery of the kick in context, as a double kick, against a punching assailant.

Figure 4.13.5

Figure 4.13.6

Figure 4.13.7

Figure 4.13.8

Figure 4.13.9

Two kicks in a row against a punch. Your timing must be perfect.

Key Points

- There is no kick without the surprise effect: you drop down suddenly from a high position.
- Do not follow your opponent if he retreats: you have to perform the kick to its set end position, and no further.
- The power of the kick does not come from your body movement, but from the muscles of the leg and posterior: don't try to put your body into the kick.

Targets

This is not a powerful kick: the head is the only valid target.

Typical Application

Figures 4.13.10 through 4.13.13 show the kick's use against a spin-back outside crescent kick (Chapter 6, Section 8). As your opponent spins back to kick, step forward and sit down on your heels while keeping up your guard. As soon as you have evaded the kick, place your hands on the floor and lift up, kicking him in the face while he's lowering his leg.

Figure 4.13.10

Figure 4.13.11

Figure 4.13.12

Figure 4.13.13

This kick will always follow an exaggerated ducking move, and therefore, is ideal against spin-back kicks

Specific Training

- Train in front of a wall (See Figures 4.13.14 and 4.13.15), placing your foot first, then kicking lightly, the double kicking. Use the wall to stay in the handstand a few more seconds to build confidence.
- Then start working on the heavy bag for full-power kicking.
- When the kick is mastered, start kicking the bag from the fighting stance at different ranges.

Figure 4.13.14
Use the wall to build confidence.

Figure 4.13.15

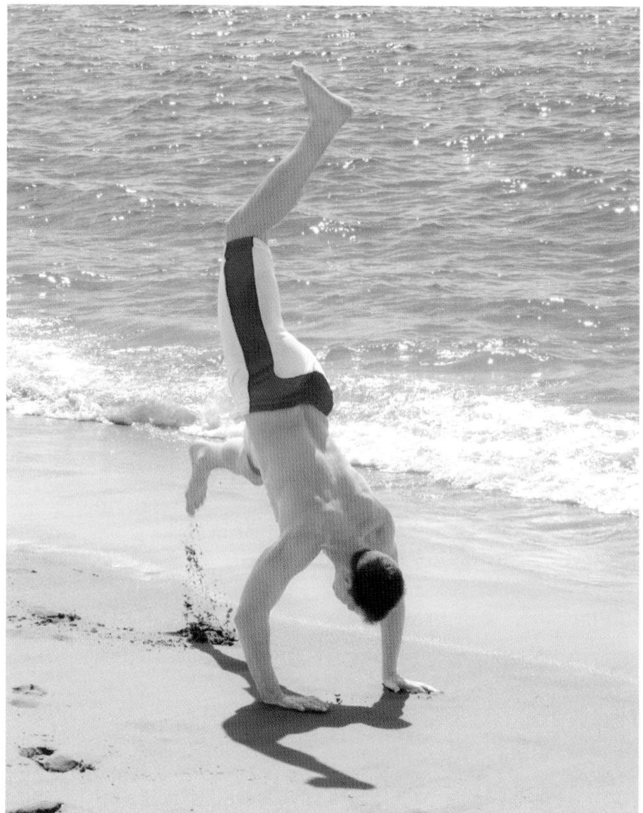

Figure 4.13.16
Practicing on sand will build confidence by removing the fear of a hard fall.

Self-defense

See Figures 4.13.17 through 4.13.20. You are attacked by a high-punching assailant. Instead of retreating, step forward and down on one knee and stop-reverse punch him in the groin. Immediately place your hands on the floor and back kick him in his unprotected face, as his hands went down to his groin.

Figure 4.13.17

Figure 4.13.18

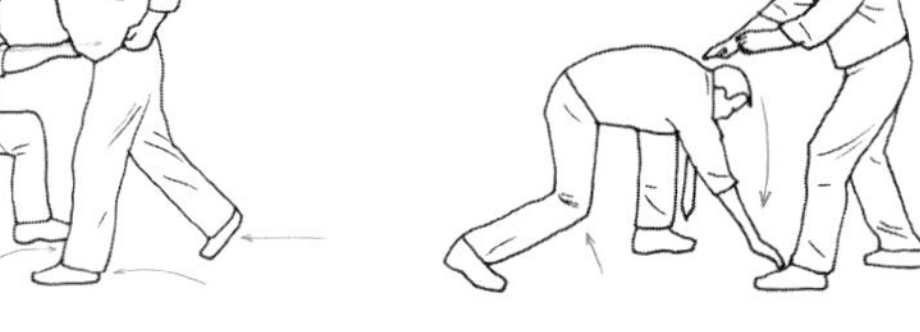

Figure 4.13.19

Figure 4.13.20

This time you duck and punch, then use your low position to deliver the kick.

4.14 The Double Drop Back Kick

Nghich ma cuoc (viet vo dao), Double mule kick (common name)

General

The double drop back kick is, in its preparatory stages, very much like the regular drop kick. You can spin back or spin forward to kick an opponent in front of you, or just directly kick back into a rear assailant. Your body weight is on your hands only, as you kick with both legs, but you use the power of the whole uncoiling body, which makes it a damaging kick. It is a kick of choice if you lose your balance for some reason. It is a very typical kick of the ground fighting styles of kung fu.

Description

See Figures 4.14.1 through 4.14.5. Here we describe the kick after a cross step forward, the rear leg coming *behind* the front leg. You then spin while crouching, and place your hands on the floor in front of you. In one move, switch your weight onto your hands and throw both legs backward into the target, while pushing with your hips and using your whole body. After impact you bend back the legs and land on the balls of your feet.

Figure 4.14.1

Figure 4.14.2

Figure 4.14.3

Figure 4.14.4

Figure 4.14.5

This kick is sometimes aptly named the double mule kick.

Figures 4.14.6 through 4.14.8 show the use of the kick against an aggressively punching opponent.

Figure 4.14.6

Figure 4.14. 7

Figure 4.14.8

The power of the kick comes out clearly in these images.

Key Points

- The kick is one uninterrupted move from the moment you start bending. You have to use the whole momentum of the body, and there is some "whipping" action between the bending and kicking.
- You must chamber back after impact, so as not to get your legs caught: bend the legs back after hitting a few inches into the target.

Targets

- Typical targets include the knees, groin, lower abdomen, solar plexus, and ribs.
- If your opponent is bent forward: chin, throat and face.

Typical Application

Figures 4.14.9 through 4.14.13 show a deliberate use of the technique from a regular standing position. Your opponent lunges toward you with a committed high punch, for example as you have left yourself open on purpose. Evade the punch by stepping forward and to his outside, while bending below the plane of the punch. You add another step forward just behind his back while placing your hands on the floor. Your opponent pivots to follow you, and as you crouch and have your back toward him, he will be under the impression that you are fleeing. You double drop back kick him in the lower belly as he prepares further punches.

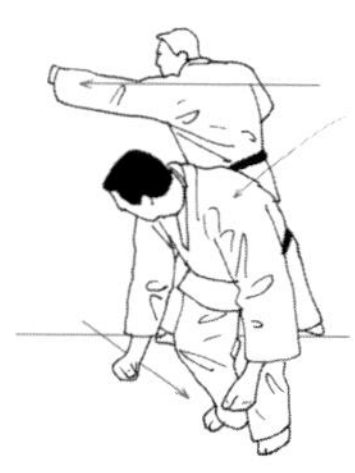

Figure 4.14.9 Figure 4.14.10 Figure 4.14.11 Figure 4.14.12 Figure 4.14.13
A typical technique from the Monkey and Drunken styles of kung fu.

Specific Training

Very much like for the other drop kicks, you have to work the footwork in front of the heavy bag. In this case, you also have to work on the kick's power on the bag. If this is a kick you "feel" and are likely to use, work it as a stop-kick, with a partner letting the heavy bag swing toward you. Perform the kick in such a way that you impact the bag with full power as it becomes vertical in its swing.

Self-defense

Figures 4.14.14 through 4.14.17 show you the use of this kick in a situation you have not created. This is, in our opinion, where the importance of this kick lies. You have been pushed forcefully backward and have somewhat lost your balance. Your opponent is coming at you to make use of this situation to punch or kick you. If you try to fight your rearward momentum to recover your balance forward, you are in danger of being hit. Therefore, just as in judo, don't fight your momentum but go in its direction, while spinning back to recover your balance away from your opponent. In the same movement, basically started by your assailant and using its power, place your hands on the floor, and then double back kick him as he is confidently closing on you.

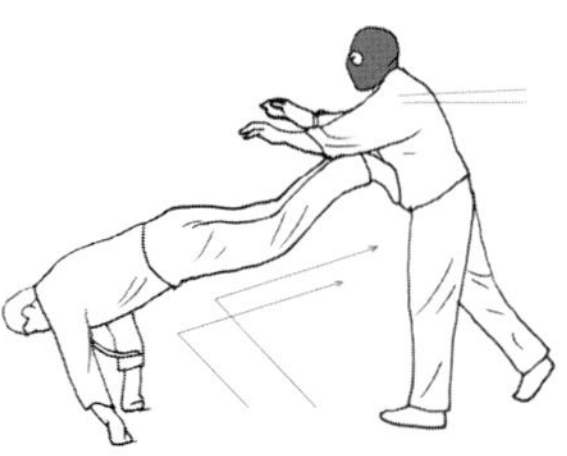

Figure 4.14.14 Figure 4.14.15 Figure 4.14.16 Figure 4.14.17
A great technique against a "pusher."

4.15 The One-legged Drop Back Kick

General

This is an important kick to practice for a kicker. This is a kick you should automatically perform if your kicking leg gets caught by your opponent. To be effective, you must perform this maneuver immediately and nearly without thinking if your foot gets caught during a kick. Automatic means, of course, a lot of training and drilling, but it is important, as standing on one leg with your other leg caught is a very dangerous and vulnerable position. You have to react before your opponent's follow-up!

Description

See Figures 4.15.1 through 4.15.6. As soon as your leg gets caught, pivot outwards on your standing leg while dropping to the floor and catching yourself on your hands. Do not try to punch your way out of this—there is no way you can be effective in the hands of a serious adversary. As soon as your hands touch the floor, and even if possible a few milliseconds before, you launch a powerful back kick with your formerly standing leg. Put everything you have into this kick—you have nothing to lose. This is basically a double drop back kick (Section 14 of this chapter) but with one leg only—the other leg is already there! Put your hips and your whole body into the kick. If he does not release your leg, keep kicking, aiming for another target; and keep kicking until he releases you.

Figure 4.15.1

Figure 4.15.2

Figure 4.15.3

This maneuver is practically the only thing you can do if your kicking leg gets caught.

Figure 4.15.4

Figure 4.15.5

Figure 4.15.6

These photos show the delivery of the kick following the catch of a front kicking leg.

Key Points

- This will only work if it is an explosive movement—the movement is uninterrupted and you do not lower yourself toward the floor, you fall as fast as possible and are already kicking.
- Start kicking as early as possible in the move and do not stop kicking until you are released. You are vulnerable to a kick, in the groin for example, although it is, ironically, your caught leg that somewhat protects you.

Targets

Typical targets include the knees, groin, lower abdomen, solar plexus, throat, and chin.

Typical Application

There is only one application to this kick—your kicking leg gets caught. This is why we will not present a self-defense application, as it is self-evident. There is one interesting variation, though, worth illustrating. This is a very sophisticated move and, frankly, unnecessary, but derived from the need in light-contact karate to "show" the referee that you have scored. This need to emphasize the points you have scored has caused tournament fighters to develop unhealthy habits, detrimental to realistic fighting and traditional arts. We shall not dwell on this, but one example of those nasty habits is staying for a few seconds with your foot on your opponent's face after having scored a high kick point. Doing so is unwise in an actual fight, although it is definitely possible if you have really caught your opponent and stunned him. The following move is therefore unnecessarily theatrical, although it can be effective. See Figures 4.15.7 through 4.15.13. You have caught your opponent in the side of the head with a high roundhouse. Rest your foot on his shoulder and pivot outwards on your standing leg, just as if your kick had been caught. The moment your hands touch the floor, your foot is already leaving his shoulder while the other leg is already back kicking him.

Figure 4.15.7 Figure 4.15.8 Figure 4.15.9
A high roundhouse caught on your opponent's shoulder. Act fast!

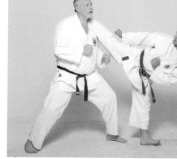

Figure 4.15.10 Figure 4.15.11 Figure 4.15.12

Specific Training

- There is no substitute to training with a partner on this one! Work on both sides, and get several kick types caught (front, side, roundhouse, and the like).
- Train for power on the heavy bag, with your "caught" leg resting on a standing bag or a stool (See Figures 4.15.14 and 4.15.15).

Figure 4.15.13
You should strive to release the "roundhouse-leg" while kicking, as illustrated here.

Figure 4.15.14
Drill until automatic!

Figure 4.15.15

More Advanced Back Kicks

What follows is a brief review of some more advanced kicks. They are not presented in detail here, as they are beyond the scope of this book.

The Flying Back Kick

The name is self-explanatory. Basically, it is a flying side kick with more "back" toward the opponent.

The Spin-back Flying Back Kick

The name gives it all again: a great kick as it is easier to execute than the spin-back flying side kick (less spin back needed).

Comparative Table

Table 1 — Comparative table of the chambering and trajectory of main back kicks.

CHAPTER FIVE

Hook Kicks

Hook kicks are another relatively modern development, as they are virtually absent from all ancient classical Chinese and Japanese styles. They are prominent in recent and eclectic styles like capoeira and sport taekwondo. Hook kicks are based on speed and they are very effective when properly executed. They are quite sneaky as they generally present themselves counter-intuitively to the recipient and follow difficult-to-track trajectories. They require flexibility, timing, and a lot of training, but hard work in mastering them pays off in the end.

This chapter presents the different ways to execute them in applications that will allow you to surprise an opponent.

5.1 The Straight Leg Hook Kick

Mawashi uchi / Ura mawashi geri (karate), *Huryeo / Kumchi dolye cha gi* (taekwondo), *Revers* (savate-boxe francaise), Sweep kick (jeet kune do), *Gancho* (capoeira)

General

The hook kick is the bread-and-butter kick of the kicking artist. It is not a very powerful kick, but it is very fast, it can be delivered from many starting positions, and it comes at an angle that makes it difficult to be seen. And one should remember that knockouts come more from the inability of the body to prepare itself for the concussion (i.e. seeing the hit coming and tensing the muscles), than from the power of the attack itself. Many knockouts, even in light-contact karate, come from an undetected hook kick to the head. Those elements also make it a great "timing" stop kick, definitely a favorite. We shall describe here the classical rear leg hook kick, a difficult kick to perform as such, although great when mastered, but the best way to train for hook kicks, especially at the beginning. It is, again, one of those important drills that will slowly teach your body how to kick from any position, even if you never use the kick itself. The kick described here is the straight leg version: As will be explained later (in Section 2 of this chapter), all hook kicks can be delivered full-range with a straight leg, straight leg with a hooking movement at the end (*Kake*—karate) just after impact, or with a bent leg during the development of the kick toward the straight leg at impact.

Description

From a fighting stance, lift the rear knee forward and up (Figure 5.1.2), and then pivot on the standing foot to present your side to the opponent, just like for a full rear leg side kick (Chapter 2, Section 1). While leaning, develop the leg at a slight oblique angle to your inside, a little bit as if side kicking an evading opponent (Figure 5.1.4). As the leg is nearly straight, use your hips to start bringing the leg back to the middle line first, and then apply more hip motion to enable you to penetrate the target a few inches. The trajectory of the foot is clearer from the overhead view (Figure 5.1.7), or from the front view (Figures 5.1.8 through 5.1.11). As soon as you have hit the target and penetrated it, bend your leg while pivoting back to the chambered position. Hit the target with the back of the heel (foot flexed) or the whole of the plant of the foot (foot extended). In Japanese, the heel is called *kakato, kibisu* or *ensho*. The plant of the foot is called *teisoku*. See Figure 5.1.14).

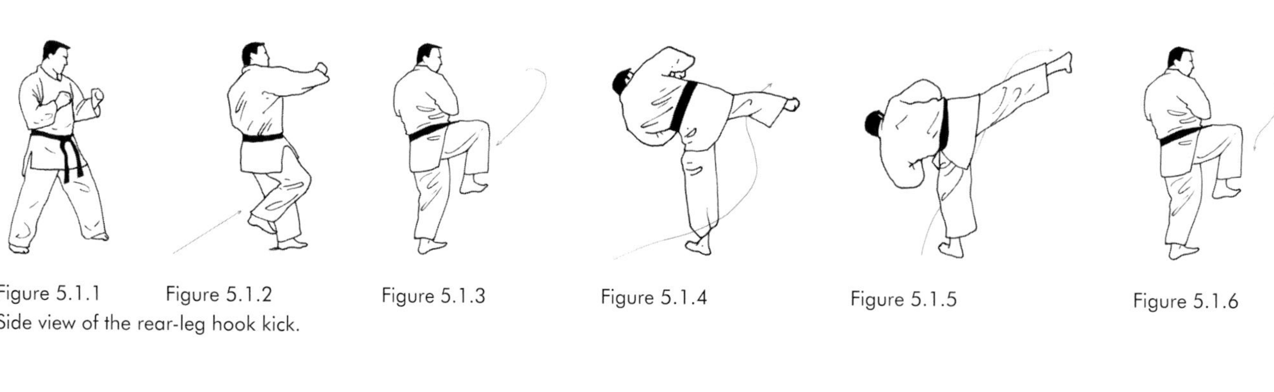

Figure 5.1.1 Figure 5.1.2 Figure 5.1.3 Figure 5.1.4 Figure 5.1.5 Figure 5.1.6
Side view of the rear-leg hook kick.

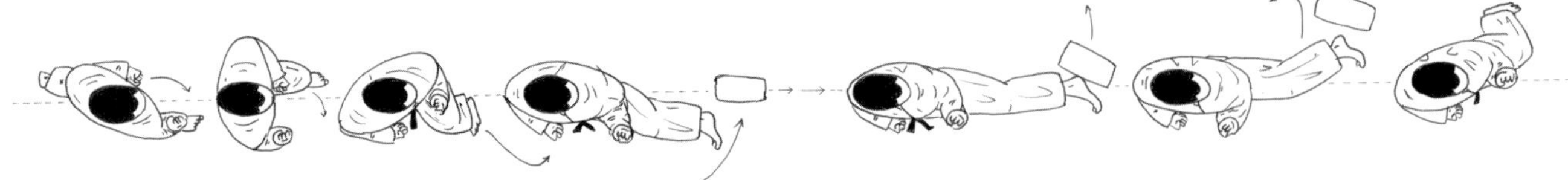

Figure 5.1.7
Overhead view of the rear-leg hook kick.

Figure 5.1.8 Figure 5.1.9 Figure 5.1.10 Figure 5.1.11 Figure 5.1.12 Figure 5.1.13
Front view of the rear-leg hook kick.

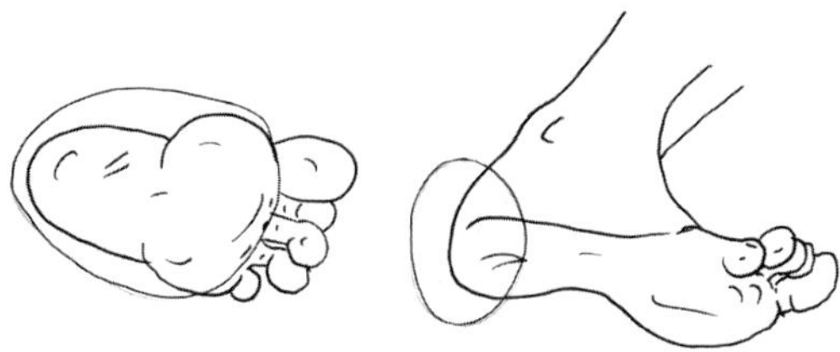

Figure 5.1.14
The parts of the foot that connect with the target.

Figures 5.1.15 to 5.1.17 show the kick delivered with the plant of the foot.

Figure 5.1.15
The other side view of the rear-leg hook kick.

Figure 5.1.16

Figure 5.1.17

Figures 5.1.18 to 5.1.24 show a natural follow-up for the kick. After impact, lower the leg behind his and twist him down while blocking his legs and hips.

Figure 5.1.18

Figure 5.1.19

Figure 5.1.20

Figure 5.1.21

Figure 5.1.22

Note how the hook kick starts at the last possible moment.

Figure 5.1.23

Figure 5.1.24

Key Points

- This is one smooth uninterrupted movement.
- Do not bob up: your head should stay at same level during the whole development of the kick.
- Develop the kick at belt level, not higher, in order to keep it undetected for as long as possible. Only when you start the move back toward the centerline, do you start lifting the leg toward the target.
- Kick a few inches through the target.
- At impact your body and leg are in alignment and the toes of your standing foot point 180 degrees from your opponent.

Targets

The rear leg version of the hook kick described here is a rather powerful kick and can be used against the knee, the kidneys, the groin, the lower ribs and the head.

Typical Application

Figures 5.1.23 to 5.1.26 show a simple but very effective combination for a rear leg classical hook kick: high outside / low outside / high inside. High lunge jab to the outside of his head, followed by a low reverse punch on his outside, aimed just below the elbow that just blocked the jab. (Classical *Kizami* / *Gyacku tsuki*—karate). Your opponent is "conditioned" to attacks to his outside, with his lead hand still controlling your low reverse punch. But your reverse punch has also been pulling your rear leg forward for a hook kick, which will be difficult for him to see coming as it develops below his line of vision and comes up at the last second.

Figure 5.1.25 Figure 5.1.26 Figure 5.1.27 Figure 5.1.28
These images illustrate a simple but very effective combination.

Specific Training

- For speed, a lot of flexibility is needed: splits and flexibility drills for the knees will yield dividends.
- It is important to work on the penetration of this kick. The best way is to have a partner holding target mitts shoulder width apart, while you practice kicking the second one through the first! (See Figures 5.1.29 and 5.1.30).

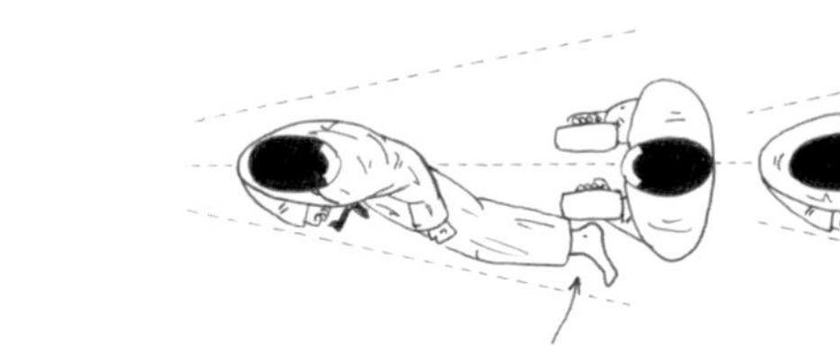

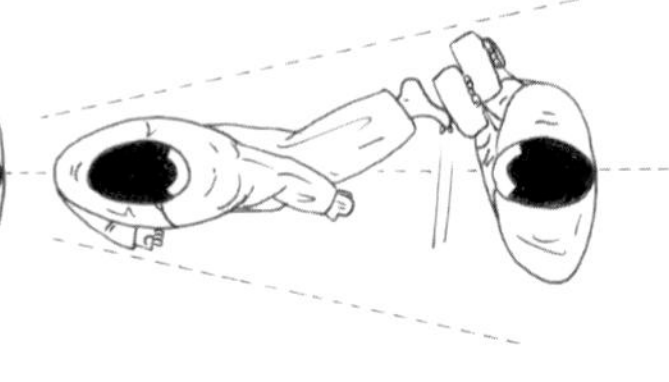

Figure 5.1.29 Figure 5.1.30
Learning to kick through a target.

- Heavy bag kicking is important to develop a feeling for distance, footwork, and impact.
- For speed, agility, and flexibility, kick over a standing bag (or a partner's extended arm). For range and penetration, kick a ball, a basketball for example, placed on the top of the standing bag (or held by a partner). See Figure 5.1.31.
- In fighting stances, hold extended rear hands with a partner and take turns slowly delivering the rear leg hook kick to the head.

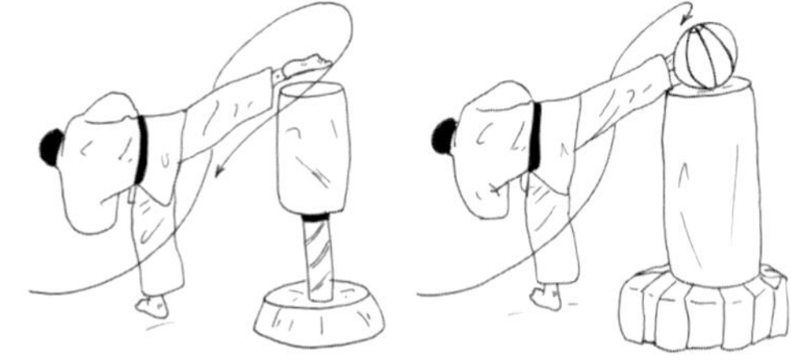

Figure 5.1.31
Drill kicking over for speed and through for power.

Self-defense

The following images illustrate an application very similar to the previous one, as it is again a follow-up to a full-hipped reverse punch (*Gyacku tsuki*—karate). It is a logical follow-up as the hip "pulls" the leg forward naturally, and it allows one to finish off the assailant from his blind side. An assailant gets a hold of your right wrist with his right hand (Figure 5.1.32). You have to act fast before he makes use of this hold to further his aggression. Pull your hand back with your hips and your whole body, while hitting his wrist in a classical downward block (*Gedan barai*—karate). See Figure 5.1.33. As soon as you're released, reverse your momentum and lean forward with a full hip spin into a powerful committed reverse punch (Figure 5.1.35). The hip pivot of the punch "pulls" your rear leg forward into a straight leg hook kick to the head on his blind outside (Figure 5.1.36).

Figure 5.1.32 Figure 5.1.33 Figure 5.1.34 Figure 5.1.35 Figure 5.1.36
A very decisive release from an aggressive wrist grab.

5.2 The Hooked Hook Kick

Ushiro mawashi kake geri (karate), *Nakka tshagy* (taekwondo)

General

All hook kicks in this chapter can be delivered either in their straight leg version, or in a "hooked" version. The hooked hook kick is simply the same kick until impact. It then hooks into the target and pulls it forward, instead of going through it. It is the same principle as the hooked back kick (Chapter 4, Section 7). The combination of the large circular movement and the little hooking forward gives this kick a little extra concussive power, similar to the whipping of the backfist. And as the kick is always using the heel as the weapon, excluding the plant of the foot, it becomes quite effective. The kick itself has a shorter range than the straight leg kick, as it uses the heel of the flexed foot and not the plant of the extended foot, and it also requires to be a little more into the opponent as it needs something to hook into. In its preferred application, the kick is even much shorter, but so effective: Instead of kicking the side of the head, hooking into it or not, you hit the back of your opponent's head with your hooking heel. This is an extraordinarily effective kick at close range, as it is totally unexpected.

Description

The kick illustrated in Figures 5.2.1 to 5.2.6 is the classical rear leg hook kick, this time with a hooking effect at the end. But as already mentioned, all hook kicks can be performed in this way. The kick is performed exactly as the straight leg version, until impact with the heel (Figure 5.2.5) of the flexed foot. You then start bending the leg forcefully while maintaining the overall circular movement into the target. The overhead view in Figure 5.2.7 shows how the range of this kick is shorter.

Figure 5.2.1 Figure 5.2.2 Figure 5.2.3 Figure 5.2.4 Figure 5.2.5 Figure 5.2.6
Side view of the hooked hook kick.

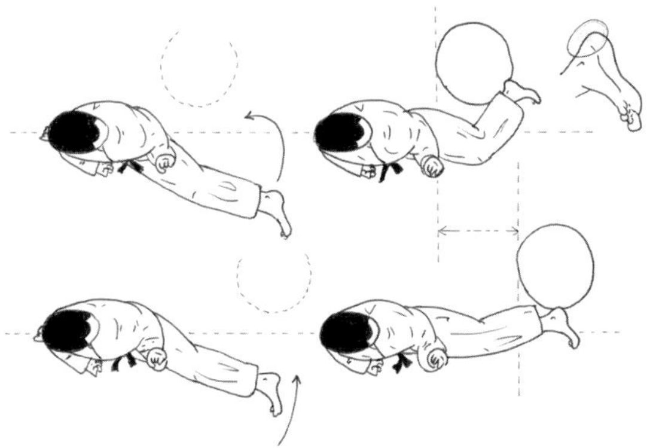

Figure 5.2.7
Overhead view of the shorter hooked hook kick finish, in comparison to the regular hook kick.

Figures 5.2.8 to 5.2.13 show the delivery of this kick, starting from a much closer position than for the straight leg hook kick and hitting the opponent *behind* the head.

Figure 5.2.8
Side view of the hooked hook kick.

Figure 5.2.9

Figure 5.2.10

Figure 5.2.11

Figure 5.2.12

Figure 5.2.13

These photos show the delivery from another angle, and the clear impact of the heel behind the head.

Key Points

- Same as the straight leg version.
- The hooking move is not chambering: You do not pivot back into chambering stance while hooking. The hooking is a short powerful kick performed while your body and leg are aligned.

Targets

The heel is a harder and more accurate weapon than the plant of the foot! The head, kidneys, neck, solar plexus, groin, sides of the thigh and knee are all effective targets.

Typical Application

Figures 5.2.14 to 5.2.17 show an offensive "back of the head" application, to be used against a standing or a "just about to attack" opponent. From your fighting stance, lunge widely and aggressively on his outside while backfisting the side of his head. Your lunge must be totally committed and take you immediately out of the centerline. Your rear leg steps up all the way to your front leg, to allow the same front leg to lift for a front leg hooked hook kick to the back of the head of your "now-turning-toward-you" opponent.

Figure 5.2.14

Figure 5.2.15

Figure 5.2.16

Figure 5.2.17

Fast footwork will position you for a difficult-to-see-coming hooked hook kick.

Specific Training

- Flexibility, just like for the straight leg hook kick.
- The hooking movement must be practiced on the speed ball, the hanging ball, and the heavy bag. Make sure your kick brings the equipment hit forward toward you. (See Figure 5.2.18).

Figure 5.2.18
Drill for speed, precision and the right "hooking" finish.

Self-defense

As already mentioned, this is a great kick for close combat. One of the best, we would add, because of its unexpectedness. In a close encounter, you expect a knee strike, or a stomp, but not a high kick on the back of the head! See Figures 5.2.19 to 5.2.22. In a clinch, you try to uppercut your opponent's chin while pivoting your hips into a side stance. Even if the uppercut is not effective, it is enough if it allows you to break the clinch and get into a leaning back side stance. With no footwork at all, lift your front leg (See Section 3 of this chapter) into a hooked hook kick to the back of his head, while leaning back as much as needed. The more flexible you are, the less you need to lean back, but leaning back is also placing your upper body away from a possible punch at close range.

Figure 5.2.19
A great clinch-breaker.

Figure 5.2.20

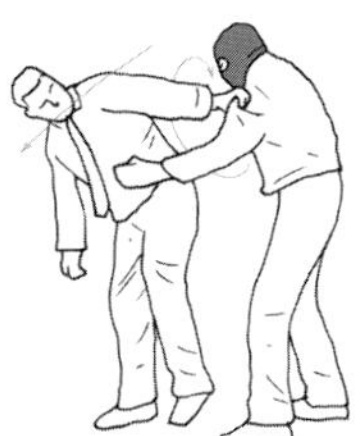

Figure 5.2.21

Figure 5.2.22

5.3 The Front Leg Hook Kick

Furyo cha gi (taekwondo)

General

This is the fast, easier to perform version of the hook kick. But we still recommend lots of practice of this kick in its classical rear leg version (Section 1 of this chapter). The kick can be delivered straight leg or hooked, like all hook kicks. It can be delivered (1) directly, just lifting the front leg, on a standing opponent, or as a "timing" stop kick to an attacking or approaching opponent; (2) after a classical cross step forward; or (3) after a forward hop where the rear foot replaces the rising front foot. The front leg hook kick is a very versatile and fast kick, coming from a generally surprising angle. But it lacks in power, when compared to the rear leg hook or spin back hook kick, and is therefore limited to groin or head attacks. Of course attacks to the legs and to the body are also possible, but preferably as feints, set-ups, harassment or distance-closing moves.

Description

Figures 5.3.1 through 5.3.9 present all 3 possibilities for the front leg hook kick, only differing in footwork. Basically, it is very much like a front leg side kick (Chapter 2, Section 3), slightly oblique in reference to the centerline, and a circular finish of the extended leg.

Figure 5.3.1 Figure 5.3.2 Figure 5.3.3 Figure 5.3.4 Figure 5.3.5 Figure 5.3.6

Figure 5.3.7 Figure 5.3.8 Figure 5.3.9

Side view of front-leg hook kicks: direct kick, cross-step kick and hopping kick, respectively.

Figures 5.3.10 through 5.3.13 shows the trajectory more clearly from a front view.

Figure 5.3.10 Figure 5.3.11 Figure 5.3.12 Figure 5.3.13

Front view of the front-leg hook kick (hopping version).

Figures 5.3.14 through 5.3.17 show the delivery of the kick in its hopping straight-leg version, connecting with the plant of the foot.

Figure 5.3.14

Figure 5.3.15

Figure 5.3.16

Figure 5.3.17

Front-leg hook kick. The hop is very clear.

Key Points

- In the front leg version the hip movement is even more important, and the body/leg alignment is key.
- The leg is mostly extended at belt level, and only lifted at the end of the trajectory, in order to alert the opponent as late as possible.

Targets

- Groin
- Head

Typical Application

The hook kick being this author's favorite kick, two typical applications will be presented here: An offensive one and a defensive one.

Figures 5.3.18 through 5.3.22 present a very effective and surprising combination, both for sport and in a self-defense situation. It is especially effective against those opponents with their guards extended away from their bodies. As your opponent's front hand cries out to be caught (Beware of traps!), try to catch it in a sudden move with your front hand, while executing a full step. Do not step before you try to catch as you'll telegraph your move: Try a sudden snatch and the stepping starts after your hand has launched. If you have not caught the hand, the technique stays the same, as all your opponent's attention will be riveted to the hand-snatching move. Follow in a smooth move with a midsection roundhouse kick. If you have got hold of his hand, you pull it to keep his abdomen open. You recoil the roundhouse and launch a hook kick to the head from his outside, without posing the leg on the floor. If you still have his hand under control, use it to keep him in range and distracted.

Figure 5.3.18 Figure 5.3.19 Figure 5.3.20 Figure 5.3.21 Figure 5.3.22

The outside hook kick is a natural follow-up to the inside roundhouse.

Figures 5.3.23 through 5.3.25 show a defensive application very much favored by this author: a "timed" stop hook kick. Keep the weight of the body on your rear leg as much as possible, without appearing to do so. As soon as your opponent launches a committed attack, lift your front leg into a hook kick to catch him in mid-move. Remember: the whole feeling of a timed stop-kick is forward—never backward. Your opponent expects you to retreat, even if only slightly, and develops his move in such a way. Your forward move will foil his plans and catch him before full power development.

Figure 5.3.23 Figure 5.3.24 Figure 5.3.25

The font-leg hook kick is the ideal kick for stop-kicking an opponent just starting an attack.

Specific Training

As this is not a powerful move, the work with the heavy bag is not for power development, but just as a firm target. Hit as powerfully as possible though.

- Work the kick on the speedball and padded targets held by a partner, for speed and accuracy.
- Practice the kick on the heavy bag with a hop forward, but place a chair in front of the bag to force you to chamber before the hop and hit high (See Figure 5.3.26).

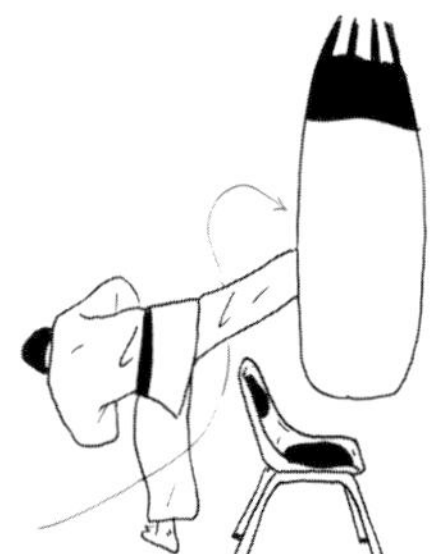

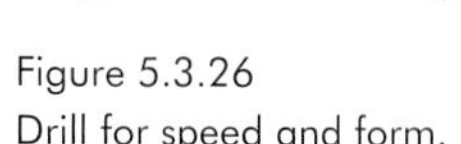

Figure 5.3.26
Drill for speed and form.

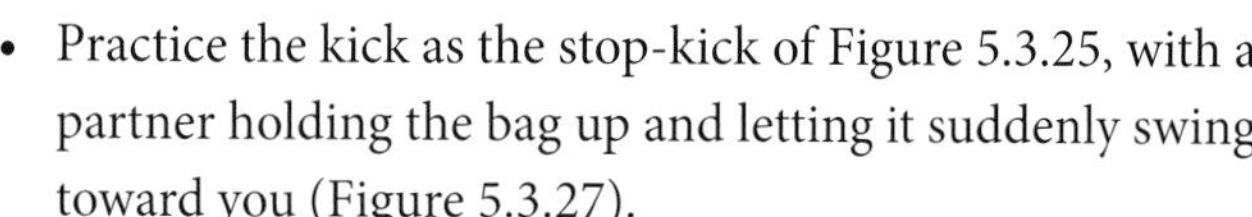

- Practice the kick as the stop-kick of Figure 5.3.25, with a partner holding the bag up and letting it suddenly swing toward you (Figure 5.3.27).

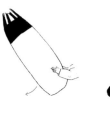

- A fast hook kick requires a lot of flexibility work!

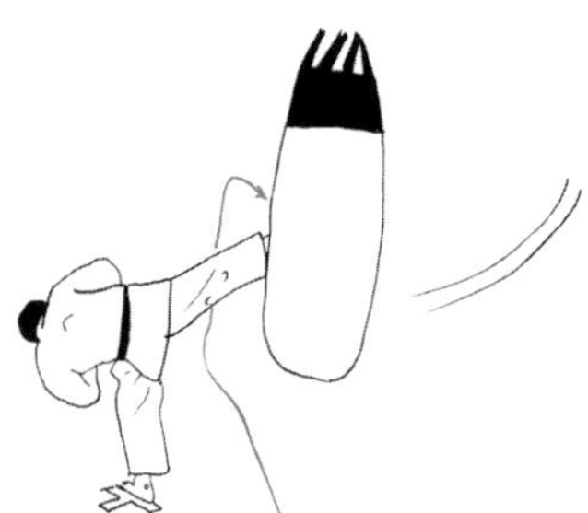

Figure 5.3.27
Drill for timing and speed.

Self-defense

Figures 5.3.28 through 5.3.31 show an important application, also interesting for tournament use, against an opponent who attacks your legs a lot, whether with sweeps or low kicks. It is a backward-forward move to be executed smoothly and with no stop in between. Your opponent attempts to low-kick your front leg: evade by pulling the leg back with a full body back evasion, eventually with a slight backward hop of the rear leg. In an uninterrupted move you switch your momentum forward and use the evading leg to hook kick your opponent's head, while hopping forward on your standing leg.

Figure 5.3.28

Figure 5.3.29

Figure 5.3.30

Figure 5.3.31

A very important back and forth evasion/counterattack move.

5.4 The Spin-back Hook Kick

Ushiro mawashi geri (karate), *Dora cha gi / Mom Dolye cha gi* (taekwondo), *Luu van cuoc* (viet vo dao), *Pai lie tui* (kung fu), *Te glab lang / Chorake fard hang* (muay thai)

General

The spin-back hook kick is the powerful version of the hook kick, obviously thanks to the centrifugal acceleration during the spin. Of course, the kick has the drawbacks of a longer path to the target, of having to turn your back to the opponent, and of a difficult-to-stop momentum. The kick is still very fast though because of the acceleration of the spin, and very surprising when well executed. It is devastating when used in self-defense against an untrained assailant or when used against an opponent unfamiliar with this type of kick. The kick can be delivered in its regular (straight leg) or in its "hooked" form. But let it be noted that the kick requires a lot of practice and training before it can be used in real fighting situations.

Description

As shown in Figures 5.4.1 through 5.4.7, the kick is basically the same hook kick but delivered with the back leg after a full 360 degrees pivot on the front foot. The principle of the spinning back is the same as for the other spin-back kicks we have seen. You start pivoting with the head first, then the shoulders, which pull the waist, and only then the leg as a coiled elastic band. But in the case of the spin-back hook kick, the circular movement must be emphasized, as it is the centrifugal force that will give the power to the kick. And unlike the spin-back back kick (Chapter 4, Section 3) for example, there is no stopping the momentum here to switch to a straight line of attack—the spin continues through the target!

Although it is powerful and therefore efficient with the legs or the body as targets, the preferred target of this kick is the head. When attacking high, it is important not to start to lift the leg early in the spin, but at the last instant (See Figure 5.4.3), so as to ensure the climbing of the leg outside the field of vision of the opponent.

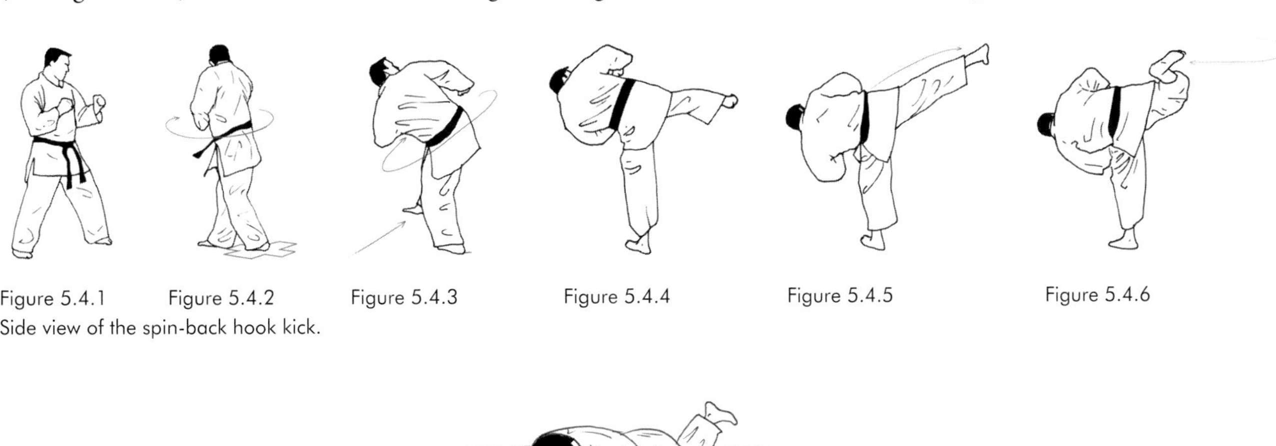

Figure 5.4.1 Figure 5.4.2 Figure 5.4.3 Figure 5.4.4 Figure 5.4.5 Figure 5.4.6
Side view of the spin-back hook kick.

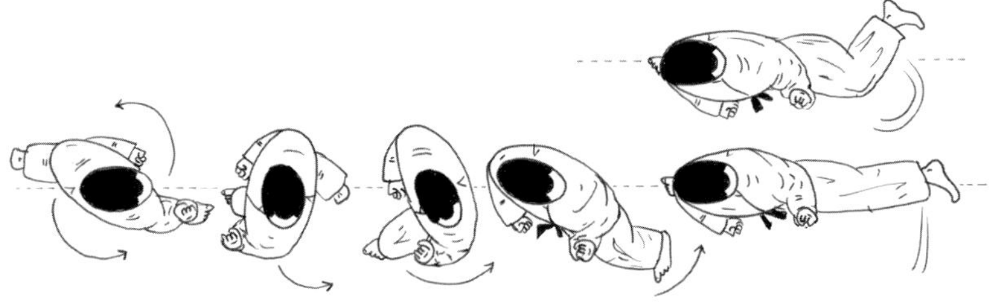

Figure 5.4.7
Overhead view of the spin-back hook kick, regular and hooked.

Figures 5.4.8 to 5.4.11 show the delivery of the kick.

Figure 5.4.8 Figure 5.4.9 Figure 5.4.10 Figure 5.4.11
Note the full twist before the leg even starts to lift!

Key Points

- Do not telegraph your move by an exaggerated spin involving the arms: Use the discreet but forceful spin of the shoulders to "pull" the waist and leg.
- Avoid stopping the spin after 360 degrees twist: You have to kick through the target, and then stop by bending the leg.
- Minimize the time you lose eye contact with the opponent.

Targets

As mentioned, the kick is very powerful from the accelerating circular movement and can be used on all possible targets. The head is preferred though, as the unexpectedness of the impact (kick not seen coming) often and easily causes knock-downs and knock-outs.

Typical Application

The spin-back hook kick is most optimally used, in our opinion, as a counterattack kick. Figures 5.4.12 through 5.4.15 shows the classic block/control of a high roundhouse, followed smoothly by a spin-back hook kick while the assailant is still lowering his kicking leg. It is to be noted that the block is already part of the spinning move.

Figure 5.4.12 Figure 5.4.13 Figure 5.4.14 Figure 5.4.15
The classic rolling into a roundhouse kick and using the momentum to pivot into the spin-back hook kick.

Specific Training

- This kick must be practiced for power on the heavy bag, and for speed and accuracy on the speedball. In order to develop the skill of kicking opponents at all ranges, it is wise to always practice both regular and hooked versions during the same training session.
- Practice on both the heavy bag and the speedball, with a chair in front: You start climbing just before you touch the chair (See Figures 5.4.16 and 5.4.17).

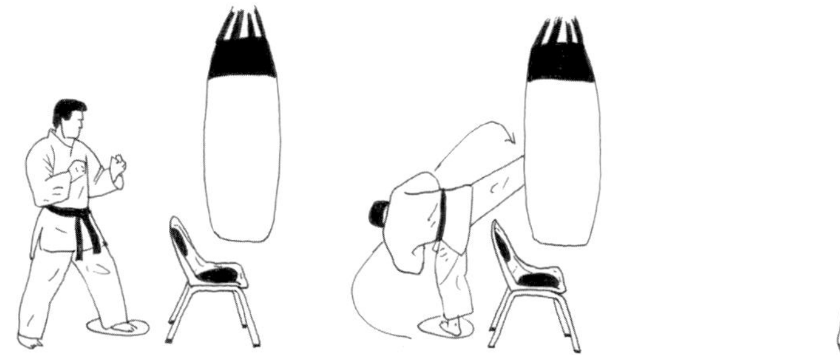

Figure 5.4.16
Straight-leg hook kick into the heavy bag.

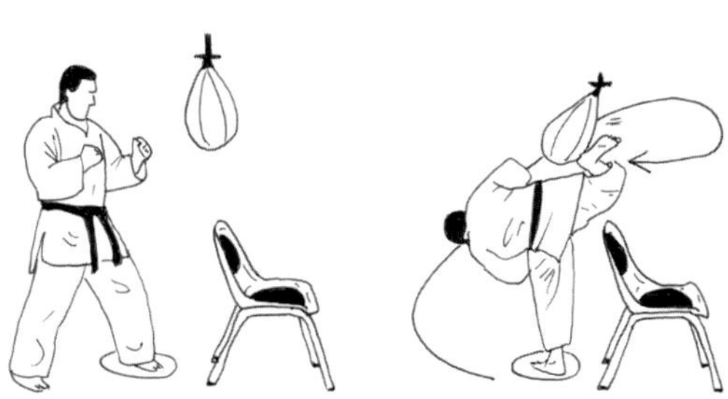

Figure 5.4.17
Hooked hook kick into the speedball.

- Figures 5.4.18 to 5.4.21 show drilling the kick with a moving partner holding a target pad.

Figure 5.4.18

Figure 5.4.19

Figure 5.4.20

Self-defense

Figures 5.4.22 through 5.4.26 show an offensive application of the kick. An offensive spin back kick is better delivered to an "immobilized" opponent, and in this case, you will put him off-balance for the time needed to kick him. Overwhelm your assailant with an aggressive jab/cross (*Kizami tsuki / Gyacku tsuki*, karate) combination to the face with a strong forward momentum. Make use of the twist of the hips to pull your rear leg into an inside kick/sweep (*Ko uchi gari / De ashi bara*—judo / karate) of his front leg to his outside. Continue this circular momentum and accelerate into a full spin-back hook kick to the head of your unbalanced assailant.

Figure 5.4.21
Kick fast and through the target.

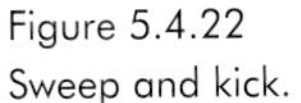

Figure 5.4.22
Sweep and kick.

Figure 5.4.23

Figure 5.4.24

Figure 5.4.25

Figure 5.4.26

5.5 The Universal Chamber Hook Kick

General

This kick, as expected, is simply the regular front leg hook kick delivered from the universal chambering position already described (Chapter 2, Section 4, and Chapter 3, Section 4) and presented once more in Figure 5.5.1. The kick has all the advantages and disadvantages of the front leg hook kick, coupled with the effect of surprise conferred by the universal chamber: The opponent does not know if the kick on its way is side, roundhouse or hook.

Figure 5.5.1
The universal chambering position.

Description

Figures 5.5.2 through 5.5.6 describe the kick preceded by a half-step with a small hop, and with a hooked finish. Of course, the footwork can be different and the finish can be straight-legged.

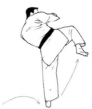

Figure 5.5.2 Figure 5.5.3 Figure 5.5.4 Figure 5.5.5 Figure 5.5.6
Side view of the universal chamber hook kick.

Key Points

- Keep the guard up.
- Perform the chamber perfectly: only a perfect technique will fool the opponent. If you "prepare" your specific kick when chambering, even slightly, you are telegraphing your intentions. It is a common mistake.
- Kick through the target.

Targets

Just like the regular front leg hook kick, this kick is not powerful. Kick only to the head or the groin.

Typical Application

Figures 5.5.7 through 5.5.12 present a very fast and efficient combination. You attack your opponent with a rather unusual reverse midsection punch/high jab (*Gyacku tsuki / Kizami tsuki*—karate) with full step and a committed forward momentum. Make sure that your high jab comes convincingly to the outside of his face to force him to overblock. Leave your jabbing hand when he blocks and try to get a hold of his hand. In any case, leave your hand in front of his face, slightly to the outside, to hide your next move as much as possible. Make use of the momentum and the hip twist of the front hand jab to "pull" the back leg forward in a slide, while lifting your forward leg into the universal chamber. Hook kick to the inside of his face while pulling on his front hand if you have it. You then chamber the leg and lower it in front of him, between his own legs, while your hand releases his to come behind his neck. Sweep his front leg from under him by lifting your front leg between his, all the while pushing him down from behind his neck (*Uchi mata*—judo). In tournament fighting you still have to make another point by hitting him while he is down.

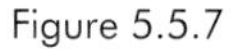

Figure 5.5.7 Figure 5.5.8 Figure 5.5.9 Figure 5.5.10

Figure 5.5.11 Figure 5.5.12
A hook kick flowing naturally into a classic throw.

Specific Training

- All universal chamber kicks must be practiced in front of the mirror.
- Always train all three types in the same session (side kick, roundhouse kick, hook kick), and train alternating them.
- Heavy bag training, from the good technical universal chamber, forces you to properly differentiate the three types.

Self-defense

Figures 5.5.13 through 5.5.19 present a "simple" front leg hook kick as a timing stop-kick, but with a universal chamber, and followed by a punishing combination suitable for real self-defense. As already mentioned, the front leg hook kick is considered by this author to be one of the best kicks for stop-kicking an advancing opponent. As your assailant starts to attack you, do not retreat but hop forward into a universal chamber, well guarded, and initiate your hook kick. Kick through the target and chamber. From the chamber, and without lowering your leg, deliver a (small) roundhouse (Chapter 3, Section 2) to his groin, and then backfist him while lowering the leg forward. Finish off with another quick front leg hook kick, but this time, hooked, to hit him behind the head. No need for a universal chamber for the last hook kick.

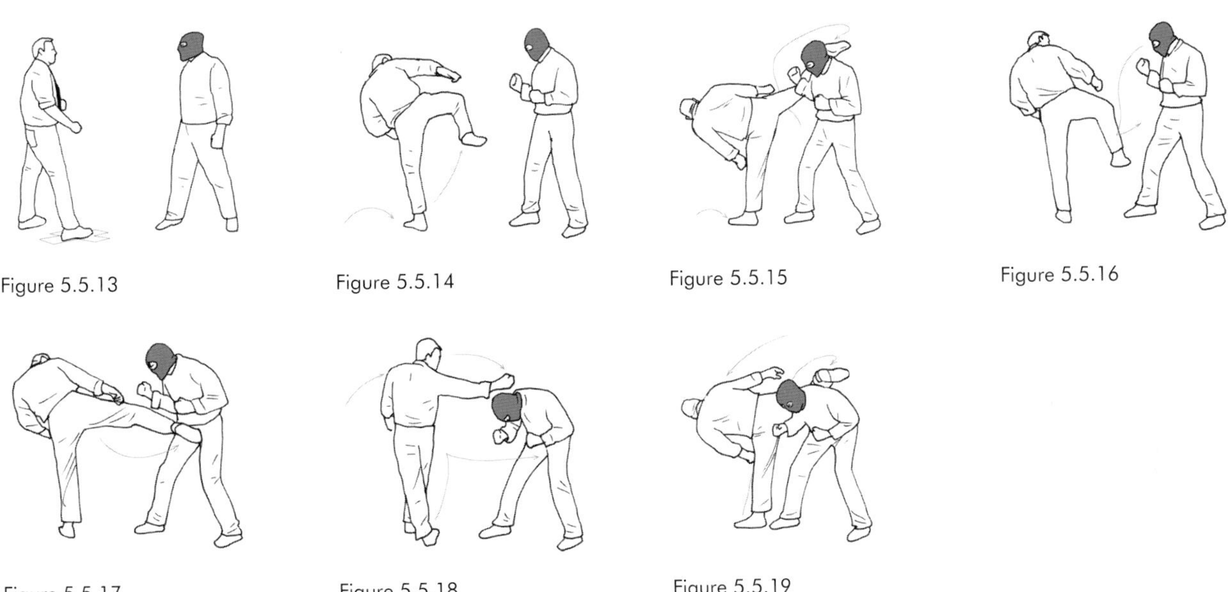

Figure 5.5.13 Figure 5.5.14 Figure 5.5.15 Figure 5.5.16

Figure 5.5.17 Figure 5.5.18 Figure 5.5.19

These images depict a very effective three-kick combination.

5.6 The Oblique Hook Kick

General

Angling the trajectory of your kicks is always a good idea: Anything out of the ordinary has a better chance to succeed by surprising your opponent. The oblique hook kick is especially suitable for an oblique delivery as it lends itself easily to a longer trajectory. It is even more powerful than the regular hook kick, as it has a longer trajectory for circular acceleration. The technique is basically a longer trajectory back leg hook kick delivered after a forward oblique half-step evasion. The half step forward can be an evasion from an incoming attack, or just footwork to better fool the opponent. We have found this technique to be very effective as it easily fools unseasoned opponents.

Description

See Figures 5.6.1 through 5.6.6. From the fighting stance, perform a half-step obliquely forward with the front foot, and so remove your body completely from the centerline (or the line of a coming assault). As soon as your foot touches the ground, chamber the rear leg for a hook kick, as if it was to be delivered to an opponent standing in front of your angled position. The hip movement involved will help fool your opponent, will protect you and will allow for a more powerful kick. Start to develop your hook kick and keep the accelerating circular momentum until you have hit through the target, which is a little bit further away than for the regular hook kick. Of course, the kick can be delivered hooked or straight-leg.

Figure 5.6.1 Figure 5.6.2 Figure 5.6.3 Figure 5.6.4 Figure 5.6.5
Front view of the oblique hook kick.

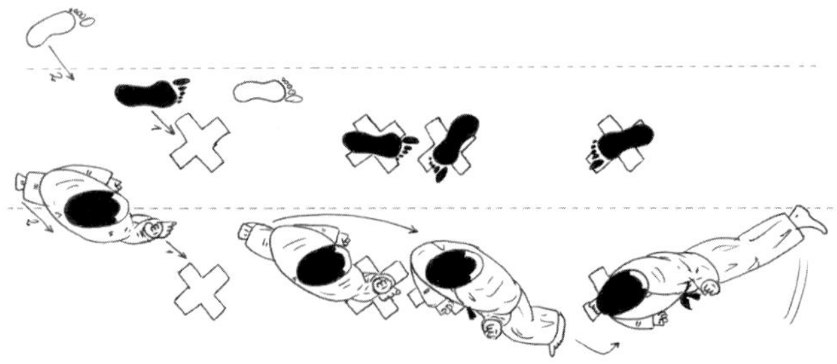

Figure 5.6.6
Overhead view of the oblique hook kick.

For better understanding, Figures 5.6.7 through 5.6.10 show the delivery of the kick against a step-punching opponent.

Figure 5.6.7

Figure 5.6.8

Figure 5.6.9

Key Points

- The kick is delivered in one smooth continuous move.
- Be careful when stepping forward and stay guarded.
- Deliver the kick as if your opponent stands diagonally 45 degrees in front of you. Picture this in your mind when training.

Targets

The kick is more powerful than the regular hook kick and can be used to kick the solar plexus or the kidneys. However, the preferred targets are still the head and the groin. The angle of attack also allows for a throat attack.

Figure 5.6.10
Front view of the oblique hook kick in action.

Typical Application

As mentioned, this kick is most suitable for delivery against an opponent committed to an attack on you. Figures 5.6.11 through 5.6.14 show the kick used against a front leg roundhouse, but it can be adapted to most attacking moves.

As your opponent starts to launch a front leg hopping roundhouse, step obliquely forward to his inside for the oblique hook kick. He did not plan for a "longer" roundhouse, but you should still keep your guard up to control it.

Figure 5.6.11 Figure 5.6.12 Figure 5.6.13 Figure 5.6.14
The oblique hook kick as a "timing" stop-kick.

Specific Training

- Mark the floor for the 45 degrees half-step and mark the bag 45 degrees to the back. Touch the marked floor with the step and hit the mark on the back of the bag in one smooth movement (see Figure 5.6.15).

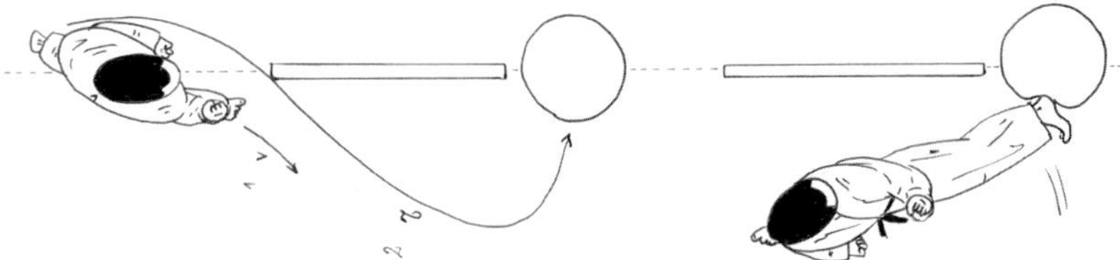

Figure 5.6.15
Training on a static bag.

- Practice the kick as a timing stop-kick, against a heavy bag swung by a partner (see Figure 5.6.16).

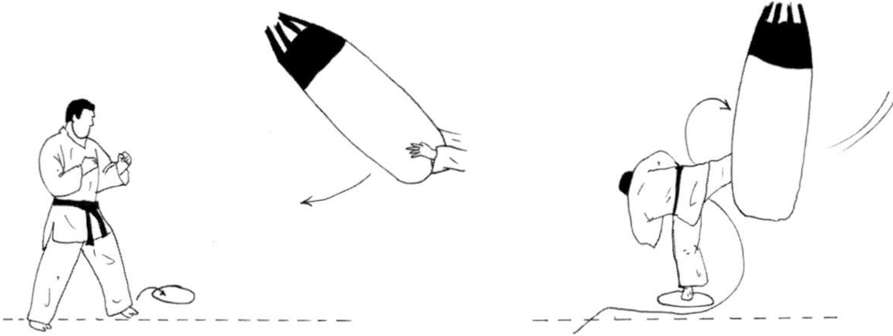

Figure 5.6.16
Training on an incoming bag.

Self-defense

Figures 5.6.17 through 5.6.20 show the forward half-step as a full-scale forward evasion against an overhead club strike. The following hook kick will catch the assailant on the back of the neck. As this is a self-defense situation, keep hitting until safe, and therefore make use of the momentum of the lowering of the leg to hit the back of his head again with a hammer fist strike.

Figure 5.6.17
Evading a club strike.

Figure 5.6.18

Figure 5.6.19

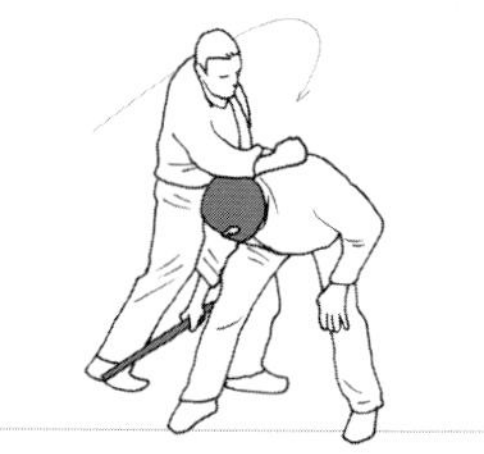

Figure 5.6.20

5.7 The Half-pivot Hook Kick

General

Just like the previous kick, this is a hook kick delivered after evasion footwork. Those kicks are presented here because the footwork changes the way the kick is performed—these are not just steps followed by the kick. The half-pivot hook kick is a hook kick delivered after a quarter of a turn pivot on the front foot that brings you to the outside of the mid-line, very much in the way of the *Tai-sabaki* of aikido. Some karate styles like Shukokai and Sankukai are very fond of those types of evasion moves, especially circular ones. This kick is nearly exclusively to be used on an attacking opponent who is committed to a straight forward momentum. However, it could be used as an angled attack in certain circumstances, but with a smaller step, which makes it close to a front-leg hook kick delivered with a cross-step. This kick requires a lot of training, but is a must to practice for the stop-kicker.

Description

Figures 5.7.1 through 5.7.4 clearly show the circular pivot on the front foot and the rear leg executing more than a 90 degrees circle. You stand perpendicular to your attacking opponent, with your rear leg "crossed" behind the front. Deliver a hook kick with the front leg into the line of attack.

Figure 5.7.1
Pivot, then kick.

Figure 5.7.2

Figure 5.7.3

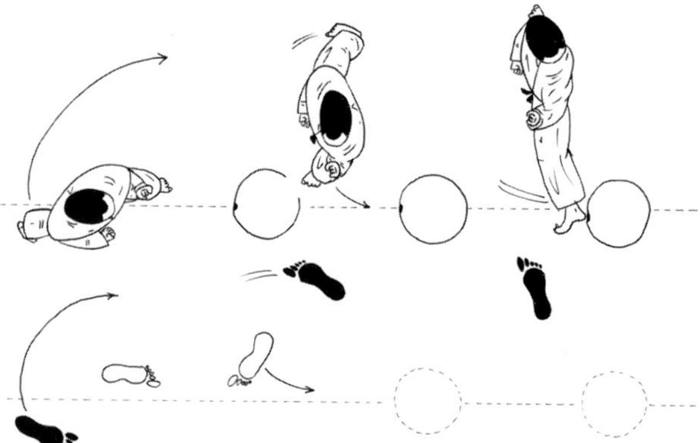

Figure 5.7.4
Overhead view of the half-pivot hook kick.

For more clarity, Figures 5.7.5 through 5.7.8 show the delivery of the kick in a hooked heel version after an evading block against a step-punching opponent.

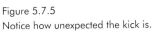

Figure 5.7.5
Notice how unexpected the kick is.

Figure 5.7.6

Figure 5.7.7

Figure 5.7.8

Key Points

- This is a continuous move. There is no pause between the footwork and the kick.
- Keep your guard up and control your opponent's momentum.

Targets

The power of the kick is multiplied by the forward momentum of the opponent, and therefore powerful enough to target the solar plexus as well. However, the preferred targets still are the head and the groin.

Typical Application

The kick being a timing stop-kick, the applications will be quite straightforward. Figures 5.7.9 through 5.7.11 show the technique against a punch, like before, but this time with no block.

Figure 5.7.9
Evasion only, no block. Timing is of the essence!

Figure 5.7.10

Figure 5.7.11

Specific Training

- Mark the heavy bag at head level and stand in front of the mark. Evade and kick the mark.
- Repeat with chair between you and the bag (see Figure 5.7.12).

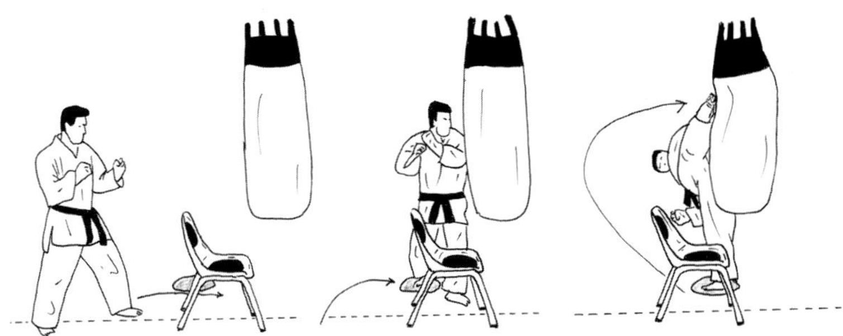

Figure 5.7.12
Train for speed and technique.

- As with all stop-kicks, work on the swinging bag.
- Work with an attacking partner using padded targets and/or protection.

Self-defense

Figures 5.7.13 through 5.7.15 show the technique used against a front-kicking assailant. Note the guard and the control of the kicking leg. The kick is delivered as the assailant lowers his leg.

Figure 5.7.13 Figure 5.7.14 Figure 5.7.15
The half-pivot hook kick against a front kick.

5.8 The Downward Hook Kick

Furyo tshagy (taekwondo)

General

The downward hook kick is a hybrid between a hook kick and a downward heel kick (hatchet kick, axe kick—see Chapter 6, Section 5). Instead of being fully circular, the kick comes down obliquely toward the target. This is sort of the counterpart of the downward roundhouse kick (Chapter 3, Section 8), but coming from the other direction. The downward hook kick has the same advantages, however, one rarely expects to be kicked from above, and the final trajectory of the kick easily surprises the opponent. This is also a great kick against ducking opponents, as you follow his downward evasion with the kick. The kick could also be considered a variation of the downward heel kick (Chapter 6, Section 5), but with your body facing sideways instead of forward. In any case, just as with all hybrid-type kicks, there are an infinite numbers of possible variations of the kick: With more or less emphasis on the "hook" or the "downward" part of the kick. The kick also allows for a more "facing" finish position, than the regular hook kick terminating with the body facing sideways with less visibility.

Description

Figures 5.8.1 through 5.8.8 show the delivery with the rear leg, although the kick can be delivered with the front leg or after any suitable footwork. The delivery of the kick is totally similar to the regular hook kick until the start of the extension of the leg. With the extension of the leg, the hips start to pivot back forward to face the opponent. At full extension, and just before impact, the foot is pointing 45 degrees toward the ceiling and the hips are diagonal in reference to the midline. The kick comes down diagonally 45 degrees through the target. The leg then recoils, while the hips continue their pivot back toward chambered position.

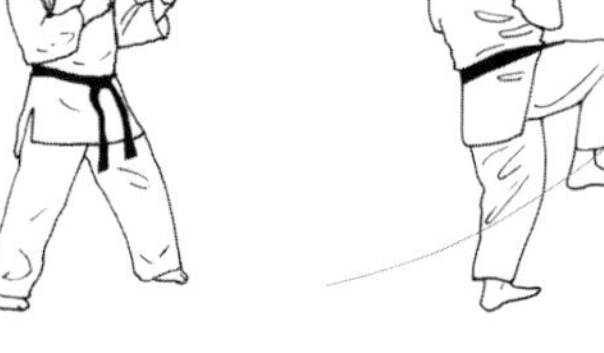

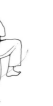

Figure 5.8.1 Figure 5.8.2 Figure 5.8.3 Figure 5.8.4 Figure 5.8.5
The kick flies sideways and down.

Figure 5.8.6

Figure 5.8.7

Figure 5.8.8

Front view of the downward hook kick in comparison to the regular hook kick.

Figures 5.8.9 through 5.8.12 show an interesting combination using this particular kick: a straight leg roundhouse to the inside of your opponent's knee joint causes him to open and kneel. You then use your kicking leg to come back with a downward hook kick to his neck while he is still down.

Figure 5.8.9

Figure 5.8.10

Figure 5.8.11

Key Points

- The kick is coming downwards and therefore must come from higher than the opponent's head.
- A lot of hip flexibility work is needed.
- The shift in the hips and start of downward movement comes as late as possible in the kick execution, so as not to telegraph your intentions.

Targets

- Head and neck
- Back of the neck
- Back and kidneys, if your opponent is bent-over.

Figure 5.8.12
The perfect relative situation for a downward hook kick.

Typical Application

Figures 5.8.13 through 5.8.17 show a great application of the kick in an offensive combination, also applicable to the regular hook kick. Feint a front leg low inside small roundhouse attack toward the front leg or the groin of your opponent. You can just feint or, preferably, get to the point where you touch the leg or the groin with a fast convincing kick. This is a great opening move against an opponent jabbing his attackers, as your slight backward tilt and high guard protect you when kicking. As soon as you get his attention to his low/inside gate, recoil the leg and pivot slightly for a high downward hook kick coming from the outside. This is especially effective if your feint has caused him to bend forward, but is equally effective if not, just because of the angle of attack.

Figure 5.8.13

Figure 5.8.14

Figure 5.8.15

Figure 5.8.16

Figure 5.8.17
Low inside to downward high outside combination.

Specific Training

- Perform a lot of hip flexibility training.
- You need to train on a target you can hit diagonally from above—a standing heavy bag, for example (see Figure 5.8.18).

Figure 5.8.18
Make sure trajectory is diagonally down.

Self-defense

Figures 5.8.19 through 5.8.24 show the use of the kick on a bending opponent. Your assailant is a counter-attacker, and you lure him into a reverse punch by launching a rear leg front kick (toward his groin) that is not totally committed and which is purposely to force him to block and counter. As soon as he blocks you recoil the leg and land the foot largely on the outside while controlling his punch. The momentum liberates your rear leg as you shift your weight forward, and in one smooth, continuous move you roundhouse kick his ribs, his solar plexus or lower belly under the punching arm. Chamber the leg back as he bends over, and without lowering the leg, deliver a downward hook kick to the back of his head or neck.

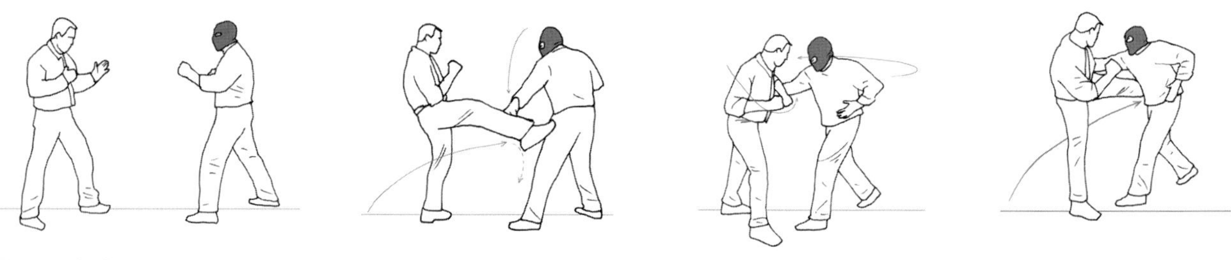

Figure 5.8.19

Figure 5.8.20

Figure 5.8.21

Figure 5.8.22

Figure 5.8.23 Figure 5.8.24
The roundhouse to the body places him in position for the downward hook kick.

5.9 The Bent-body Hook Kick

General

The bent-body hook kick is a very simply a hook kick delivered with the upper body bent sideways, more than warranted by flexibility: The body is nearly parallel to the floor. It is presented as a separate kick because its delivery is slightly different, and the kick is very useful in practice. The orthodox delivery of the kick calls for the body to bend during the extension of the leg, just like for the regular kick, but to a greater degree. In practice, the kick is often delivered from an already bent position, as will be illustrated in the applications. The obvious advantage of the kick is upper body evasion—kick while keeping your upper body away from an attack or a potential attack/counterattack. This is an extremely effective and versatile kick, as it is fast and very safe to deliver. This kick allows for kicking a very close opponent, in a very unexpected manner. It allows less flexible artists to kick high to the head, by bending the body very low, even to the extent of placing the hand to the floor (See Section 11 of this chapter). We have seen this kick used by a great master like Shotokan's Kanazawa, and referred to as the "scorpion" kick. In its delivery from very close, a less flexible practitioner can use the forward ankle or thigh of the opponent as a support (See Figures 5.9.1 through 5.9.4)

Figure 5.9.1 Figure 5.9.2 Figure 5.9.3 Figure 5.9.4
Using the opponent's leg as support.

Description

Figures 5.9.5 through 5.9.8 show the orthodox delivery of the rear leg version of the bent-body hook kick. You just bend over with the upper body during the development of a regular hook kick. The kick can, of course, be practiced in its front leg version, and with or without a "hooked" finish.

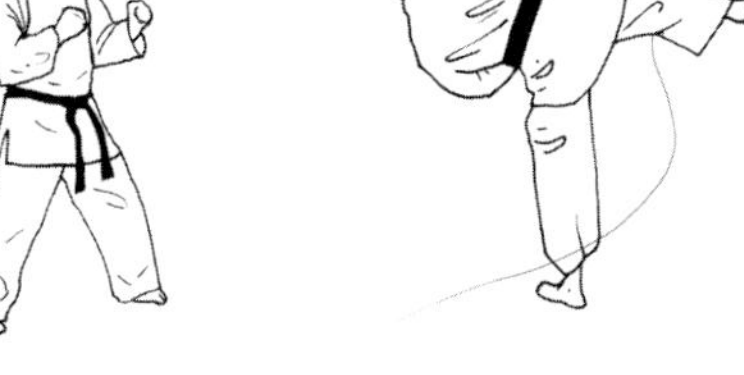

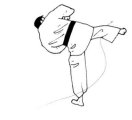

Figure 5.9.5 Figure 5.9.6 Figure 5.9.7 Figure 5.9.8
Lowering the upper body also helps to kick higher.

Figure 5.9.9 shows how the kick scores while the upper body is out of reach of a punch by the opponent.

Figures 5.9.10 through 5.9.13 show the same advantage against a stop-punching opponent, in a front-leg high bent-body hook kick.

Figure 5.9.9
A very safe-to-deliver kick.

Figure 5.9.10

Figure 5.9.11

Figure 5.9.12

Key Points

- Slightly bend the standing leg for even more reach.
- Keep your eyes on the opponent at all times.

Targets

- Head
- Groin

Figure 5.9.13
A winning technique: Step in to cause the opponent to start a stop-punch, then kick.

Typical Application

Figures 5.9.15 through 5.9.19 present a very special application of this kick, which was automatically used by this author against those fighters who tried to "time-stop" his attacks with the once very popular jumping backfist strike (Figure 5.9.14). This maneuver is not really a kick in the sense that the kick itself does not cause harm or hurt where it strikes; but the kick causes a hard fall to the opponent and allows for an effective follow-up.

Feint with a half-step forward and a fake body move, to convince your opponent that you are launching a committed punching attack. As he jumps up (and slightly forward) start to bend away from him while bringing your rear leg half a step forward for a hopping front leg hook kick. Deliver the straight leg hook kick to his upper thighs while he is still in the air (but cannot reach your face as you are bending away), removing the support on which he expected to land. This is a hard fall, and you make use of his distress to score as soon as he slams the floor: You can heel kick him, or even just punch.

Figure 5.9.14
The jumping backfist strike

Figure 5.9.15

Figure 5.9.16

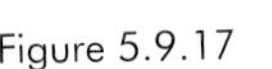

Figure 5.9.17

Figure 5.9.18

Figure 5.9.19
This is a very nasty fall! Practice carefully and exclusively on a mat.

Specific Training

- Train for flexibility and practice the regular hook kick.
- Train with a partner in punching position (Figure 5.9.9)—kick while keeping away from the fist.
- Train with a punching partner: You evade his punch by bending and hook kicking.

Self-defense

Figures 5.9.20 through 5.9.23 show an application in which the kick is unorthodox as it starts from a bent position. This is a follow-up of a blocked front kick, and is valid whether the kick is a purposeful feint or has failed. Deliver a forceful and forward committed penetrating front kick. Your assailant evades the kick from the outside and diverts it to your inside. In order to avoid the coming counterattack, lower your kicking foot as far away from him on your inside as possible while you bend forward. Remain bent forward while switching your weight to the front leg and starting a hook kick to his head from the rear leg.

Figure 5.9.20

Figure 5.9.21

Practice as an automatic counter to your kicking leg being thrown aside.

Figure 5.9.22

Figure 5.9.23

5.10 The Bent-body Spin-back Hook Kick

Meia lua de compasso / Chibata / Rabo de arraia (capoeira)

General

This is, of course, the spin-back version of the body bent hook kick. This is a kick very much in use in capoeira, and their typical variation is illustrated in Figure 5.10.10: a very large circular movement and with the upper body totally bent, as to allow looking at the opponent from down under. The advantage of the bent-body spin-back hook kick comes from being away from the opponent as much as possible, combined with the power of the centrifugal force of the spin back rotation. The bending of the upper body while pivoting adds to the power of the circular movement. Of course, bending the upper body also allows for higher kicking if flexibility limits the height of your kicks.

Description

Figures 5.10.1 through 5.10.4 show the orthodox way to practice the kick. You start just like for a regular spin-back hook kick (Section 4 of this chapter) by turning the head and shoulders first, then the hips. As soon as you start pivoting on your foot and turning the hips, you also start bending the upper body. At the apex of the kick, your body is about parallel to the floor.

Figure 5.10.1

Figure 5.10.2
Bending over helps the speed and power of the kick.

Figure 5.10.3

Figure 5.10.4

Figures 5.10.5 through 5.10.7 show the delivery of the kick with a partner.

Figure 5.10.5
Note how bending over makes this a very safe kick.

Figure 5.10.6

Figure 5.10.7

Key Points

- Kick through the target.
- Speed is key to the power of the kick: practice for a smooth accelerating kick. Muscles of the leg must be relaxed for speed and flexibility.
- Keep maximum eye contact with the opponent: regain eye contact as early as possible in the spin.

Targets

Preferable targets are the head and the groin. But this is a powerful kick, so the kidneys, solar plexus, middle of the back, side of the thigh, and the knee are good alternative targets.

Typical Application

Figures 5.10.8 through 5.10.11 show a capoeira-style application of the kick. Spin and bend fully while still on both of your feet, then kick while completing the spin. Look at your opponent from down under. In the application, the kick is used against a counter-puncher: You feint with half a reverse punch to provoke his reverse punching. You then reverse your momentum and the direction of the pivot of the hips, bending while spinning back to use the full momentum of the spin and bend to throw a fast kick.

Figure 5.10.8 Figure 5.10.9 Figure 5.10.10 Figure 5.10.11

The trap: lure your opponent into a counterpunch and kick him.

Specific Training

- This kick must be practiced on the heavy bag, but for speed.
- Practice with a partner roundhouse-punching at head level to force you to bend.

Self-defense

The following illustrations show an example of the kick in its more punishing "hooked" form, and as a natural follow-up to a classic *tai-sabaki* type of evasion as practiced in aikido or in karate styles such as Sankukai or Wado ryu. The body-bending is used to keep the body away from the assailant, as he is armed with a knife. You are suddenly attacked by an assailant stabbing with a knife toward your belly, and turn naturally to his outside while evading the middle line (Figure 5.10.13). Your naturally-hanging arm blocks and controls the attacking arm while you make use of the momentum of your circular movement (*Tai-sabaki*) and accelerate into a spin-back. You start bending as early as possible while delivering the kick to the back of his head (Figure 5.10.14). As you are staying very close to him while evading to his back and away from the straight line of attack, you must hook the finishing part of the hook kick. Continue your pivot while lowering the leg and regain control of his attacking arm. If possible, you can hit his elbow joint with your open hand while hitting his wrist from the inside, as illustrated (Figure 5.10.15). In any case, you keep control of his armed arm, while inverting your circular momentum, pushing him backward by pressing his throat and sweeping his front leg in an outer reap throw (*O soto gari*—judo). See Figure 5.10.16.

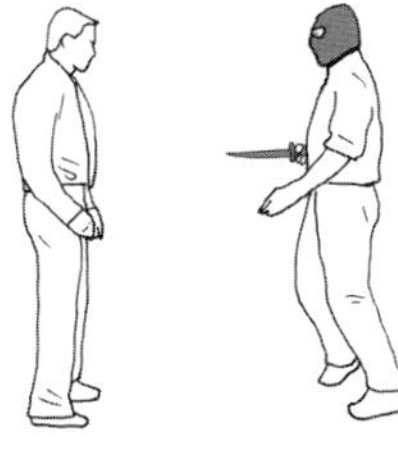

Figure 5.10.12 Figure 5.10.13 Figure 5.10.14 Figure 5.10.15 Figure 5.10.16

Circular moves against a knife attack.

5.11 The Hand-on-the-floor Hook Kick

General

This kick is the natural evolution of the bent-body hook kick, taken a little bit further. It is presented separately though, because of the way that the hand touches the floor, which allows for a slightly different delivery. As part of the body weight can be switched to the hand, the kick is lighter, faster and better anchored. The kick has the same advantage as the bent-body hook kick: the body is away from the opponent while the kick is fast, surprising and easy to perform high.

The way that the hand is firmly on the floor allows for more stability and fast combinations. The kick can, of course, be delivered with the front or the rear leg, and in its regular or "hooked" form.

Description

Figures 5.11.1 through 5.11.4 show the kick delivered as a front leg hopping kick. You front leg hop, and as soon as the kicking leg starts to rise like a regular hook kick, start to bend the upper body back. The hand should get to the floor just before the kick gets to full extension and scores. After hitting, you can follow up from the hand-on-floor position or chamber back into an upright position.

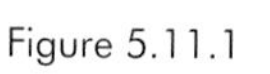

Figure 5.11.1 Figure 5.11.2 Figure 5.11.3 Figure 5.11.4
Bending toward the floor helps lift the leg higher if needed.

Figures 5.11.5 and 5.11.6 show how this kick can be delivered to the head even at zero range, in an extremely surprising way.

Key Points

- The hand leans firmly on the floor and takes on part of the body weight.
- Use your "lighter" weight on your foot to accelerate the circular kicking motion.
- Keep your eyes on your opponent at all times.
- Lean back up with your hands in guard.

Figure 5.11.5
The hook kick in very close combat.

Figure 5.11.6

Targets

- Preferably the head.
- Possibly the groin and knee.

Typical Application

Figures 5.11.7 through 5.11.10 show the use of the kick as a "counterattack trap." This is an excellent move to use against a "wait, block and counter" type of opponent, especially if he is not easily fooled by fake half-punches. You launch a fully committed rear leg roundhouse to his kidneys, keeping your upper body relaxed and your head leveled. This kick is difficult to block, and the combination stays the same whether your kick connects, is blocked, or partially blocked. You chamber back while keeping your momentum to lower the leg back crossed-legged in front of you. As your opponent launches his reverse punch counter, you bend down (same momentum!) and launch back the hook kick with the same leg, while laying the opposite hand on the floor. Your body is away from his punch, but your foot easily reaches his head from an unexpected angle.

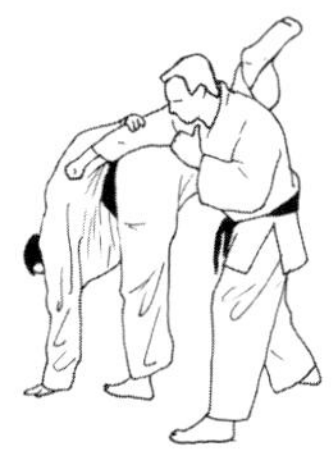

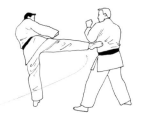

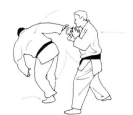

Figure 5.11.7 Figure 5.11.8 Figure 5.11.9 Figure 5.11.10

This technique is based on the bending over to evade the counterpunch.

Specific Training

- Practice on the heavy bag, or any target, for form and speed. There is no need to work on power.
- Practice on heavy bag with chair between you and the bag.
- Practice with a partner counterpunching when you start kicking, to force you to bend and evade (See Figure 5.11.10).
- Alternate with the regular hook kick and its hand-on-floor version.

Self-defense

Figures 5.11.11 through 5.11.14 show one of the best self-defense applications for kick use in close combat. This can be applied to many situations. In this example, you block/evade a punch on the outside of your assailant, always an advantageous position. You follow up in a classic circular move to his solar plexus, smoothly passing under his punching arm, and hitting with the ridge or the hand (*Haito uchi*—karate) or the closed fist. You keep the momentum to start a rear leg hook kick. As you are close, the hook kick is better and safer with the hand on the floor and with a "hooked" finish to the back of his head.

Figure 5.11.11 Figure 5.11.12 Figure 5.11.13 Figure 5.11.14

A very naturally-flowing combination.

5.12 The Hand-on-the-floor Spinning Back Hook Kick

Meia lua de compasso (capoeira)

General

We have given this kick its capoeira name as it is typical of this art and very frequently used in their *jogo* (game). The capoeira version of this kick is delivered in a different way, more specific to the emphasis of this style, and we will show both deliveries. The kick in itself is the natural continuation of the principles behind the bent-body spinning back hook kick (Section 10 of this chapter), just a little farther away with the upper body until the hand lies on the floor. Again, the advantages of the kick are the same: faster because of some body weight on the hand, safer as upper body is away from opponent, surprising effect because the kick is unorthodox and easier to deliver high for less flexible people.

Description

Figures 5.12.1 through 5.12.5 show the more orthodox delivery, which is closer to the Japanese and Korean traditional kicking arts. As you start pivoting on yourself just like for a regular spin back hook kick (Section 4 of this chapter), you immediately combine the spinning with a downward move of the upper body until your hand lies on the floor. Your hand should touch the floor and take on some of your weight, just before you leg gets at full extension and hits the target after a 360 degrees turn, at full centrifugal force.

Figure 5.12.1 Figure 5.12.2 Figure 5.12.3 Figure 5.12.4 Figure 5.12.5
Fast and flourishingly beautiful kick.

Figures 5.12.6 through 5.12.10 show the capoeira-like version of the kick, lighter on your feet, faster, more relaxed and "jumpy." Spin back and bend simultaneously in order to achieve, as quickly as possible, a fully bent position, with one or two hands firmly on the floor, and with your back to the opponent. Of course, you do not stop in this position and it is only a milestone in a continuous and accelerating movement. From there, keep your circular spin-back momentum and switch some weight onto the hand(s) to start a straight leg hook kick with what was your rear leg. Kick through the target and continue with your circular movement while standing up.

Figure 5.12.6 Figure 5.12.7 Figure 5.12.8 Figure 5.12.9 Figure 5.12.10
Front view of the capoeira-like version of the kick.

Key Points

- This is a smooth and continuous movement.
- Power comes from speed and therefore muscles must be relaxed.
- Acceleration of the kick comes from starting the pivot from the head down, and relieving the standing leg from some of the body weight.
- Always kick through the target.

Targets

Centrifugal force turns this kick in an extremely powerful one. Kick the head or groin preferably, but back, kidney, solar plexus, lower belly, knees, thighs are great targets if you use the heel as connecting surface.

Typical Application

Figures 5.12.11 through 5.12.14 show an interesting example of the kick as a follow-up to an outside lower block (*Gedan barai*—karate) to an incoming committed front kick attack. As you evade the kick forward and on the outside of the opponent while he has to lower his kicking leg, you are close enough for a punch follow-up. Therefore you bend away from the opponent while delivering the kick upward from below his punching arm. This is an extremely successful and surprising maneuver against a front kicker.

Figure 5.12.11

Figure 5.12.12

Figure 5.12.13

Figure 5.12.14

The bending keeps you safe and the circular move allows for an accelerating kick.

Specific Training

Refer to *Specific Training* for the bent-body spin back hook kick (Section 10 of this chapter) and hand-on-floor hook kick (Section 11 of this chapter).

Self-defense

The following images illustrate a more capoeira-like delivery of the kick, but in an application suitable for regular delivery as well. This is a great kick to use against a fighter waiting to time-stop you with a front leg roundhouse kick. After you have ascertained that it is his special fighting technique, feint half a reverse punch to provoke him into starting his kick (Figure 5.12.16). Reverse your hip momentum and spin-back bend to place your hands on the floor (Figure 5.12.17). You are already below his chambering leg. Continue your spin back momentum to deliver a high hook kick just as he completes his kick into void. Kick through his head before you start straightening up (Figure 5.12.18).

Figure 5.12.15

Figure 5.12.16

Figure 5.12.17

Figure 5.12.18

Lure your opponent into a counter you'll evade while kicking.

5.13 The Oblique Spin-back Hook Kick

General

This is simply a spin-back hook kick preceded by evading footwork. It is presented separately as a kick because the footwork causes some differences in the delivery of the kick, as the arc traveled by the kick is shorter than with a regular spin-back hook kick. Because of the starting position of the kick, the foot travels less than a full half-circle to reach the target. The move in itself is very confusing to the opponent, as you fully leave the mid-line, or the eventual line of attack, to finally kick from an unexpected angle. The evading footwork can be used either as an attack or as an evasion from a straight attack. Practicing this version of the hook kick is important, as it helps build your ability to kick from many different positions relative to your opponent.

Description

Figures 5.13.1 through 5.13.5 show how to perform a long step forward at an inside 45 degrees with your front foot, and so removing your body from the mid-line. You then switch your weight onto the front foot and bend a little more out of the mid-line, while starting your spin-back. Pivot from the head down, like a regular spin-back hook kick and finally kick through the target, which is still on the mid-line. The spin back is shorter, which makes the kick faster, more surprising, but also less powerful.

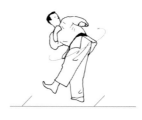

Figure 5.13.1 Figure 5.13.2 Figure 5.13.3 Figure 5.13.4
Side view of the shorter oblique spin-back hook kick.

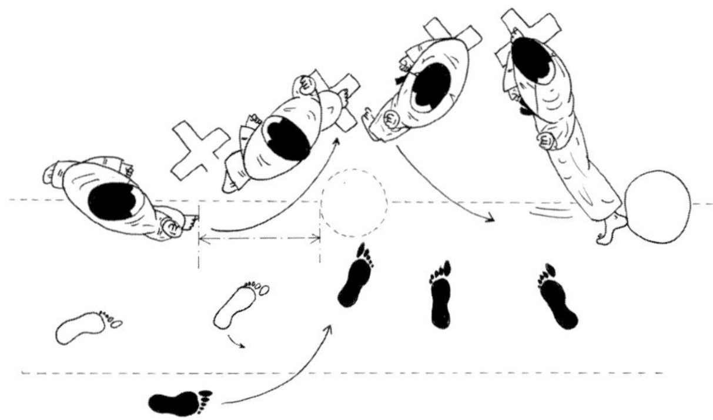

Figure 5.13.5
Overhead view of the oblique spin-back hook kick. Note the centerline.

Figures 5.13.6 through 5.13.9 show the delivery of the kick in a combination starting with an out-of-centerline lunging backfist on the outside of the opponent, laying the groundwork for the kick coming on his inside.

Figure 5.13.6

Figure 5.13.7

Figure 5.13.8

Key Points

- The key to the success of the technique is the evading step forward, which must be fast, untelegraphed (same head height), and long enough to take you immediately out of the line of attack.
- Keep your eyes on the opponent while stepping and start bending together with the step.
- Make it one smooth move—the kick starts with the step and the spin back starts as soon as the stepping foot touches the floor.

Targets

Typical targets include the head and the groin. The kick is less powerful than the regular spin-back hook kick, but still powerful enough for use to the solar plexus or the knees.

Figure 5.13.9
Note the backfist while getting out of the centerline.

Typical Application

Figures 5.13.10 through 5.13.12 show the use of the kick as an attack, following one of our preferred opening moves: a fast backfist attack delivered while lunging forward and to the outside of the opponent. The forward lunge must be untelegraphed and long, while you try to land your forward foot behind his own, on the outside. To avoid telegraphing, the backfist starts toward his head a few milliseconds before you start your lunge. As you land, you are in the natural position to lunge your oblique spin-back hook kick from his blind angle!

Figure 5.13.10

Figure 5.13.11

Figure 5.13.12

The same offensive combination seen from the other side.

Specific Training

- It is useful to practice the kick on the heavy bag, with the midline indicated on the floor, as well as a taped cross signaling the step to be taken. You'll then start from a fighting stance farther and farther away from the cross.
- Repeat the exercise with a chair between you and the bag. This will force you to take a full lunge step, and lift the leg early in the kick. (Figure 5.13.13)
- Always practice the regular spin-back hook kick after working on the oblique version!

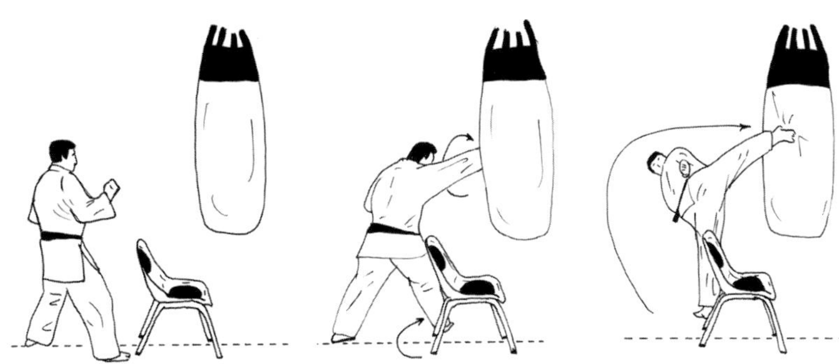

Figure 5.13.13
Exaggerate the side step while practicing.

Self-defense

Figures 5.13.14 through 5.13.17 show a defensive application of the kick blending naturally in the evading move. As you are assailed by a telegraphed front kick, you evade to your outside, while blocking/controlling your attacker's leg from the inside. If possible, control the leg to slightly overextend his kick into an off-balanced landing. All the while you deliver your oblique spin-back hook kick, on which he will practically impale himself. Natural follow-ups to the kick are a backfist to the face, and a low stomping side kick to the inside of his knee.

Figure 5.13.14

Figure 5.13.15

Figure 5.13.16

Figure 5.13.17

Extremely effective: your kick flies into his forward momentum!

5.14 The Drop Hook Kick

General

The drop hook kick is not a very powerful kick, and therefore not very much in use. Well-timed and executed it can still be an interesting weapon in your arsenal. In order to be able to use the kick in real situations, you will need to practice it a lot to allow for speed, deception, as much power as possible, and accuracy. The kick can be useful as a sweep to throw down your opponent, or as a "timing" stop kick to the groin coming in the opposite direction of the adversary's kick (See Figure 5.14.18). We shall still consider the kick used as a "sweep," a real kick, because it is always best delivered so: hit as hard as possible, with the heel, in order to inflict damage to the side of the knee, the calf or the side of the ankle; the fall of the opponent is a positive by-product.

Description

Figures 5.14.1 through 5.14.5 show the orthodox delivery of the kick: As the kick is not suitable for an attack, you need to step back and bend to the floor, pivoting on your rear foot. This is basically a downward/rear evasion. Place your hands and what was your back knee on the floor, and start kicking with your "previously front leg that stepped back" and that is now free of your body weight. This is very much a rebounding of the foot, as soon as your hands and knee lean on the floor. The development of the kick is circular, parallel to the floor.

Figure 5.14.1 Figure 5.14.2 Figure 5.14.3 Figure 5.14.4 Figure 5.14.5
Drop down and kick at knee or groin level.

Figures 5.14.6 through 5.14.8 show the delivery of the kick to the side of the knee joint.

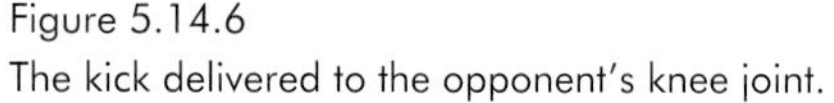

Figure 5.14.6
The kick delivered to the opponent's knee joint.

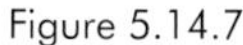

Figure 5.14.7

Figure 5.14.8

Key Points

- The power of the kick comes exclusively from the accelerating circular movement: You therefore need to lift and straighten the leg early and make the largest circular move possible.
- Keep your eyes on your opponent at all times.
- Kick through the target, but do not overstretch your kick, as you then become extremely vulnerable.
- Strike with the heel—not the calf or the sole of the foot.

Figure 5.14.9
The drop hook kick delivered to the thigh.

Targets

- Groin
- Thigh (see Figure 5.14.9)
- Knee
- Calf
- Ankle

Typical Application

Although it is not very much used in attacks, we present an exception, in order to show the opposite footwork which gets us in the same coiled position: Instead of step-pivoting back with the front leg, you can cross-step forward with your rear foot behind the front and bend down to the floor. The combination illustrated in Figures 5.14.10 through 5.14.13 will be efficient if you have drilled the kick a lot and if you make sure you kick with the heel onto sensitive points of your opponent's leg (The side of the knee is ideal).
The stepping forward to get into coiled position is possible by your simultaneously delivery of a feinted backfist that will keep him busy and slightly off-balance. A feinted backfist is a continuous movement starting as a convincing straight punch toward the groin that turns into a high outside backfist. As soon as the backfist is delivered, forcefully drop to the floor into a coiled position and kick the side of his knee. Kick through to ensure pain and the fall of the opponent.

Figure 5.14.10

Figure 5.14.11

Figure 5.14.12

Figure 5.14.13

These images depict an offensive combination, resulting in a takedown when delivered with precision.

Specific Training

- The best way to drill the kick as a real punishing low kick is to deliver it to a medicine-ball (as heavy as possible) for power and a basketball for speed and accuracy. See Figure 5.14.14. Make sure you hit with the heel, as hard as possible (Sending the ball as far as possible).

Figure 5.14.14
A great and fun drill.

- Practice the kick at groin level on the heavy bag: Touch the bag in fighting stance and deliver the kick, while emphasizing the spring-like rebounding of the kicking foot off the floor. See Figure 5.14.15.

Figure 5.14.15
Speed and timing drill.

Self-defense

Figures 5.14.16 through 5.14.18 present the classic use of the kick against a high roundhouse (Chapter 3, Section 1), with the orthodox step-back footwork. The kick is very efficient because of the target (groin) and the opposite directions of the two circular movements.

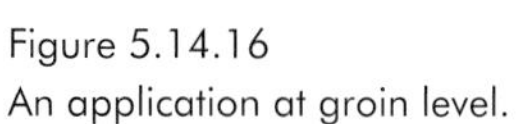

Figure 5.14.16
An application at groin level.

Figure 5.14.17

Figure 5.14.18

5.15 The Drop Spin-back Hook Kick

Hadan dora cha gi (taekwondo), *Hao so tung toy* (kung fu), *Rasteira giratoria* (capoeira)

General

The drop spin-back hook kick is much more powerful than the simple drop hook kick, thanks to the centrifugal force and acceleration of the circular movement. Of course, it takes longer and there is some loss of eye contact during the spin back. This kick is very much in use, especially in Chinese arts as a sweep of the front leg or the standing leg during a kick. The delivery of the sweep and the kick being the same, it is recommended to always deliver it "kick-minded" and to try to always connect with the heel onto sensitive anatomical points. The result will be the same felling of the opponent, but with added punishment. Just like the simple drop hook, this kick is great to use against the open groin of a high-kicking opponent.

Another advantage of this kick, when compared to the simple drop hook kick (Section 14 of this chapter), is that the bending down and footwork is already part of the kick itself and adds to the momentum of the circular movement.

Description

Figures 5.15.1 through 5.15.5 show the delivery of the kick. Start a regular spin-back, but immediately bend down with the legs and upper body. Continue the circular movement while the knee of the front leg and the hands reach the the floor. As soon as the body weight shifts from the rear leg, lift it and start kicking, while still spinning back with your hips.

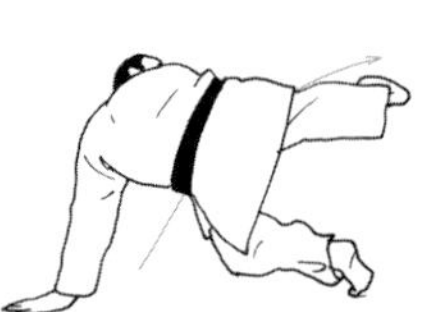

Figure 5.15.1

Figure 5.15.2
Notice the spin starts already while you're dropping.

Figure 5.15.3

Figure 5.15.4

Figure 5.15.5

Figures 5.15.6 through 5.15.9 show the delivery of the kick as a sweeping takedown against the standing leg of a high roundhouse kicking opponent.

Figure 5.15.6

Figure 5.15.7

Figure 5.15.8

Key Points

- Bend down in a circular movement.
- Start kicking as early as possible, and in an arc as large as possible.
- Kick through the target.
- Connect with the heel.

Targets

- Groin
- Knee
- Thigh
- Ankle
- If your opponent bends over, the head is a target. The kick is usually too weak for body targets.

Figure 5.15.9
Note how timing is of the essence for success with this kick.

Typical Application

Figures 5.15.10 through 5.15.12 show the classic use against a kicking opponent, as mentioned previously. This is an easy kick to score against a kicker, provided you have drilled it a lot, and time it perfectly. The drop into "coiled" position must be fast and forceful, nearly a "fall" into position. This move has the advantage of a total downward evasion of the kick without any need for footwork: you just drop in place into a position where you are not very vulnerable.

Figure 5.15.10

Figure 5.15.11

Figure 5.15.12

These images depict a devastating stop kick if executed with the right timing.

Figures 5.15.13 through 5.15.18 show a classic "sweep" combination including this kick, used a lot in tournaments of all styles. The move is great against fighters who lift the front leg and close their guards against all attacks, covering themselves and stopping the body attacks on their limbs, waiting to counterattack. It is also a great combination attack in itself against all fighters—those who stand their ground, or those backing away.

According to the fighter in front of you, you attack the standing leg, the front leg of a retreating opponent or even both legs. Just remember: always treat this as a kick, and not as a gentle sweep. And always follow up onto your falling opponent—a falling opponent is not vanquished yet!

Attack your opponent with a high reverse punch to put him off-balance and block his field of vision. Use the hip momentum to throw a low sweeping kick to his forward ankle. Whether you succeed in hitting his ankle, or he succeeds in lifting his knee, the combination stays the same. Lower the kicking foot while you keep the circular momentum into a drop spin-back hook kick. Kick the side of the knee of the rear leg on which he his standing or where he has his body weight, and follow-up.

Figure 5.15.13

Figure 5.15.14

Figure 5.15.15

Figure 5.15.16

Figure 5.15.17

Figure 5.15.18

These images illustrate a classic combination leading to a sweep kick.

Specific Training

- Train on the heavy bag, but for speed, hitting at marked groin level.
- Practice kicking a medicine-ball and/or a basketball: Kick fast to send it as far as possible (See Figure 5.15.19).

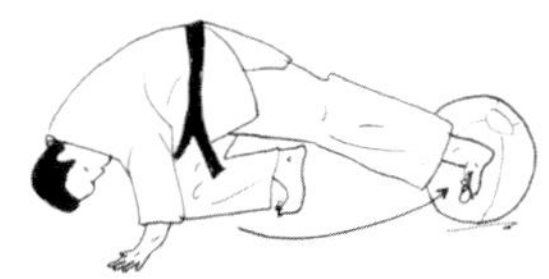

Figure 5.15.19
Drill for speed, power and precision. Hard, but fun!

Self-defense

Figures 5.15.20 through 5.15.24 show an interesting use of the kick when you are yourself attacked with a low kick: Either you have been hit by a classical low-kick (Chapter 3, Section 7 and Chapter 8, Section 6) that bent your knee, or you have managed to partially absorb the kick by twisting and bending the knee and getting down on it. In any case, you find yourself spinning back into coiled position for the drop spin-back hook kick. To make use of maximum power you kick the vital points on his rear leg with your heel: the knee, the calf or the ankle. Follow-up with body or head kicks when he falls down.

Figure 5.15.20

Figure 5.15.21

Figure 5.15.22

Figure 5.15.23

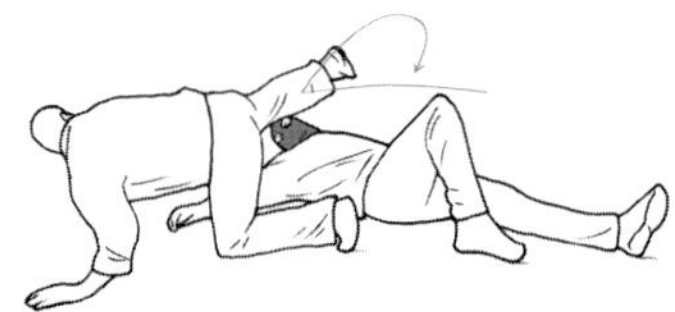

Figure 5.15.24
A great counter to a low kick.

5.16 The Drop Spin-back Downward High Hook Kick

General

This kick is very similar to the previous drop spin-back hook kick, with the difference being that the trajectory of the kick switches to downwards just before impact. This requires changes in the preparation of the kick: a lower body, a higher leg and a longer twist of the hips during the kick. The kick is not easy to perform, and needs a lot of training to become powerful. It is, however, an extremely surprising kick, and useful for agile fighters who feel comfortable ground fighting. It is a close-combat kick, to the head but from the ground, which needs fast and committed body movements to allow for enough power to inflict damage.

Description

Figures 5.16.1 through 5.16.7 show that in the beginning of the kick—which is identical to that of a regular drop spin-back hook kick—you twist back and go down on the front knee in one smooth, uninterrupted and fast move. The rest of the kick, though, is one bursting and springy twist performed in an explosive way, very much like a flying kick. Just before your knee touches the floor, you already twist in the air in a high circular hook kick, while simultaneously receiving yourself on the hands and keeping the twisting momentum until you find yourself nearly on your back. The apex of the kick is just before connecting with the target, and the heel strikes downward through the target.

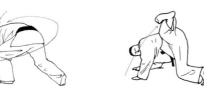

Figure 5.16.1 Figure 5.16.2 Figure 5.16.3 Figure 5.16.4 Figure 5.16.5
Side view of the drop spin-back downward hook kick.

Figure 5.16.6 Figure 5.16.7
Front view: compare the regular and the downward hook kicks.

Key Points

- Try to practice the kick as a jumping kick: the twist is in the air.
- The twisting, kicking and falling down are one simultaneous movement.
- You kick down through the target and use the momentum of your body twist to power the trajectory.
- Always follow-up after the kick, as you are in a vulnerable position. His groin will usually be exposed to further kicking (see Figures 5.16.8 through 5.16.13).
- Always hit with the heel.

Targets

The downward trajectory limits the targets to the vulnerable points of the head alone. The back of the neck is also a target, if the opponent is bent-over.

Typical Application

Figures 5.16.8 through 5.16.13 show the typical offensive application: Make use of an appropriate offensive momentum in close combat. Attack your opponent with an un-telegraphed hopping front leg small roundhouse kick (Chapter 3, Section 2 and Chapter 3, Section 3) to the groin. Whether you score or just cause him to lower his guard is irrelevant to the rest of the combination. As you recoil and lower your kicking leg behind his front leg (using your forward and circular momentum), simultaneously jab his now unguarded face. Whether you connect or just keep him busy lifting back his hands is not important to the rest of the combination: As soon as your foot reaches the floor, throw yourself into the kick, aiming for his face. As your other leg blocks at least his front leg, he will fall to the floor. Keep the twisting momentum of the kick to roll onto your back and kick him in the groin with the other leg while he is still falling.

Figure 5.16.8 Figure 5.16.9 Figure 5.16.10 Figure 5.16.11

Figure 5.16.12 Figure 5.16.13

These images depict a fantastic offensive combination for the springy fighter.

Specific Training

- This kick must be practiced (quite a bit) on a standing bag, in order to drill the twist in the air and the downward trajectory. The standing bag can be held by a partner.
- Always alternate with a regular drop spin-back hook kick (Section 15 of this chapter) when you practice the kick!
- When you have mastered the move on the bag, you must practice on a protected partner or one holding foam focus pads, in order to drill the move at the right distance and on a realistic opponent.

Self-defense

Figures 5.16.14 through 5.16.17 show the use of the kick in defensive mode, after a downward evasion. Evade a power-punching opponent's attack by suddenly twisting down and landing, after your spin-back, onto your front knee. You are already, of course, delivering the drop downward high spin-back hook kick to his face. As this time, you find yourself on the inside of his feet. You don't provoke his fall, but keep your twisting momentum, and, from your back-on-the-floor position, launch a roundhouse kick to his head with the other leg.

Figure 5.16.14

Figure 5.16.15

Figure 5.16.16

Figure 5.16.17

The momentum of the kick allows you to follow up with a powerful ground roundhouse kick.

5.17 The Small Heel Back Hook Kick

General

This is a very simple but effective back kick, although conceivable as a variation of a short spin back hook kick too. It is encountered in some kung fu and pencak silat styles. Basically, it is a short bent leg "hooked-finish" hook kick, delivered usually to the groin of an opponent standing behind you. As the kick comes with a twist of the hips, it is also generally powerful enough to be used toward the solar plexus or the kidneys of an opponent. It is an important and easy kick to master, great for self-defense and close combat. It also teaches you to kick from any range and any position. Is your opponent too close for an efficient hook kick? Hit him with a short one!

Description

Figures 5.17.1 through 5.17.7 show the classic delivery of the kick, as a back kick: You look back and lift the bent leg directly behind you, a little bit like a short back kick. The trajectory of the foot is up and around. Your hips pivot toward the opponent while you hit the target horizontally, and hook into the target.

Figure 5.17.1 Figure 5.17.2 Figure 5.17.3
The side view of the kick.

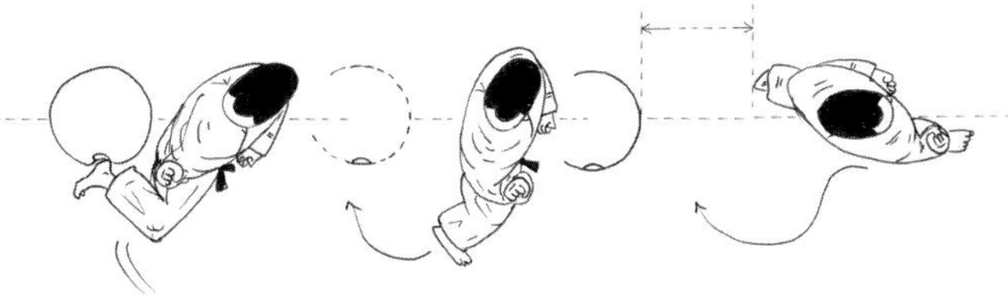

Figure 5.17.4
Overhead view of the kick clearly showing the trajectory.

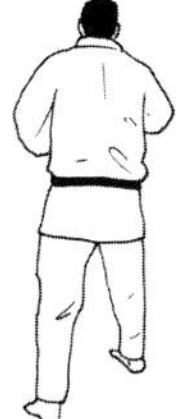

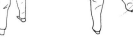

Figure 5.17.5 Figure 5.17.6 Figure 5.17.7
Back view of the kick. Notice how un-telegraphed the kick can be.

Figures 5.17.8 through 5.17.11 show the use of a spin-back variation of the kick after a high backfist to raise the guard.

Figure 5.17.8 Figure 5.17.9 Figure 5.17.10 Figure 5.17.11
Notice how close you are to your opponent at the end of the spin.

Key Points

- You lift the leg back as it is, with no chambering: This is a fast, un-telegraphed kick.
- Most of the power of the kick comes from the hip movement: the leg stays half-bent up to the end. This is very much like a hook punch driven by the body.
- Only at impact do you start hooking the kick into the target.
- Use the heel only as the striking surface.

Targets

- Preferably the groin.
- If the kick has been mastered and is powerful: the solar plexus and the kidneys. It then must be accurate and use the heel only.

Typical Application

Figures 5.17.12 through 5.17.15 show the use of the kick when you find yourself with your back, even if only partially, toward an attacking or counterattacking opponent. For example, your opponent has evaded your high roundhouse by leaning back and has succeeded in putting you off-balance by accelerating your momentum and pushing down your kicking leg. Or, as illustrated, he simply blocks your high hook kick. You find yourself with your back to him as he prepares to counterattack with a reverse punch. Use your accelerated momentum to let your kicking leg rebound off the floor, as if it has hit a spring, and hit your advancing opponent's groin with a small heel back hook kick.

Figure 5.17.12 Figure 5.17.13
These images depict a fast double kick. Let your foot rebound off the floor.

Figure 5.17.14

Figure 5.17.15

Specific Training

It is important to practice this kick on the heavy bag for power and the sense of distance: Stand in fighting stance with your back to the bag but touching it with your front hand extended backward. Explode into the kick, in one move, with no telegraphing, as powerfully as possible (Figures 5.17.16 and 5.17.17).

Figure 5.17.16 Figure 5.17.17
Try to do the drill without looking, but just gauging the distance with the hand.

Self-defense

Of course, as a back kick, it is ideal to use in self-defense situations, when attacked from behind. Figures 5.17.18 through 5.17.20 show the use of the kick against an assailant coming behind you. The kick is fast and easy, and can be used as soon as you have turned your head and seen him. As soon as you have hit his groin, you complete your twist while backfisting him in the now unprotected head.

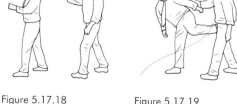

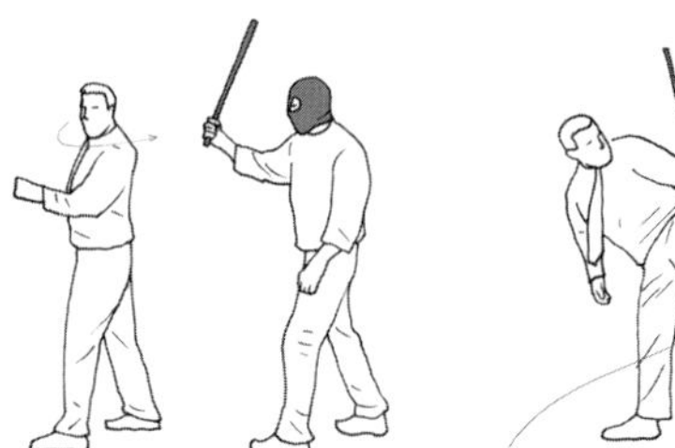

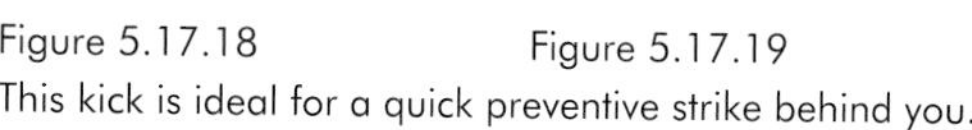

Figure 5.17.18 Figure 5.17.19
This kick is ideal for a quick preventive strike behind you.

Figure 5.17.20

More Advanced Hook Kicks

What follows is a brief review of some more advanced kicks. They are not presented in detail here, as they are beyond the scope of this book.

The Flying Hook Kick

Mawashi ushi tobi geri (karate)

The name of the kick is self-explanatory: it is basically a front leg hook kick delivered while jumping. As with all "flying" kicks, the jumping is not necessarily as high as possible, but also forward, or even backward. This kick is not very powerful, but its angle of attack can be relatively surprising.

A flying hook kick.

The Flying Spin Back Hook Kick

Ura mawashi tobi geri (karate)

This very spectacular and powerful kick is a favorite of action movies, and the bread-and-butter of Taekwondo tournaments, it is a very powerful because of the centrifugal force of a twisting body freed from the constraints of the ground.

The Sacrifice Spin Back Hook Kick

Although very similar to the drop spin-back downward high hook kick (Section 16 of this chapter), this scissor-type kick entails dropping to the floor from very close to the opponent. It is more of a takedown than a full-powered kick.

The Roundhouse Chamber Hook Kick

This is a great feint kick. It is an important kick to master for the kicking fighter, as it keeps the opponent on edge and guessing which kick will develop from any chambered position. The feinting move is self-explanatory here.

The Roundhouse to Spin Back Hook Kick Combination

This is, of course, a natural combination keeping the same circular momentum and accelerating it while kicking with one leg after the other. This is a must-practice combination.

Comparative Tables

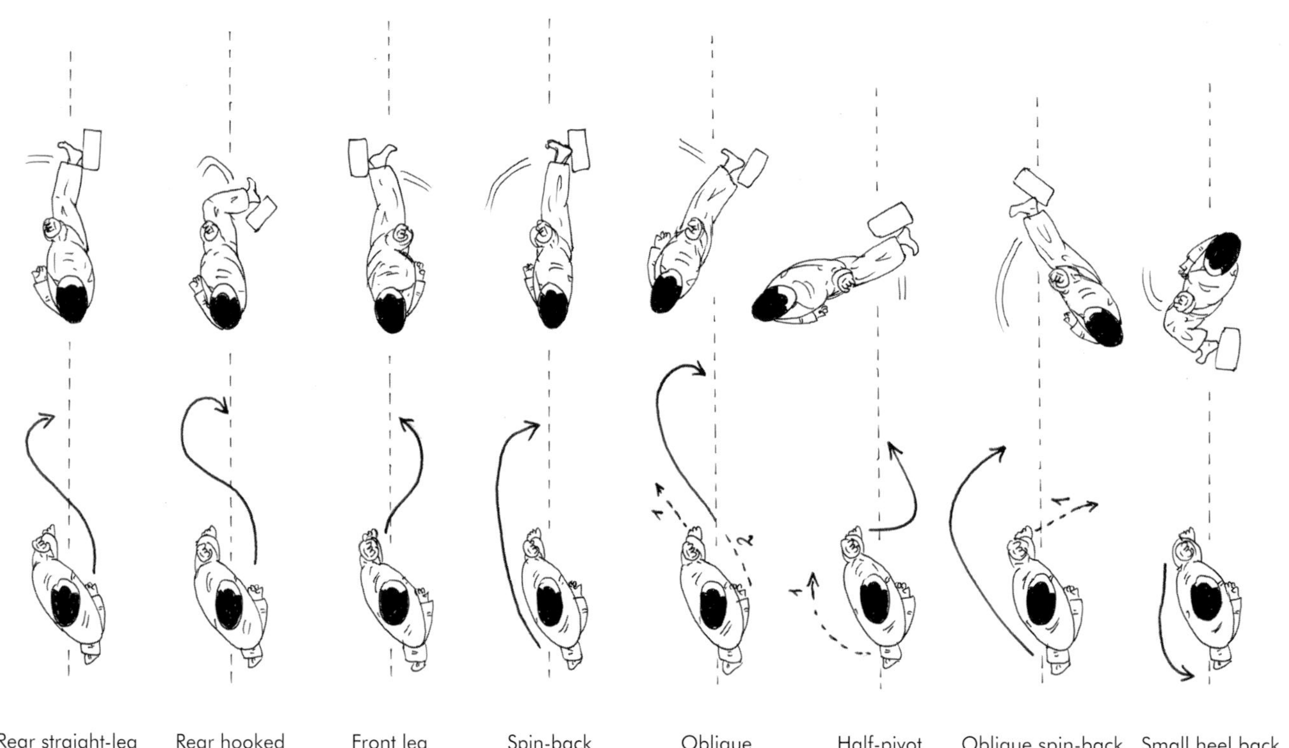

Table 1 — Comparative trajectories of main hook kicks—overhead view.

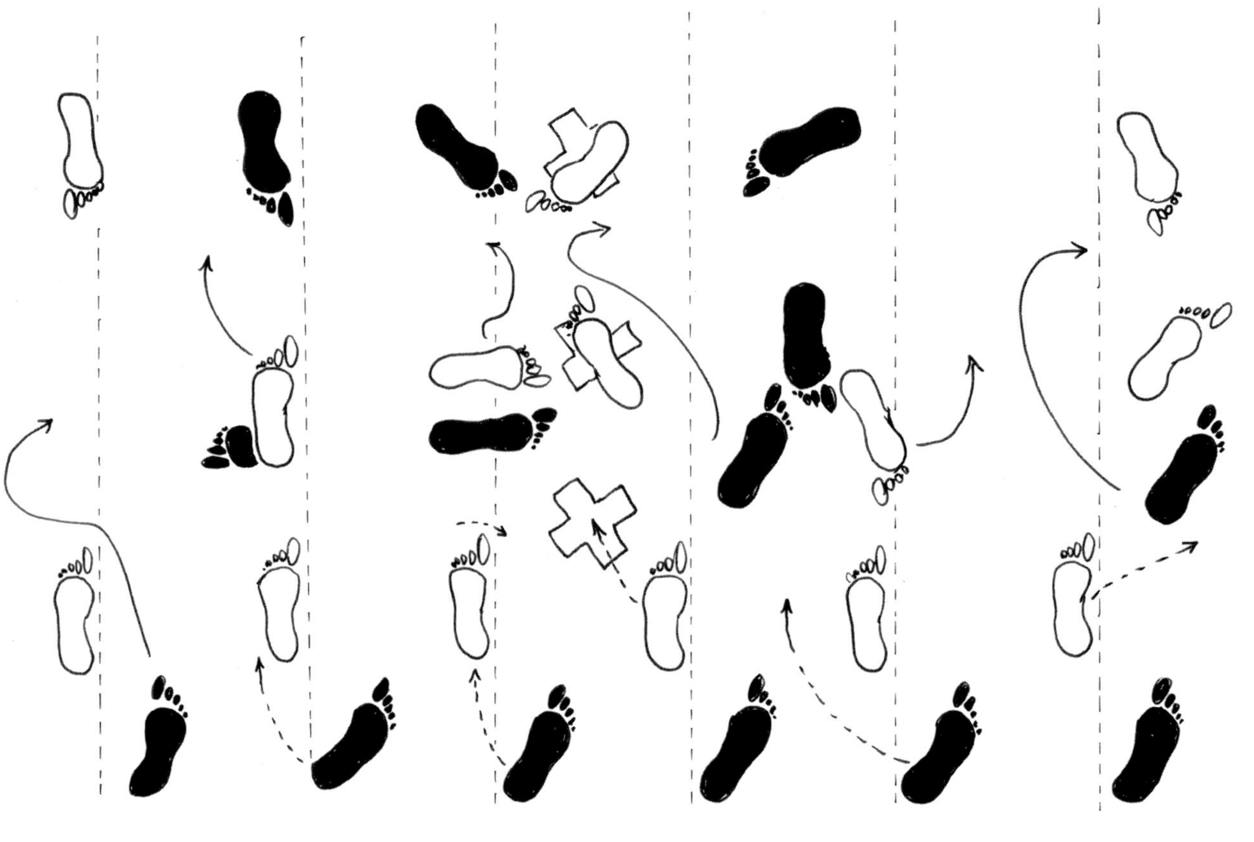

Table 2 — Comparative footwork of various hook kicks.

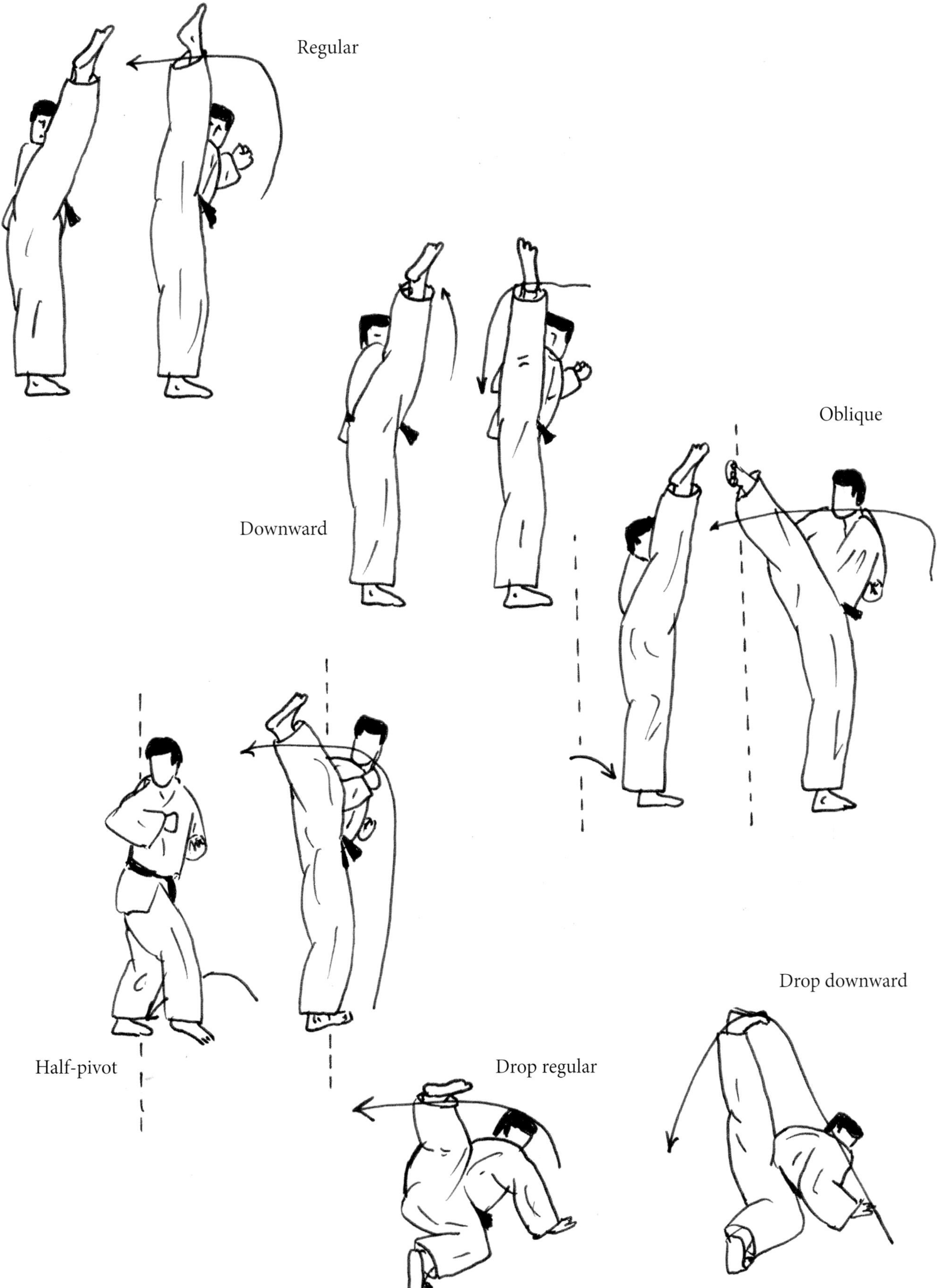

Table 3 — Comparative trajectories of various hook kicks—front view.

CHAPTER SIX

Crescent Kicks

This chapter presents crescent kicks, outside crescent kicks and straight-leg downward kicks. All these kicks are straight leg kicks surprisingly coming to the opponent from his side or overhead. These kicks are common to all ancient traditional styles, but not very much in use in modern sporting events. However, they are very useful kicks—fast and powerful, especially at close range—and wrongly underused. Of course, their close combat applications make them perfect kicks for self-defense.

Some of the typical uses presented will suggest practical applications for the reader's practice.

6.1 The Crescent Kick

Mikazuki geri / Soto mikazuki geri / Aori geri (karate), *Nae mandal / Bandal cha gi* (taekwondo), *Yue liang jiao* (kung fu), *Meia lua de frente* (capoeira), *Thuong dao son / Dao phuong cuoc* (viet vo dao)

General

The crescent kick is found in nearly all fighting styles, as it is probably the most versatile of all kicks: It can be used against a very close opponent, or at regular kicking distance. It can be delivered as a full power kick, with a 180 degree pivot of the hips, or as a fast, nearly straight front leg kick. It can be used as a full-fledged attack, or as a block of an incoming punch or kick (See Figures 6.1.27 through 6.1.29). It can be used to open or weaken an opponent's guard. It can be used against nearly all targets, from the face down to the groin, and including the limbs. It is a very common kick in most styles, ever-present in the capoeira "game" and taekwondo contests, very frequent in many kung fu styles, and the third most-encountered kick in traditional karate forms, after the front and side kick.

Figures 6.1.1 through 6.1.10 show the way it is practiced in the *Heian Sandan* and *Heian Godan* forms of Shotokan-ryu karate.

Figure 6.1.1

Figure 6.1.2

Figure 6.1.3

Figure 6.1.4

Figure 6.1.5

This kata excerpt shows a crescent kick found in the Heian Sandan kata.

Figure 6.1.6

Figure 6.1.7

Figure 6.1.8

Figure 6.1.9

Figure 6.1.10

This kata excerpt shows two crescent kicks found in the Heian Godan kata.

This is also the way, in our opinion, that it should be practiced in the beginning, in order to impart the right feeling of how to use the hips to generate power in this kick (Figures 6.1.11 through 6.1.16). Later on, the skilled practitioner will use the same power generating principles in a much shorter and faster kick (See Figures 6.1.18 through 6.1.26).

Description

Figures 6.1.11 through 6.1.17 show the traditional full-power crescent kick: From a side horse stance (*Kiba dachi*—karate, *Ma bu*—kung fu), extend the lead hand forward and hit the palm of the hand with the plant of the foot in a straight movement, while pivoting 180 degrees with the hips. When you lower the leg, you are in a side horse stance again, but with the other side forward.

Figure 6.1.11

Figure 6.1.12

Figure 6.1.13

Figure 6.1.14

Figure 6.1.15

Figure 6.1.16

These illustrations depict a front and side view of a crescent kick.

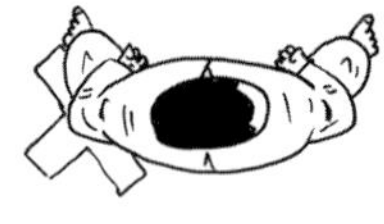

Figure 6.1.17
An overhead view of the crescent kick.

Once you have "mastered" the full-power traditional kick, start working on the following variation (of course, keep practicing the traditional one as well!). You now start from a fighting stance and launch your rear leg forward, nearly straight, in an arc with an apex that occurs just as it passes in front of your mid-line (see Figures 6.1.19 through 6.1.22 and 6.1.24 through 6.1.26). You hit the target from the side, outward to inwards. You kick through the target, and after impact start to bend the leg, which can then be lowered in front, or into its original rear position. The wideness of the arc traveled by the foot is up to you: The wider it is, the more power you pack into the kick, but the longer it has to travel and the earlier it can be detected. If the arc is minimal, like a straight leg front kick with an added small sideward shift at the end, the kick will be less powerful, but very fast and very difficult to detect because its trajectory is mostly out of your opponent's vision range. It is key for the kicking fighter to practice both extremes, and be able to choose in a fight the amount of "arc" suitable to the situation.

Figure 6.1.18 Figure 6.1.19 Figure 6.1.20 Figure 6.1.21 Figure 6.1.22
The front view of the accelerated crescent kick.

Figure 6.1.23 Figure 6.1.24 Figure 6.1.25 Figure 6.1.26
The side view of the accelerated crescent kick.

As already mentioned, the kick is great to attack extended limbs. Figures 6.1.27 through 6.1.29 show its use to open an opponent's guard by hurting the elbow joint, to stop and block a front kick by attacking the knee joint, and to block a punch while inflicting pain to the arm muscles. Certain styles, capoeira among them, emphasize a coiling of the plant of the foot when attacking the arm, in such a way that the foot somewhat molds itself around the attacked limb and "catches" it slightly.

Figure 6.1.27 Figure 6.1.28 Figure 6.1.29
Three different crescent kick limb attacks.

Figures 6.1.30 through 6.1.33 show the execution of the kick to attack the guard of the opponent.

Figure 6.1.30 Figure 6.1.31 Figure 6.1.32 Figure 6.1.33
These images show a crescent kick being used to attack an opponent's guard.

Figures 6.1.34 and 6.1.35 illustrate how close to the opponent this kick can be effectively delivered.

Figure 6.1.34 Figure 6.1.35
These images show the crescent kick's efficacy in close-quarters fighting.

Key Points

- The hips are generating the power of the kick; the leg is just the extension of the hips. Always use the hips to pack as much power as possible into the kick, even if it is a "fast" kick.
- Pivot on your standing foot while kicking: from a 1/4 turn pivot in the "fast" kick, to a 1/2 turn pivot in the traditional execution.
- Always kick through the target. This is a kick that lends itself too easily to a "slapping" version with no follow-through impact.
- This kick brings you closer to the opponent than most kicks: Keep your guard up.

Targets

As mentioned, the crescent kick can be used on most targets, especially in its powerful version: the head from all sides, the upper and lower back, the ribs and solar plexus, the groin, the knees, the arms from all sides from the wrists to the shoulders, and more.

Typical Application

The following images show a very efficient application that we like very much, one that is very efficient against a "standing" opponent, or one who likes to time-jab an incoming opponent. This application also shows how the crescent kick can be used against a very close opponent. The key to this combination lies in the explosiveness of your sudden lunge forward, as you stand in opposite stance to your opponent. As you burst forward, you use your front hand to control his lead hand, negate any possibility of a jab, and keep his attention focused there (Figure 6.1.37). While still in your forward momentum, you launch a full power rear leg crescent kick to the side of his face (Figure 6.1.38). You kick through and use your kicking momentum to keep pivoting while lowering your leg (Figure 6.1.39). Keep turning and accelerating to deliver a spin-back knife hand (or hammer fist) strike to the side of his neck (Figure 6.1.40). Hit through and keep turning with your momentum (Figure 6.1.41) to finish him off with a roundhouse kick (same leg as the crescent kick), which is basically a very powerful 360 spin-back roundhouse kick (Chapter 3, Section 11). See Figure 6.1.42.

Figure 6.1.36

Figure 6.1.37

Figure 6.1.38

Figure 6.1.39

Figure 6.1.40 Figure 6.1.41 Figure 6.1.42
Your explosive advance will allow you to control your opponent while you set up your crescent kick. A quick succession of different follow-up attacks will allow you to press your advantage.

As this kick is very versatile, here is another typical application, showing its use as a guard-opening, joint-attacking technique. One should keep in mind that attacks to the guard or limbs will tire the opponent and cause his guard to lower or to recoil from further attacks. The following images show such an application, especially useful against opponents with a guard reaching "far out." You attack his elbow straight out from the fighting stance, making sure you do not telegraph your intentions (Figure 6.1.44). You recoil the leg, without lowering it, into a side kick chambering (Figure 6.1.45), and you deliver a *hopping* side kick or back side kick to the body (Figure 6.1.46). If your opponent has stepped back enough to dilute the power of the kick, you find yourself, after lowering the kicking leg, facing him in the same stance, but with the other side forward (Figure 6.1.47). You immediately launch the same crescent kick attack, with the other leg, and to his other elbow (Figure 6.1.48). Rare are the fighters able to learn from their mistakes in the middle of a fight! This time, lower the leg while keeping the circular momentum (Figure 6.1.49), and start a spin-back hook kick to the head (Figure 6.1.50).

Figure 6.1.43 Figure 6.1.44 Figure 6.1.45 Figure 6.1.46

Figure 6.1.47 Figure 6.1.48 Figure 6.1.49 Figure 6.1.50
The crescent kick is an effective guard-opening, joint-attacking technique. An effectively delivered technique can often be successfully repeated in the heat of a fight.

Specific Training

- This kick requires a lot of training in order to impart maximum power in all the kick's variations. It is important to train at several ranges, and with a wide and a narrow circular trajectory.
- Always practice the traditional full power crescent kick as a part of your crescent kick training routines.
- Figures 6.1.51 through 6.1.53 show several possible drills: kicking over a partner's extended arm at several heights for height, speed and technique; kicking the heavy bag for power; kicking the speed ball over a chair for wide arc and precision; kicking a medicine-ball over a standing bag or held by partner for height, precision and power.

Figure 6.1.51

Figure 6.1.52

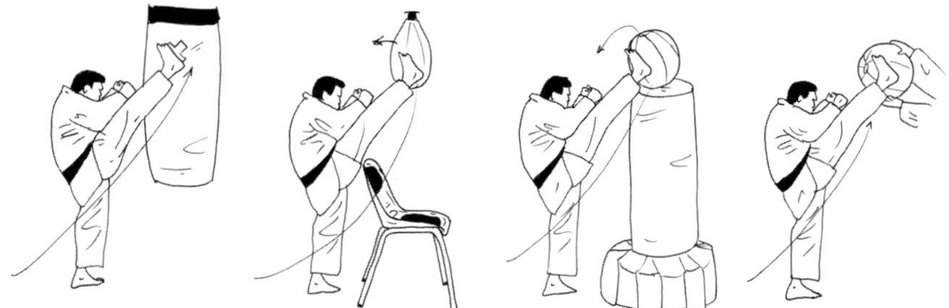

Figure 6.1.53
These illustrations show a variety of drills designed to improve a range of attributes.

- Figure 6.1.54 shows a drill for speed and distance management: touch the heavy bag with the extended front hand and kick an imaginary, very close opponent with maximum speed, *without touching the bag.*

Figure 6.1.54
This is a drill for improving speed and distance management.

- Figure 6.1.55 shows a drill for the feeling of maximum power into the kick: kick the bag with a 270 degrees circular crescent kick, from a side position with the heavy bag on your outside. This is also a drill for kicking from all positions.

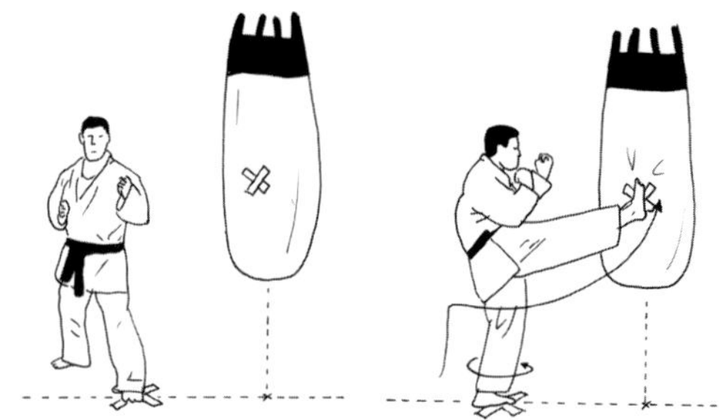

Figure 6.1.55
This is a drill for developing power.

Self-defense

Here again, because of the versatility of the kick, we present two applications of the crescent kick. The images that follow illustrate the classic use of the crescent kick against the knife-wielding arm of an assailant. This is not an easy move to succeed with—always remember that handling an armed opponent is extremely dangerous! Taking the initiative and being aggressive does give you an important element of surprise, however. You attack the wrist or elbow of the knife hand with a full power crescent kick, using the side of the shoe for maximum damage (Figure 6.1.57). The full power of the kick will take you into a spin-back that is critical to develop as far as possible from the opponent. Lower the leg close to you (Figure 6.1.58), and not close to the assailant! You then deliver a spin-back bent-body side kick (Chapter 2, Section 5, and Chapter 2, Section 9), with the other leg, to his forward knee (Figure 6.1.59). Keep the body away and kick through the knee to inflict real damage (Figure 6.1.60). Lower the leg and continue the circular momentum to deliver a full power low kick (low straight-leg roundhouse, Chapter 3, Section 7) to the side of the same knee (Figure 6.1.61).

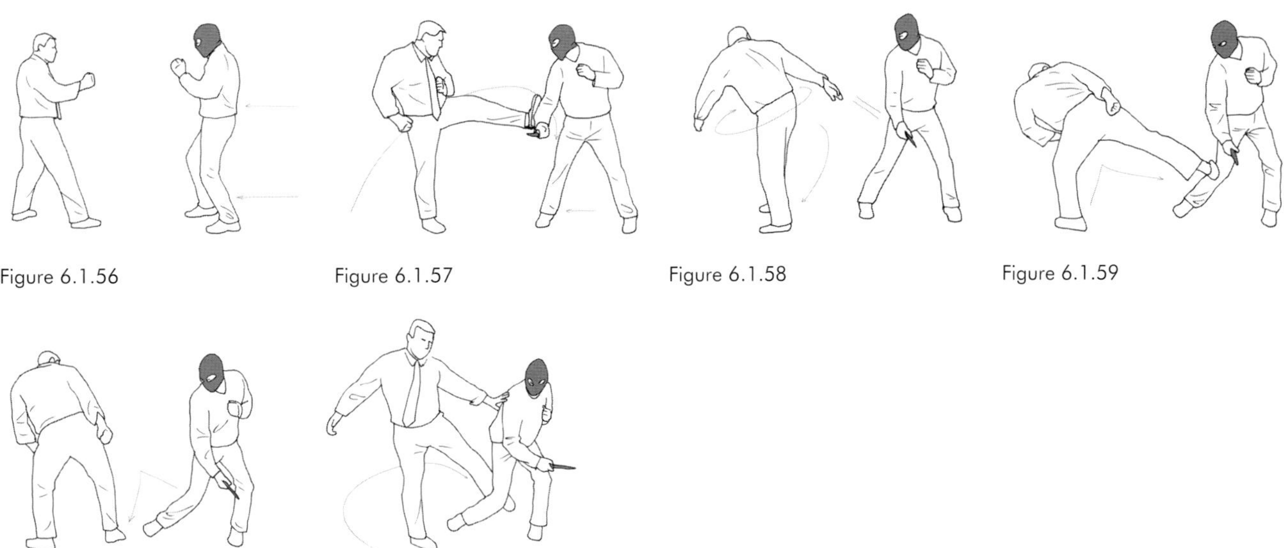

Figure 6.1.56 Figure 6.1.57 Figure 6.1.58 Figure 6.1.59

Figure 6.1.60 Figure 6.1.61

Focus first on the attacker's weapon hand with a classic crescent kick, and then deliver a spin-back bent body side kick to the attacker's knee.

The second application, illustrated in the following images, shows the use of the kick in very close combat. The use of high kicks at very close range is always a surprise. You duck your assailant's jab with a small side-step/duck to the outside, while block-trapping the attacking hand for control (Figures 6.1.63 and 6.1.64). In an uninterrupted movement, you are already launching a high crescent kick to the side of his head (Figure 6.1.65). This is a short and fast move.

Figure 6.1.62 Figure 6.1.63 Figure 6.1.64 Figure 6.1.65

This quick move contains the element of surprise, as a high kick is not expected in close quarters fighting.

6.2 The Front Leg Crescent Kick

General

The front leg crescent kick is a very fast and useful kick, but it is much less powerful than the traditional rear leg crescent kick. It is easy to understand, as the arc is much narrower and there is no room for a lot of hip pivot. It is, however, a very efficient kick for starting a combination attack, to feint and harass, or to wear down an opponent's guard. The kick, because of its lack of power, is only effective as a block, a guard mover or a head kick. It scores easily, but is generally not enough in itself.

Description

The traditional way to practice the front leg crescent kick is as follows. Bring your rear foot forward in a small step that brings it to the front foot level or a little bit further forward (Figure 6.2.2). Immediately launch the formerly front leg in a straight arc toward the head level of an imaginary opponent in front of you (Figure 6.2.3). Kick through and start bending and lowering the leg (Figure 6.2.4). Of course, like all front leg kicks, the kick can be delivered with a hop instead of a step, with the rear foot replacing the raising front foot. Like the regular crescent kick, the wideness of the arc can be varied according to the circumstances, but much less as the hips are already in position from the beginning.

Figure 6.2.1 Figure 6.2.2 Figure 6.2.3 Figure 6.2.4
These illustrations depict a front view of a front leg crescent kick.

Figure 6.2.5 Figure 6.2.6 Figure 6.2.7
These illustrations depict a side view of a front leg crescent kick.

Key Points

- Do not telegraph your step/hop forward. Especially keep head level steady, and "explode" forward with no warning.
- As the kick lacks in power, it is extremely important to kick through the target.
- Although the range is limited, do use the hips in the kick as much as possible.
- You are close to the opponent—keep your guard up.
- Always follow-up—this is generally not a single kick move.

Targets

The only worthwhile targets are the head and groin, as well as the upper limb joints (for harassment).

Typical Application

The following illustrations show a very typical use of the kick. In opposite stances, feint a reverse punch while hopping forward, in order to draw your opponent's attention to his lower inside and to give your own hips some pivoting room. Hit his guard from the outside with your front leg crescent kick (Figure 6.2.9). Lower your kicking leg forcefully in a rebounding motion: the foot hits the floor as if it was a spring and lifts right back (Figure 6.2.10). Your hips pivot back while your leg lifts in an *outside crescent kick* (Section 3 of this chapter) to the side of his face (Figure 6.2.11). If necessary, hop forward *while* kicking to close the distance. Hit through the target and lower your leg to his outside. Note that you are covered even if he tries to jab you. Simultaneously with your lowering the leg, keep the momentum and deliver a power reverse punch to his face with full hip pivot (Figure 6.2.12). You then sweep his front leg, in the direction of his toes (*De ashi barai*—judo), while controlling his lead arm and use it to pull him down (Figure 6.2.13). While he's falling, lift your other leg for a stomp kick, or a downward heel kick (Section 5 of this chapter). See Figure 6.2.14.

Figure 6.2.8

Figure 6.2.9

Figure 6.2.10

Figure 6.2.11

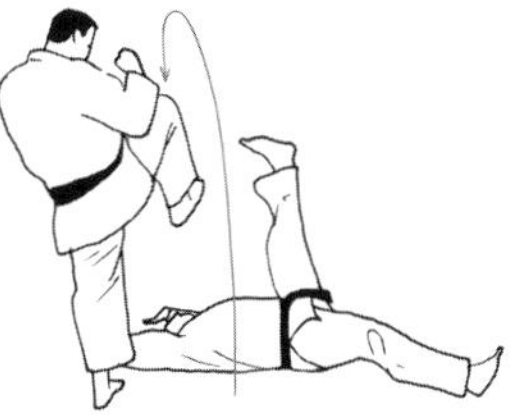

Figure 6.2.12 Figure 6.2.13 Figure 6.2.14
Pairing two opposing front leg crescent kicks in series is a typical (and effective) application of this kick.

Specific Training

- The kick must be practiced for speed on the heavy bag, while starting from different ranges.
- Flexibility is key for speed in this kick: work on the front splits and back stretch for example.
- As the kick is not stand-alone, practice combinations (see Figures 6.2.8 through 6.2.14) in shadow boxing, with a partner and on the bag.

Self-defense

The following illustrations show a very efficient and surprising use of the kick at very close range and a very painful follow-up. As an assailant gets a hold of your hand (with his same hand), always react immediately, as he is probably following up with something nastier and has limited your ability to react (Figure 6.2.15). Rotate your hand clockwise up around his wrist in the classic hold reversal, while moving slightly to his outside (Figure 6.2.16). Immediately launch a crescent kick to the (blind) side of his head, while keeping hold of his wrist (Figure 6.2.17). Lower your leg forcefully *over* his extended arm while pulling his wrist. "Sit" (horse stance) on his extended arm while using his wrist to place his elbow joint up. Pull up on the wrist while sitting down on the elbow to control him or dislocate the joint (Figure 6.2.18). You can then upward hook back kick him in the face (Chapter 4, Section 7). See Figure 6.2.19.

Figure 6.2.15 Figure 6.2.16 Figure 6.2.17 Figure 6.2.18 Figure 6.2.19
Turn the tables on a wrist-grabbing opponent with a hold reversal and immediately launch a front leg crescent kick to his head, continuing down with your leg to trap and control his arm. Finish up with an upward hook back kick to his face.

6.3 The Outside Crescent Kick

Gyacku mikazuki geri / Sokuto mikazuki geri / Ura mikazuki geri / Uchi mikazuki geri (karate), *Biteulo / Mandal cha gi* (taekwondo), *Queixada* (capoeira), *Thuong tao phong* (viet vo dao), *Pan toi* (kung fu)

General

The outside crescent kick just travels the inverse trajectory of the crescent kick and strikes the target in front of you from your inside to your outside. In its "short and fast" version, it is more powerful than the fast crescent kick because of the hip movement always necessary to perform the kick. It is also a surprising kick, as it comes from outside your opponent's vision field if delivered from close enough, and comes in an "unnatural" direction. Just like for the crescent kick, the outside crescent can be delivered with a wide or a narrow arc, and all variations in between. The kick connects with the blade and/or the upper part of the foot. Just like with the crescent kick, the outside crescent can also be used to block, to harass or remove a guard or to attack the limbs; it is used from afar or in close combat.

Description

The following illustrations show the kick in its traditional way: You bring your rear leg forward just like for an oblique front kick (Chapter 1 Section 12), knee chambered high, but with the leg and hips turned to your inside (Figure 6.3.2). You already pivot on your foot while extending the kicking leg to your inside (Figure 6.3.3). You then pivot back with your hips while completing the extension of the leg and kicking from your inside outwards (Figure 6.3.4). The full extension of the leg and the apex of your circular movement should coincide with impact, just as the leg passes in front of you. You kick through the target and then start to bend and lower the leg (Figure 6.3.5).

Figure 6.3.1 Figure 6.3.2 Figure 6.3.3 Figure 6.3.4 Figure 6.3.5
These illustrations depict a front view of an outside crescent kick.

Figure 6.3.6 Figure 6.3.7 Figure 6.3.8 Figure 6.3.9
These illustrations depict a side view of an outside crescent kick.

Figure 6.3.10 Figure 6.3.11
These images show the crescent kick's efficacy in close-quarters fighting.

Figures 6.3.12 through 6.3.15 show the delivery of the kick against an opponent's guard.

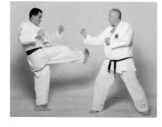

Figure 6.3.12 Figure 6.3.13 Figure 6.3.14 Figure 6.3.15
These images show an outside crescent kick used against an opponent's guard.

Figures 6.3.16 through 6.3.18 show the use of the kick as an attack to the head from a close distance.

Figure 6.3.16

Figure 6.3.17

Figure 6.3.18

These images show a close-range outside crescent kick used to attack an opponent's head.

Key Points

- The leg is an extension of the hips: the circular movement comes from the hips.
- Keep your guard up as it is a kick that brings you closer to your opponent than most kicks.
- Always kick through the target.
- You need to pivot on your standing foot to allow for the hip movement.
- Practice the wide and the narrow arc versions.

Targets

Typical targets include the limbs, the face and the groin. With a wide arc, the upper and lower back are also targets.

Typical Application

The following illustrations show a perfect set-up for this kick, which brings it as it should: from up close and from an unexpected direction. Get close to the opponent with a classic jab/cross combination (*Kizami tsuki / Gyacku tsuki*—karate) to the face (Figures 6.3.20 and 6.3.21). Your high reverse punch (cross) is delivered purposely to the outside of his head to cause him to overblock, and your fist lingers more than necessary to block his field of vision while keeping his attention to his outside (Figure 6.3.22). This reverse punch (*Gyacku tsuki*—karate) also frees your hips and rear leg for an outside crescent kick to the inside of his head (Figure 6.3.23).

Figure 6.3.19

Figure 6.3.20

Figure 6.3.21

Figure 6.3.22

Figure 6.3.23

This outside crescent kick application is launched from close quarters and will be an unpleasant surprise for the opponent who has been misdirected by your initial jab/cross combination.

Specific Training

- All training tips for the crescent kicks are valid, just performed in the opposite direction. Figure 6.3.24 shows the kicking over a partner's hand drill, the heavy bag kicking over a chair drill, and medicine ball kicking drill.

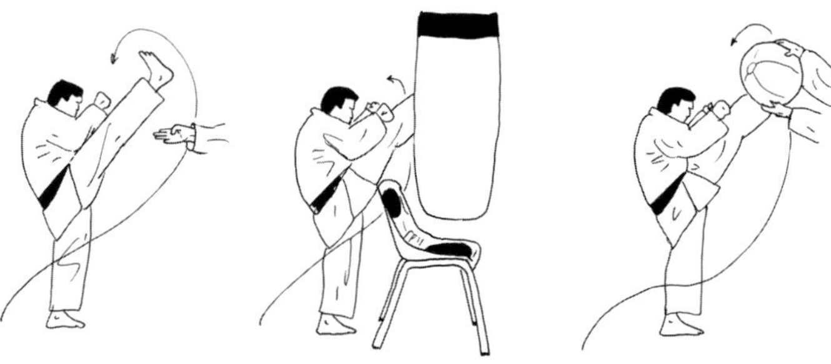

Figure 6.3.24
These illustrations show a small selection of training techniques that will help you develop your outside crescent kick aptitude.

- Always practice the narrow and wide arc variations.
- Figures 6.3.25 through 6.3.28 show a fighter practicing the kick on striking pads held by a moving partner.

Figure 6.3.25

Figure 6.3.26

Figure 6.3.27

Figure 6.3.28

Have a partner hold striking pads so that you can practice the kick at full strength to develop power and speed.

Self-defense

The following illustrations show a limb attack to open an assailant's guard and weaken his hold on a weapon. The side of a shoe is usually hard and can cause pain and damage. As mentioned, the kick is surprising as your rear leg, situated on his outside, suddenly attacks his lead hand from *his inside*, the opposite direction it should come from (Figure 6.3.30). Make use of the momentum to lower your leg while freeing your weight from your other leg and keep the general circular direction with a rear leg roundhouse (Chapter 3, Sections 1 and 2) to his groin (Figure 6.3.31). Lower the kicking leg to his inside, while controlling his armed elbow from the outside and punching him in his open kidneys or lower ribs (Figure 6.3.32). Keep pivoting while launching a crescent kick (Section 1 of this chapter) if he stays erect or a downward heel kick (Section 5 of this chapter) if he bends down (Figure 6.3.33).

Figure 6.3.29

Figure 6.3.30

Figure 6.3.31

Figure 6.3.32

Figure 6.3.33
Use an outside crescent kick to unexpectedly knock your opponent's weapon away and open him up for a series of devastating strikes.

6.4 The Front Leg Outside Crescent Kick

General

The front leg version of the outside crescent kick is very fast and generally unexpected, but of course lacks in power. However, this is a great kick for feinting, harassing and opening the guard, and as a first kick in a combination. All what was said about the front leg crescent kick is true here as well.

Like all front leg kicks, the outside crescent kick can be delivered after different footwork patterns. As a direct front leg kick from the fighting stance, it is not very effective.

Description

Figures 6.4.1 through 6.4.5 show the kick delivered after half-a-step: the rear foot comes forward at the front foot level, and then the front leg goes up into the kick.

Figure 6.4.1

Figure 6.4.2

Figure 6.4.3

Figure 6.4.4

Figure 6.4.5

These illustrations depict a front view of a front leg outside crescent kick.

Figures 6.4.6 through 6.4.9 show the classical forward hop in which the rear foot comes to replace the already lifting front foot. Fast, but make sure you do not jump *up*!

Figure 6.4.6

Figure 6.4.7

Figure 6.4.8

Figure 6.4.9

These illustrations depict a side view of a front leg outside crescent kick, featuring a hop.

Figures 6.4.10 through 6.4.12 show the cross step which is slower, but allows for a more powerful kick with the hips pivot and a wider arc. You step with the rear foot behind the front foot!

Figure 6.4.10

Figure 6.4.11

Figure 6.4.12

These illustrations depict a side view of a front leg outside crescent kick, featuring a cross step.

Figures 6.4.13 through 6.4.17 show the use of the kick in its narrow arc version to open the guard of an opposite stance opponent, and then using the distraction and the momentum of the kick to deliver a ridgehand strike (*Haito uchi*—karate) to the neck.

Figure 6.4.13

Figure 6.4.14

Figure 6.4.15

Figure 6.4.16

Figure 6.4.17

These images show a front leg outside crescent kick used to open the guard of an opposite stance opponent.

Key Points

All key points are similar to those of the front leg crescent kick (see Section 2 of this chapter) and those of the regular outside crescent kick (see Section 3 of this chapter).

Remember that when stepping/hopping forward, it is imperative not to telegraph your move by changing your head height or moving any part of your upper body.

Targets

Primary targets are the head or groin. The limbs may be targeted for harassment and guard opening purposes.

Typical Application

The following images show a great combination using the front leg outside crescent kick as a feint and guard opener. From an opposite stance to your opponent you surge forward with a hopping front leg outside crescent kick to the inside of his front arm (Figure 6.4.19). Always kick hard, as a kick and not as a sweep! This should hurt. As you lower the leg, you jab to the now guard-less face (Figure 6.4.20), and immediately re-launch an identical front leg outside crescent kick to the face or guard of the retreating opponent (Figure 6.4.21). This time, make use of the arc of the circular kick to turn the kick into a front leg sweep, ideally without lowering to the floor: You simply continue the arc downward and sweep the front leg of your hurt and/or retreating opponent (Figure 6.4.22). This maneuver (*De ashi barai*—judo) is usually easy to perform, as the opponent is leaning backward from your assault and does not have his weight on the front leg. Your sweep has, at least, lifted his front leg while setting him off-balance. Lower your sweeping foot and jab him again (*Kizami tsuki*—karate) and immediately reverse punch him (*Gyacku tsuki*—karate) in the face (Figure 6.4.23). Grip him with your punching hand, and go forward with your rear leg to execute a full sweep of the leg he is still standing on (*O soto gari*—judo). See Figure 6.4.25. As he falls down, hard, use the same leg for a downward heel kick (see Section 5 of this chapter).

Figure 6.4.18 Figure 6.4.19 Figure 6.4.20 Figure 6.4.21

Figure 6.4.22 Figure 6.4.23 Figure 6.4.24 Figure 6.4.25

Open your opponent's guard with a front leg outside crescent kick, and follow up with a jab to the unguarded face. Fire off another front leg outside crescent kick to the face or guard before transitioning to an off-balancing sweep. Place another jab and punch before taking him down with a second sweep. Optionally finish the confrontation with a downward heel kick.

Specific Training

All drills of the front leg crescent kick and of the rear leg outside crescent kick are relevant here. Remember that the kick is a speed kick: you have to work on flexibility, footwork and speed.

Practice on the heavy bag for speed and lack of telegraphing (burst out!), from different ranges, marked on the floor.

Self-defense

The following illustrations show a self-defense application of the principles that the kick is fast, can be used surprisingly at close range, and should be the first of a combination. As your assailant steps in to punch you, hop forward in opposite stance (to his inside) and block instead of retreating as he expects (Figure 6.4.27). Your hop liberates the front leg for a close-range outside crescent kick to the head (Figure 6.4.28). Kick through and make use of the momentum to lower the leg behind you and continue the circular movement into a spin-back. As you lower the leg and continue to pivot, deliver a circular punch to the side of his face, basically a front hand hook delivered from the hips and with the whole body (*Mawashi tsuki*—karate). See Figure 6.4.29. Punch through, continue the spin-back into a bent-body (as you are close) spin-back hook kick to the head (Figure 6.4.30).

Figure 6.4.26 Figure 6.4.27 Figure 6.4.28 Figure 6.4.29 Figure 6.4.30

Intercept a punch with an unexpected advancing block, and counter with a close-range front leg outside crescent kick to the head. Follow up with a hook to the face, and finish the confrontation with a spin back hook kick to the head.

6.5 The Downward Heel Kick

Kakato otoshi geri (karate), *Naeryeo chagi* (taekwondo), *Te kook* (muay thai), Axe kick / Hatchet kick (common names), *Ono geri* (Ninjutsu)

General

The downward heel kick is a somewhat denigrated kick which does not receive the interest it deserves. It is basically a straight leg kick striking downwards from the apex of the highest leg lift possible. It is of course the ideal kick to hit a bent, kneeling, falling or prone opponent, as the maximum power will be achieved after longest possible acceleration (See Figures 6.5.1 and 6.5.2). This kick is the most used finishing move after a sweep or takedown in karate competition. It was a very typical move of the great French champion of the 1970s, Dominique Valera. The kick is also useful though on a standing opponent, as it is very surprising and difficult to deal with: standing fighters do not expect to be *kicked* from above, as a matter of routine. In that case, the kick is generally the first kick of a combination, a harassing tactic, a feint, a guard opener or an attack to the joints and limbs. In order to execute the downward kicking move, the leg must be lifted swiftly and straight (maximum power at maximum distance from the hips); This can be executed either as a crescent arc, an outside crescent arc, or a straight leg front lift. In general, the front lift is not relevant, as the target to be hit is likely in the way of the raising leg. Needless to point out then, that the downward heel kick is the ideal kick coming after a crescent kick or an outside crescent kick.

Figure 6.5.1

Figure 6.5.2

The downward heel kick is an ideal kick to hit a bent, kneeling, falling or prone opponent.

Description

The following images show the delivery of the kick from a crescent lift and from an outside crescent lift. You should hit with the back of the heel, and always kick through the target. Slow the acceleration of the downward momentum only *after* you have hit through the target. As mentioned, the kick at its maximum power, as a finishing or one-is-enough-kick, will only be when delivered to a "lower" opponent: Figures 6.5.3 through 6.5.6 depict the kick on a kneeling or standing up opponent, and Figures 6.5.7 through 6.5.10 depict the kick on a falling/prone opponent.

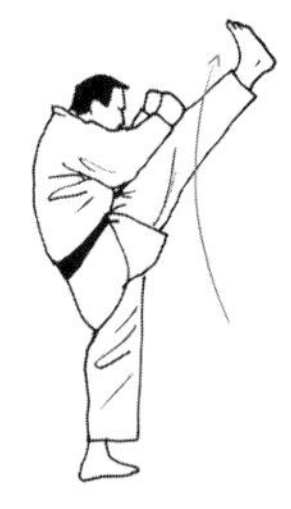

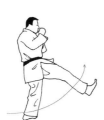

Figure 6.5.3 Figure 6.5.4 Figure 6.5.5 Figure 6.5.6

Side view of the downward heel kick geared toward striking a kneeling or standing opponent.

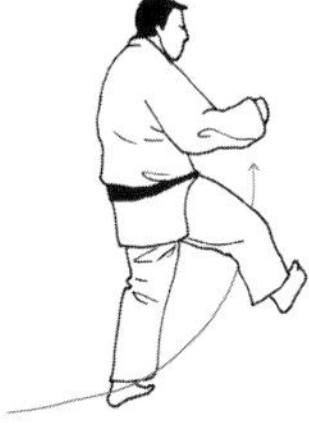

Figure 6.5.7 Figure 6.5.8 Figure 6.5.9 Figure 6.5.10

Side view of the downward heel kick geared toward striking a falling or prone opponent.

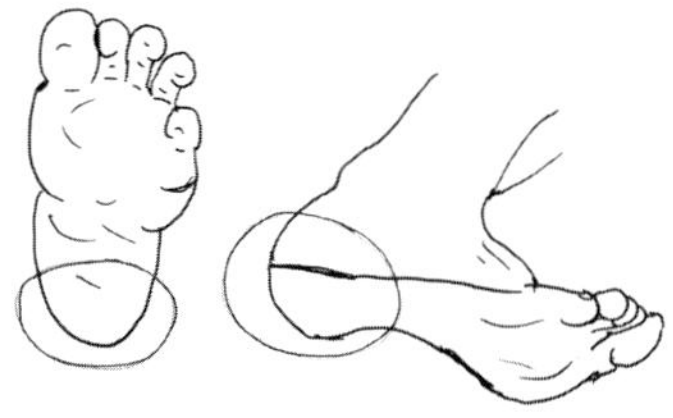

Figure 6.5.11
This is the part of the foot that makes contact during the execution of a downward heel kick.

Figures 6.5.12 through 6.5.15 show a classical use of the kick on a bent-over opponent: In opposite stances, you attack with a rear leg roundhouse to the groin or solar plexus of your opponent, then switch legs to deliver an outside crescent downward heel kick to his exposed neck or back.

Figure 6.5.12 Figure 6.5.13 Figure 6.5.14 Figure 6.5.15
These images show a classical use of the downward heel kick on a bent-over opponent.

Figures 6.5.16 through 6.5.22 show the other classic situation for the use of this kick: A prone opponent. In this combination, you avoid and deflect an oncoming front kick, overextending your opponent to place him off-balance as he lands. You then sweep his landing leg to take him down. As he is still falling down, you already prepare your downward heel kick by lifting the sweeping leg in an outside crescent as high as possible. It is imperative not to stop between the two moves and start the kick as soon as he starts falling.

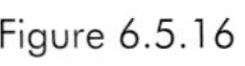

Figure 6.5.16 Figure 6.5.17 Figure 6.5.18 Figure 6.5.19

Figure 6.5.20 Figure 6.5.21 Figure 6.5.22
These images show a classical use of the downward heel kick on a prone opponent.

Key Points

- You can only lift high and fast a leg with relaxed muscles.
- Kick through the target.
- Do not slow the leg descent before the kick has hit.
- Keep your guard up as you lower the leg, as the hit itself can cause some off-balancing and put you in a vulnerable position.

Targets

- Targets on a standing opponent include: the head and face, the clavicle, the joints of the upper limbs: shoulders, elbows and wrists from all sides.
- Targets on a bent opponent include: the head, neck, upper and lower back.
- Targets on a prone opponent encompass the whole body from ankles to head.

Typical Application

As mentioned, on a standing opponent, the kick is not effective for a single attack. The following images show its use as a timed stop kick against a roundhouse, where it is good enough for inflicting serious damage and to knock down the opponent. From an opposite stance, avoid a full rear leg roundhouse of your opponent by twisting forward and on your outside, while keeping your hand up to control the kick (Figure 6.5.24). Lift your "liberated" rear leg into an outside crescent lift and strike downwards to the face or clavicle of your opponent (Figure 6.5.26).

Figure 6.5.23

Figure 6.5.24

Figure 6.5.25

Figure 6.5.26

Avoid your opponent's roundhouse and follow up with a downward heel kick.

Specific Training

- Work on your flexibility, especially splits and leg raises.
- Practice the straight leg upward kick (see Chapter 1, Section 3), as high as possible.
- This kick needs a lot of training to achieve speed, power and the right feeling of accelerating until having hit through. The kick needs to be practiced with both leg lifts: inside crescent and outside crescent. It must be drilled to hit at all heights: head, back of bent opponent, and prone opponent.
- Kick a medicine ball held by a partner at several heights, a standing bag, a striking pad held by a partner at various heights (Figures 6.5.27 and 6.5.28), a lying bag, a speed-ball as the face of a standing opponent, and a used tire held by a partner. See Figures 6.5.29 through 6.5.34.

Figure 6.5.27

Figure 6.5.28

Practice the downward heel kick on a striking pad held by a partner.

Figure 6.5.29

Figure 6.5.30

Figure 6.5.31

Figure 6.5.32

Figure 6.5.33 Figure 6.5.34

These illustrations depict a variety of training aids that are available to help you practice your downward heel kick.

Self-defense

Here, we present two applications of the kick: one as a crescent lift to hit and finish off a bent opponent, and the other as an outside crescent lift and the first kick in an aggressive combination.

The following figures show the use of the kick to get out of a clinch. As your assailant grabs you in close combat and gets into a boxing clinch (Figure 6.5.35), get one hand on the back of his head to keep him bent down, while you control his hand by grabbing it at the elbow with your other hand (Figure 6.5.36). Push him away with both hands, while continuing to push his neck down and distancing your hips from him. Launch the leg of your "neck" hand into a crescent lift and keep your hand on his neck for as long as possible (Figure 6.5.37). Strike down on his neck or back with a downward heel kick (Figure 6.5.38).

Figure 6.5.35 Figure 6.5.36 Figure 6.5.37 Figure 6.5.38

Break free of a clinch, and then bring a downward heel kick to bear on your opponent's neck or back.

Figures 6.5.40 and 6.5.41 show the use of a hopping, front leg, outside crescent lift, downward heel kick to feint or open the guard of an opponent in the same stance. As he retreats, lower your leg forward (Figure 6.5.42) and immediately launch a full power straight leg roundhouse (Chapter 3, Section 7) to *both* his legs at knee level (Figure 6.5.43). As he falls, downward heel kick him again in the body (Figure 6.5.45).

Figure 6.5.39 Figure 6.5.40 Figure 6.5.41 Figure 6.5.42 Figure 6.5.43

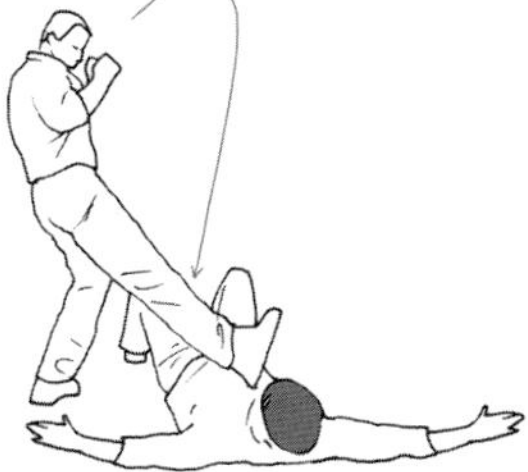

Figure 6.5.44 Figure 6.5.45

Employ a downward heel kick to open your opponent's guard, and then launch a roundhouse to sweep his legs out from under him. Finish the confrontation with a downward heel kick to the body.

6.6 The Switch Downward Heel Kick

General

Nearly all kick types can be delivered as switch kicks; this is only a matter of preceding footwork: you jump while switching legs (rear to front and vice-versa) and immediately launch the relevant kick with the "new" rear leg. We present it here, because the downward heel kick is especially adapted, and usually successful, as a switch kick. The switch allows you to use the front leg to kick, with the power of a rear leg kick. It also baffles your opponent, usually as he comes toward you: you jump and move, but basically stay (more or less) in the same place.

The switch downward heel kick is most of the time a stop kick or counter-attack kick, as it is excellent for close combat.

Description

Figures 6.6.1 through 6.6.5 show the switch, the rebound of the kicking leg and the delivery of the kick, just as a regular downward heel, from a crescent or an outward crescent lift.

Figure 6.6.1 Figure 6.6.2 Figure 6.6.3 Figure 6.6.4 Figure 6.6.5
Side view of the switch downward heel kick.

Figures 6.6.6 through 6.6.10 show a great example of application of the kick: the switch serves to gather power, but also to avoid an attack to your front knee. As the assailant launches a front leg low kick (straight roundhouse) toward your inside knee, you jump/switch legs while moving slightly backward. Your formerly front leg rebounds off the floor into a full powered outward crescent downward heel kick to your assailant's head.

Figure 6.6.6

Figure 6.6.7

Figure 6.6.8

Figure 6.6.9

Figure 6.6.10

Figure 6.6.11

Gather power and avoid a front knee attack in the same movement when you switch legs.

Key Points

All key points mentioned for the regular downward heel kick apply:

- You can only lift high and fast a leg with relaxed muscles.
- Kick through the target.
- Do not slow the leg descent before the kick has hit.
- Keep your guard up as you lower the leg, as the hit itself can cause some off-balancing and put you into a vulnerable position.

In addition:

- It is important to make the kicking foot rebound off the floor at the end of the switching hop, as if hitting a spring: down, and immediately up at full speed.

Targets

As listed for the regular downward heel kick, the following targets apply:

- Targets on a standing opponent include: the head and face, the clavicle, the joints of the upper limbs: shoulders, elbows and wrists from all sides.
- Targets on a bent opponent include: the head, neck, upper and lower back.
- Targets on a prone opponent encompass the whole body from ankles to head.

Typical Application

Figures 6.6.12 through 6.6.17 depict a great use of the kick against an opponent waiting for a move on your part to stop-reverse punch you. You switch, slightly forward, while extending your lead hand in a convincing jab. Immediately launch your now rear leg on the outside of his incoming punch, with an outside crescent lift, and downward heel kick him.

Figure 6.6.12 Figure 6.6.13 Figure 6.6.14 Figure 6.6.15

Figure 6.6.16 Figure 6.6.17

A typical application of the switch downward heel kick.

Specific Training

Train just like you would for the regular downward heel kick, but with the switch. Switch in place, and switch while purposely edging slightly forward or backward. Work on the speedball, striking pads, standing bags, and tires.

Self-defense

The following illustrations depict the use of the kick as a counter to a spin-back kick, when starting in reverse stances. When attacked with a spin back kick, always move forward, never backward, as the centrifugal power is at its maximum at the foot end and is negated close to the assailant's body. As your assailant attacks you with a spin-back hook kick from an opposite guard, do not retreat, but switch while edging slightly forward and to your inside, blocking or controlling the kick (Figure 6.6.19). Use your rear leg to deliver an outside crescent lifted downward heel kick (Figure 6.6.21).

Figure 6.6.18 Figure 6.6.19 Figure 6.6.20 Figure 6.6.21
Move in to block your opponent's spin-back hook kick, and then execute the switch downward heel kick.

6.7 The Outward Ghost Groin Kick

General

This is a fantastic kick this author first saw in a Wing-Chun kung fu practice. Like all groin kicks, it is ideal for self-defense. It is an easy kick to perform, very unexpected and suitable for close combat. You deliver the kick while turning away from the opponent, in place, and lifting the foot directly from its position to the groin of the adversary.

Description

The move is easier to understand if you look at the illustrations to the right. You pivot inwards on your front foot, while lifting the slightly bent rear leg directly to the target, *with no other movement of the upper body* (see Figure 6.7.2). The upper and lower portions of your body must be disconnected with no hint that you are doing anything other than pivoting. Use your momentum and leg muscles to put power into the kick and strike with the edge (blade) of the foot (Figure 6.7.3).

Figure 6.7.1 Figure 6.7.2 Figure 6.7.3
Side view of the outward ghost groin kick.

Figures 6.7.4 through 6.7.6 show the use of the kick in a simultaneous forward evasion of a straight jab. In self-defense, you would hit the groin and not the abdomen.

Figure 6.7.4 Figure 6.7.5 Figure 6.7.6
In close quarters, evade a jab while kicking.

Key Points

- For success, it is imperative not to telegraph: Keep your upper body relaxed.
- You need to work on the flexibility of the knee.
- The muscles of the striking leg are relaxed also: it is the speed that brings power to the kick.
- You are in close quarters: Keep your guard up.

Targets

The targets are the groin and the face of a bent opponent, exclusively.

Typical Application

The following illustrations depict a typical application of the kick. You use it when a combination has brought you close to your opponent. You can also kick him and take back your distance with no danger. Attack your opponent with a high reverse punch/front leg front kick to the opened midsection (Figures 6.6.8 and 6.6.9). Your opponent steps back and you reverse punch him to the face while lowering your kicking leg, whether you have hit him or not (Figure 6.6.10). You find yourself close to your opponent, in opposite stance, and with the rear leg free of weight. Deliver the outward ghost groin kick while keeping your guard up! See Figure 6.6.11.

Figure 6.7.7 Figure 6.7.8 Figure 6.7.9 Figure 6.7.10

Figure 6.7.11
A typical application of the outward ghost groin kick.

Specific Training

- The kick is easy to perform, but requires drilling to get the "feel" of it, to learn to gauge the distance and to use it naturally.
- Practice on the heavy bag with its bottom at groin height, from various ranges. Concentrate on relaxed upper body and kicking leg, and give no telegraphing moves.
- Work on the knee joint flexibility: runner stretches, lotus and hero's poses.
- Figures 6.7.12 and 6.7.13 show the drilling of the kick with a moving partner holding a striking pad.

Figure 6.7.12 Figure 6.7.13
Practice the outward ghost groin kick with a moving partner holding a striking pad.

Self-defense

The following illustrations depict the use of the kick as a fast, immediate response to a wrist grab. When grabbed, always react immediately: the grab puts you in a vulnerable position and with your attention away from your assailant's next move. Your assailant has gotten a hold of your right wrist from the outside, with his right hand, in order to pull you into a left punch (Figure 6.7.14). Pivot away from the punch while delivering the outward ghost groin kick (Figure 6.7.15). As soon as he is hit, circle his wrist to get a hold of it, and pull while you pivot back and punch him in the face (Figure 6.7.16). Use your other leg to stomp the back of his knee, while keeping a hold and twisting his wrist (Figure 6.7.17). You can now hit his exposed elbow joint, or armlock him.

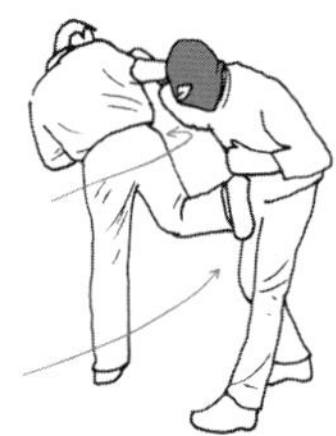

Figure 6.7.14 Figure 6.7.15 Figure 6.7.16 Figure 6.7.17
If your wrist has been grabbed from the outside and your opponent begins to pull you into a punch, pivot away from the punch and deliver an outward ghost groin kick.

6.8 The Spin-back Outside Crescent Kick

Armada (capoeira)

General

We gave this kick its capoeira name as it is a very visible and much used kick in their "game." But the kick is also omnipresent in taekwondo contests and other contact sports. We complained earlier about the lack of power of the regular outside crescent kick (Section 3 of this chapter)—what better way to remedy that than a spin-back? The spin-back allows for plenty of acceleration before hitting the target. It is therefore a very powerful kick, with the drawbacks of the spin-back kicks: more time and distance to travel, and some loss of eye contact when spinning back.

Description

The following illustrations show the delivery of the kick. As for all spin-backs, the head turns first, pulling the shoulders and then the hips (Figure 6.8.2). The hips then pull the kicking leg with all the stored energy of the twist (Figure 6.8.3). Accelerate until you have kicked through the target, and lower the leg (Figure 6.7.6).

Figure 6.8.1 Figure 6.8.2 Figure 6.8.3 Figure 6.8.4 Figure 6.8.5 Figure 6.8.6
Side view of the spin-back outside crescent kick.

Figure 6.8.7 Figure 6.8.8 Figure 6.8.9 Figure 6.8.10
Front view of the spin-back outside crescent kick.

Figures 6.8.11 through 6.8.14 show the delivery of the kick as a counterattack to a full step punch (*Oie tsuki*—karate).

Figure 6.8.11 Figure 6.8.12 Figure 6.8.13 Figure 6.8.14
The spin-back outside crescent kick as a counter to a full step punch.

Figures 6.8.15 through 6.8.18 show the delivery of the kick in an attacking combination: lunge jab, feint of a spin-back high backfist, and then the outside crescent kick at the last moment.

Figure 6.8.15 Figure 6.8.16 Figure 6.8.17 Figure 6.8.18
An attacking combination: lunge jab, feint of a spin-back high backfist, and then the spin-back outside crescent kick.

Key Points

- Kick through the target, do not decelerate before you hit.
- Minimize the no-eye contact period, and keep your guard up.
- You must totally commit to the kick to succeed.

Targets

This is a powerful kick: Most targets are valid, although head and groin are preferred. The upper and lower back, as well as the solar plexus are great targets to inflict paralyzing pain to the opponent. The kick trajectory does not make it a good kick to attack the legs (A spin-back hook kick—see Chapter 5, Section 4—would be preferable).

Typical Application

The following illustrations show the classical and natural combination for the use of this kick: In opposite stance, rear leg-crescent kick (Section 1 of this chapter) your opponent's lead arm elbow, opening his guard and pushing it to the outside (Figures 6.8.20 and 6.8.21). You have kicked through, inflicting pain, and kept the circular momentum. As soon as you lower your leg in front, keep pivoting to deliver a spin-back outside crescent kick to his unguarded head with the other leg (Figure 6.8.23).

Figure 6.8.19 Figure 6.8.20 Figure 6.8.21 Figure 6.8.22 Figure 6.8.23
Apply a crescent kick to your opponent's elbow to open up his guard, and then follow-up with a spin-back outside crescent kick.

Specific Training

- Train for speed, precision and distance—not for power.
- Flexibility training is required.
- Kick the speed-bag over a chair (See Figure 6.8.24).
- Kick the heavy bag from different ranges (See Figure 6.8.25).
- Drill with a moving partner, protected by a striking pad.

Figure 6.8.24
When kicking the speed-bag, use a chair to train yourself to deliver high, crisp crescent kicks.

Figure 6.8.25
Kick the bag from different ranges to simulate the unregulated movements of an opponent.

Self-defense

The following illustrations depict the use of the kick against a front kick attack. On top of the power of the accelerating spin-back, the successful combination gives you the added bonus of having the assailant impaling himself on your incoming kick. You are attacked, in opposite stance, with a fully committed penetrating front kick, which you avoid by evading forward and to the outside of the kick. Block or control the kicking leg while starting the spin-back (Figure 6.8.27). If you have caught the kicking leg, pull it slightly forward to accentuate the loss of balance of your attacker. Deliver your spin-back outside crescent kick to his head, as he lowers (falls forward) his kicking leg (Figure 6.8.29). Kick through the target, keeping your circular momentum, and lower your leg at your rear, presenting your side toward the assailant (Figure 6.8.30). Adjust distance if necessary, and use the other leg (front) to sweep his front leg, while grabbing his shoulder and pulling him down (*O soto gari*—judo). See Figure 6.8.31. Downward heel kick (Section 5 of this chapter) him once he is on the ground.

Figure 6.8.26

Figure 6.8.27

Figure 6.8.28

Figure 6.8.29

Figure 6.8.30

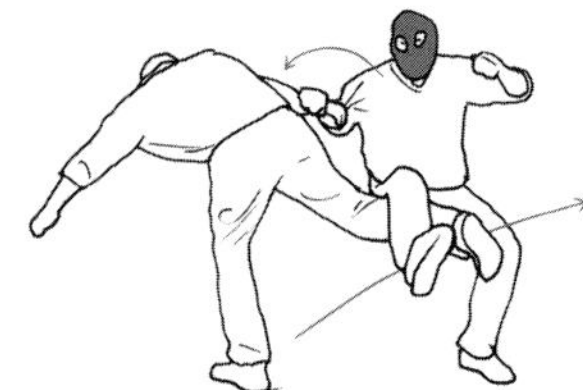

Figure 6.8.31
Evade your opponent's front kick, and apply your spin-back outside crescent kick to his head.
Follow through with a leg sweep and end the confrontation with a downward heel kick.

6.9 The Spin-back Downward Heel Kick

General

The spin back downward heel kick is adding to the power of the leg muscles and the power of gravity, the power of the centrifugal acceleration of the spin-back pivot. It is, therefore, a very powerful kick, but hard to control. Because of the spin-back, the kick is not really a pure downward heel kick, but more of a hybrid downward heel/outside crescent kick. The momentum of the spin-back, combined with the downward kick, results in a diagonal downward kick, ideal to strike the side of the face and neck, and the clavicle, with extreme force. The kick is, of course, ideal for close combat.

Description

Figures 6.9.1 through 6.9.4 show the delivery: Just like a spin-back outside crescent kick (Section 8 of this chapter), this kick reaches as high as possible, and with the apex just *before* completing the spin-back. The downward movement starts *before* you have completed the 180 degrees pivot. Keep both the pivoting momentum and the downward move at full speed until you have hit through the target.

Figure 6.9.1

Figure 6.9.2

Figure 6.9.3

Figure 6.9.4

Front view of the spin-back downward heel kick.

Figures 6.9.5 through 6.9.9 show the use of the kick as a natural follow-up to a leg block: You block a low kick with a circular raised knee block and make use of the momentum to spin back. As your opponent lowers his body to recoil away from the coming spin-back kick, your outside crescent kick becomes a downward heel kick.

Figure 6.9.5

Figure 6.9.6

Figure 6.9.7

Figure 6.9.8

Figure 6.9.9

The spin-back downward heel kick is a natural follow-up to a leg block.

Key Points

- Control the lift of the leg during spin back, to make sure the apex of the lift is before you have completed the spin-back—you must allow for some more pivot while the leg is going down.
- Keep your guard up: you are close to your opponent.
- Kick through the target and do not decelerate before.

Targets

Targets include: the side of the face, the side and back of the neck, the clavicle, the back, if the opponent is bent down, and the upper limbs.

Typical Application

The following illustrations show a typical application in close combat. As your opponent jabs you with commitment, you do not retreat but slip forward to his inside while initiating your spinning (Figures 6.9.11 and 6.9.12). Keep your hands up for protection and deliver the kick to the side of his neck (Figure 6.9.14). You could also hit him with a hammerfist strike as you spin back and before delivering the kick.

Figure 6.9.10

Figure 6.9.11

Figure 6.9.12

Figure 6.9.13

Figure 6.9.14

Step to the inside as your opponent attempts a jab. Deliver the spin-back downward heel kick to the side of his neck.

Specific Training

- Because of the angle of the kick, it is difficult to train on bags and balls. Try a standing bag that has a top that's at shoulder-level.
- The best drill is kicking a standing, and then moving trained opponent, who holds a good striking pad (Figure 6.9.15). The kicker must still be very careful, as the kick is devastating.

Figure 6.9.15
Have a partner hold a striking pad to help you develop skill in the spin-back downward heel kick.

- This is a great kick, but it must be practiced a lot. Train at full speed, and train often.

Self-defense

The following illustrations show the use of the kick in a close combat situation, after a great and very effective opening. Your assailant is an aggressive puncher and you surprise him by evading him downward, very low, and forward, toward him, with a reverse circular elbow strike (*Gyacku ushi mawashi Empi uchi*—karate) to the groin (Figure 6.9.17). Stand up, fully guarded, on his outside, while he bends from the pain, and start your spinning pivot with a hook to the head (Figure 6.9.19). Keep the circular momentum in your full spin-back downward heel kick and hit him in the back or the back of the neck according to his position and level of bending (Figure 6.9.22). After lowering the kicking leg, you can keep the momentum and deliver, with the other leg, a straight leg roundhouse (Section 7 of this chapter) to his thigh or back of the knee (Figure 6.9.23).

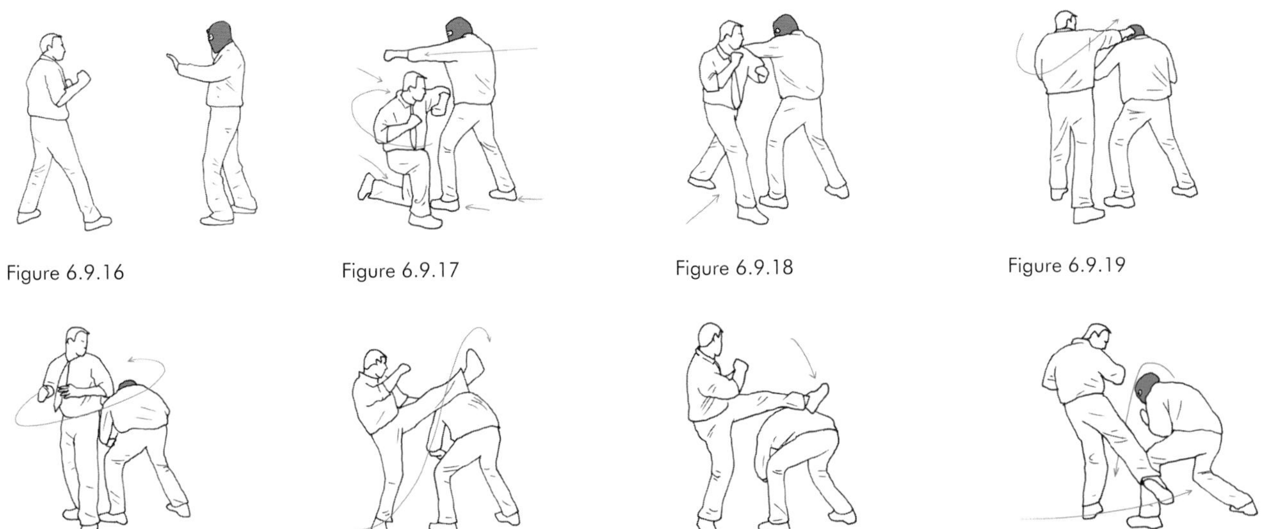

Figure 6.9.16 Figure 6.9.17 Figure 6.9.18 Figure 6.9.19

Figure 6.9.20 Figure 6.9.21 Figure 6.9.22 Figure 6.9.23

Surprise your opponent with an elbow to the groin. After delivering a hook to the head, follow up with a spin-back downward heel kick to the head or back. Finish the exchange with a straight leg roundhouse kick to his thigh or back of the knee.

6.10 The 360 Spin Crescent Kick

General

For those who complain about the lack of power of the crescent kick, here comes the solution: a crescent kick delivered after a full circle of acceleration. The kick, of course takes longer to hit the target, but it is so strong that it is difficult to block. Although it is much telegraphed, it is still surprising because it is rarely used, and somewhat counter-intuitive: You kick with your front leg, but still do a full 360 degree circle before hitting the target! The kick can be delivered as an offensive kick where you step forward toward your opponent and as a defensive/counterattack kick with footwork taking you away from your opponent.

Description

The following illustrations show the kick in both applications (offensive, and defensive/counterattack), with the first stage being identical: you pivot on your rear leg in a classical spin-back motion.

In the defensive kick, keep pivoting while taking a full step away with your front leg. Continue pivoting, and with the same leg (which is now the rear leg), deliver a regular crescent kick, using the full power of the uninterrupted pivot. See Figures 6.10.1 through 6.10.4.

Figure 6.10.1 Figure 6.10.2 Figure 6.10.3 Figure 6.10.4

Side view of the 360 spin crescent kick, used defensively.

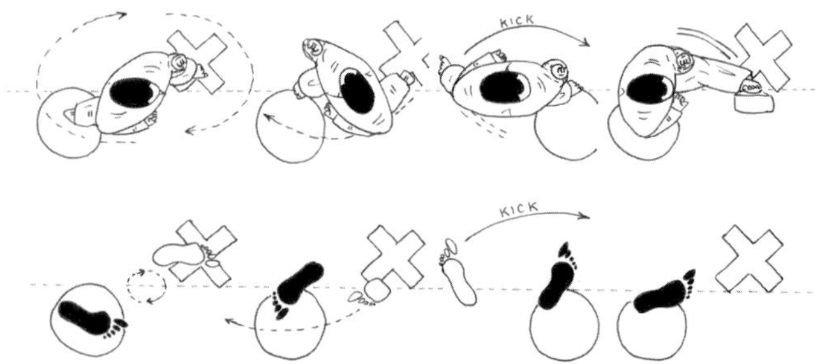

Figure 6.10.5
Overhead view of the 360 spin crescent kick in the defensive mode (top) and a diagram of the associated footwork (bottom).

In the offensive kick (Figures 6.10.6 through 6.10.9), you bring your rear leg forward toward your opponent in the same circular spinning movement, and keep pivoting on this now front foot. You keep the momentum while delivering a full crescent kick with the (now) rear leg.

Figure 6.10.6 Figure 6.10.7 Figure 6.10.8 Figure 6.10.9
Side view of the 360 spin crescent kick, used offensively.

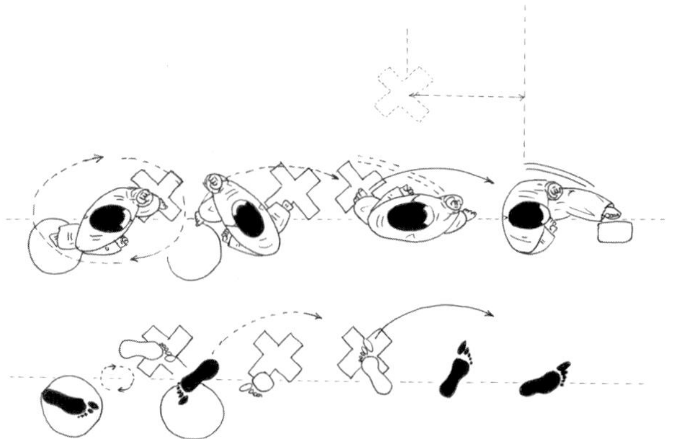

Figure 6.10.10
Overhead view of the 360 spin crescent kick in the offensive mode (top) and a diagram of the associated footwork (bottom).

Figures 6.10.11 through 6.10.16 show the delivery of the kick in an attack combination: lunge jab, spin-back backfist, step-in, take control of your close opponent's guard, and then the full powered crescent kick packing all the energy from the spin-back step.

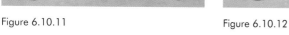

Figure 6.10.11

Figure 6.10.12

Figure 6.10.13

Figure 6.10.14

Figure 6.10.15

Figure 6.10.16

An example of the 360 spin crescent kick used as part of an attack combination.

Key Points

- The kick is one smooth, uninterrupted spin—no stopping.
- Keep your guard up and minimize the loss of eye contact while spinning back.
- Use the wide arc version of the crescent kick for maximum power.
- The spin-back is head first, then shoulders, then hips.
- Kick through the target, and do not decelerate before impact.

Targets

The kick is very powerful and everything goes: from the thigh to the head, including the arms.

Typical Application

The kick being very much "telegraphed," it is not really suitable as an offensive opening move. The following illustrations show its use in an offensive combination, making use of the circular movement. You feint a low reverse punch (Figure 6.10.18), in order to start your lunging combination of a high jab (Figure 6.10.19) to high spin-back backfist. While spinning back with the backfist punch (Figure 6.10.21), bring your rear leg forward and keep the circular/forward momentum, which will pull your (now) rear leg into a full crescent kick to his face (Figure 6.10.22). If your backfist has contacted his lead hand attempting to block, try to grab and control it while completing the kick. Kick "through" the head and lower the leg, *while keeping the circular momentum alive.* Keep pivoting and deliver a spin-back outside crescent kick (Section 8 of this chapter) with the other leg (Figure 6.10.25).

Figure 6.10.17 Figure 6.10.18 Figure 6.10.19 Figure 6.10.20

Figure 6.10.21 Figure 6.10.22 Figure 6.10.23 Figure 6.10.24 Figure 6.10.25

Use the circular momentum from a high crescent kick to power a follow-up spin-back outside crescent kick.

Specific Training

- This kick must be drilled for power: full power on the heavy bag!
- The power comes from speed and acceleration: Drill for speed on the speedball.
- This kick needs a lot of range training: Practice both forms (offensive and defensive) on the heavy bag from various distances, marked on the floor.

Self-defense

The following illustrations depict, purposely, an application of the kick in a form that is neither offensive nor defensive. As already mentioned many times, the number of possible nuances for any kick is infinite. This shows the use of the kick, in place, after the opponent has been stunned and is not moving. As your assailant starts his front leg side kick attack, jam his lifting leg with a hopping front-leg side stop-kick (Figure 6.10.27). Without lowering the leg, deliver a hopping high roundhouse to his face (Figure 6.10.28). Lower the kicking leg close to your rear leg, while starting your spin-back pivot, and use *the same leg again* for your 360 spin-back crescent kick (Figure 6.10.31). Kick through the target and lower the kicking leg behind his front leg. As a follow up, you can grab his shoulder while sweeping his leg with an inside reap (*Uchi mata*—judo). See Figure 6.10.33.

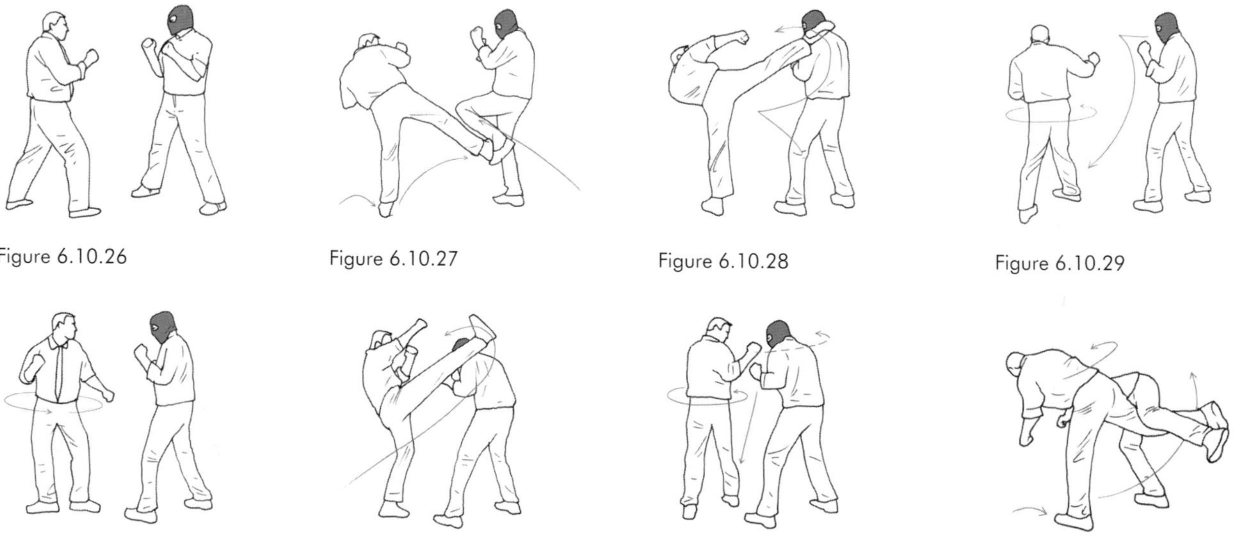

Figure 6.10.26 Figure 6.10.27 Figure 6.10.28 Figure 6.10.29

Figure 6.10.30 Figure 6.10.31 Figure 6.10.32 Figure 6.10.33

Interrupt your opponent's side kick with a stop-kick, then immediately deliver a high roundhouse to his face. Follow up with a 360 spin-back crescent kick, and then sweep him to the floor.

More Advanced Crescent Kicks

What follows is a brief review of some more advanced crescent kicks. They are not presented in detail here, as they are beyond the scope of this book.

The Flying Crescent Kick

Mikazuki tobi geri (karate)

The flying version of the crescent kick is not very commonly used, as the kick does not lend itself especially well to the jumping version. The jumping does not add anything to the momentum of the kick. It is good to practice though, as jumping forward, instead of up, can be of help to adjust the range of the crescent kick.

The Flying Outside Crescent Kick

Gyacku mikazuki tobi geri (karate)

The flying version of the outside crescent kick is much more common, but basically with a narrow arc. The jumping does not add a lot to the circular momentum of the kick itself, and the kick used is usually a narrow arc kick, close to a hybrid front kick/outside crescent. It is, though, coming at a surprising angle and is quite efficient: The jumping adds some power to the normally weak kick.

A spin-back outside crescent flying kick.

The Spin-back Flying Crescent Kick

The spin back flying crescent kick is a very powerful version of the crescent kick, as the liberation of the constraints of the floor allow for a fast spin, and therefore acceleration. It is basically a front leg kick, following a full 360 spin. Like all flying kicks, it can be delivered jumping forward, backward or in place, according to the relative position of the opponent. It can be performed jumping high or low and far. The spin-back flying crescent kick is more of a defensive/counterattack kick.

The Spin-back Outside Crescent Flying Kick

The flying version of the spin-back outside crescent kick is pretty straightforward. It is a very fast and powerful kick, used a lot in high kicking styles like taekwondo. It is more suitable to defensive and timing moves, or combinations, as it is a "short" kick. The jumping allows for closing the distance, however.

The Spin-back Flying Downward Heel Kick

The flying version of the spin-back downward heel kick is even more powerful, as the spinning back is free from the constraints of standing on the ground, and therefore faster. This is a great "timing" stop kick in close combat, but, like all flying kicks, can be performed jumping offensively forward or defensively backward. The angled trajectory is even more pronounced than in the regular spin-back downward heel kick, as the spinning momentum cannot be slowed before landing back on the ground: It should really be an "oblique angled downward" kick.

The 360 Spin-back Flying Downward Heel Kick

This is already a much more complex kick, quite acrobatic, and not for everyone. However, it is a great kick, and we have seen it performed successfully in Korean styles, rich in high and flying kicks. It basically is a spin-back downward heel kick delivered with the *front* leg. It is identical to the regular spin-back flying downward heel kick, but is preceded by a switch of the legs, in the air, at the outset of the jump. The switch can be forward or backward, but the kick is better suited as a defensive stop-kick.

The Double Spin-back Outward Crescent Kick

This is, very simply, two spin-back outward crescent kicks delivered in a row, one after the other, with the same leg, and making use of the uninterrupted circular momentum. This is a very effective combination, whether the first kick has scored or missed: You hit the already stunned opponent, or the counterattacking one. It is also a great drill for learning to kick from all positions and to understand the "feel" of the importance of acceleration in circular kicks.

The Spin-back Hook Feint to Downward Heel Kick

This kick is basically a hybrid kick between the spin-back hook kick (Chapter 5, Section 4) and the spin-back downward heel kick (Section 9 of this chapter). The spin back hook kick is purposely emphasized, in order to squeeze a block from the opponent, but at the last possible instant, the hips rotate to allow for an unexpected climbing surge of the foot, and a downward kick. Well executed, the feint is extremely compelling, and the kick is extremely surprising.

Afterword

As mentioned in the introduction,We are aware of the limitations of a first comprehensive compilation work and apologize for the intrinsic imperfections deriving from choices that had to be made.

We welcome comments and constructive criticism: noted omissions, foreign languages orthographic corrections, anecdotes, full-fledged mistake reports, additional kicks or variations, specific school's idiosyncrasies, classification remarks, relevant historical photographs, and more: all relevant and constructive input will be appreciated.

Please email us at:

martialartkicks@gmail.com

About the Authors

Marc De Bremaeker has been involved in martial arts for over forty-five years. Once a successful competitor renowned for flashy kicking, he has since been teaching in the Shi Heun organization and doing some research into the common root and principles uniting martial arts. He holds black belts in several Japanese Arts and has been training in other fighting methods on several continents.

Roy Faige is today the head of the Shi Heun style founded by his late father. He used to be a fierce competitor with numerous international tournament titles to his name, and held the positions of captain and then coach for the Israeli National team for more than ten years. Roy is also an officer in the most elite of commando units of the Israeli Army, and co-founded the ShayKiDo Institute where a combination of martial arts training and professional psychotherapy is used to help children, teenagers and adults who suffer from difficulties in self-regulation.

Shahar Navot is a renowned illustrator and caricaturist published in leading periodicals. He is also an enthusiastic martial artist with a second degree black belt in the Shi Heun karate style.